The Capital Punishment Dilemma

1950-1977

A Subject Bibliography

The Capital Punishment Dilemma

1950-1977

A Subject Bibliography

by

Charles W. Triche III

The Whitston Publishing Company
Troy, New York
1979

TABLE OF CONTENTS

PREFACE

Capital punishment is an extremely emotively charged issue. The courts, clergy, and citizenry alike often seem preoccupied with the subject. Glamourized cases, such as that of the recent Gary Gilmore incident, shove the issue into the forefront of public concern. People wonder whether society has the right to take the life of another human being no matter what the crime.

The aim of this bibliography on capital punishment is to assemble in one souce much of the literature from 1950 to 1977. The information listed reflects published data in books, essays, pamphlets, periodicals, government publications and newspapers. It is divided into three sections with each section indexing a different type of literature.

In section number one, the "Books, Essays, Pamphlets, and Government Publications" section, entries are listed alphabetically by author when an author has been given. Anonymous works are listed within the same alphabet by article title.

Arrangement of the second section, the "Subject Index to Periodical Literature", is alphabetical by subject heading and then by title within these subject headings. Journal and newspaper articles are included in this section. Newspaper articles pertaining to a given subject are listed at the end of each respective section in alphabetical order by title. In instances where the material contained in a particular article crosses disciplines, the entry for the article is repeated in each section to which the material relates. Additionally, when the material in one section largely overlaps the material in another section, the researcher is referred to added headings through a *See Also* cross reference. Approximately 170 subject headings and cross references enhance the usefulness of this bibliography.

Section three, the "Author Index", is an alphabetical listing of the authors whose works are cited in sections one and two.

While compiling this bibliography, approximately thirty indexing and abstracting services, as well as numerous bibliographies in books and periodical articles, were consulted. Some of the major sources of information are: *The Applied Science and Technology Index, Bibliographic Index, British Books in Print, Business Periodicals Index, Canadian Books in Print, Education Index, Essay and General Literature Index, Humanities Index, Index to Legal Periodicals, Index to the Christian Science Monitor, Index to U.S. Government Periodicals, Industrial Arts Index, International Index to Periodicals, Library of Congress Catalog: Books—Subjects, Monthly Catalog of United States Government Publications, The National Observer Index, New York Times Index, Psychological Abstracts, Public Affairs Information Service. Bulletin, (PAIS), Reader's Guide to Periodical Literature, Social Sciences and Humanities Index, Social Sciences Index, Subject Guide to Books in Print,* and the *Verticle File Index.*

Complete journal titles have been provided. Also, a list of all subject headings and cross references used in this bibliography appears within the preliminary pages.

I would like to especially thank Anna Jane Marks of the University of Southwestern Louisiana Library for her very valuable assistance.

Charles W. Triche III

SUBJECT HEADINGS AND CROSS REFERENCES

viii

BOOKS AND ESSAYS

Abdel Fattah, Ezzat. A STUDY OF THE DETERRENT EFFECT OF CAPITAL PUNISHMENT WITH SPECIAL REFERENCE TO THE CANADIAN SITUATION. Ottawa: Information Canada, 1972.

—. UNE ÉTUDE DE L'EFFET INTIMIDANT DE LA PEINE DE MORT A PARTIR DE LA SITUATION CANADIENNE. Ottawa: Information Canada, 1972.

Allen, E. J. "Capital punishment: your protection and mine," THE DEATH PENALTY IN AMERICA edited by H. A. Bedau. Chicago: Aldine Pub., 1964. pp. 135-146.

Alomar Esteve, Gabriel. LA PENA DE MORT. Palma de Mallorca: J. Mascaro Pasarius, 1972.

Alt, Hans Peter. DAS PROBLEM DER TODESSTRAFE. München: C. Kaiser, 1960.

Althaus, Paul. DIE TODESSTRAFE ALS PROBLEM DER CHRIST-LICHEN ETHIK. München: Verlag der Bayerischen Akademie der Wissenschaften in Kommission bei C. H. Beck, 1955.

Alvarez Ganoza, Pedro L. ORIGEN Y TRAYECTORIA DE LA APLICA-CION DE LA PENA DE MUERTE EN LA HISTORIA DEL DERECHO PERUANO, ÉPOCA REPUBLICANA 1821-1937 Y ALGUNOS ANTE-DEDENTES COLONIALES. Lima: Editorial Dorhca, 1974. p. 207.

American Academy of Political and Social Science. MURDER AND THE PENALTY OF DEATH edited by Thorsten Sellin. Philadelphia: The Academy, 1952.

The American Institute of Public Opinion. "Public opinion and the death penalty," THE DEATH PENALTY IN AMERICA edited by H. A. Bedau. Chicago: Aldine Pub., 1964. pp. 236-241.

American Jewish Committee. Institute of Human Relations. THE DEATH PENALTY FOR ECONOMIC OFFENSES IN THE SOVIET UNION. N.P.: The Committee, 1962.

Ancel, Marc. CAPITAL PUNISHMENT. New York: United Nations Economic and Social Affairs Department, 1962.

Anderson, Frank W. A CONCISE HISTORY OF CAPITAL PUNISHMENT IN CANADA. Calgary: Frontier Pub., 1973.

Arévalo Barillas, Alberto. LA PENA DE MUERTE. Granada: Nicaragus, 1946.

Artigas Orce Pereyra, E. LA PENA DE MUERTE EN EL URUGUAY: EL FUSILAMIENTO DE PAEZ Y GONZALEZ EN MALDONADO: ANALISIS HISTORICO-SOCIAL. San Carlos: s.n., 1973.

Association française contre la peine de mort. CONTRE LA PEINE DE MORT, RÉUNION D'INFORMATION ORGANISÉE PAR L'ASSOCIATION FRANÇAISE CONTRE LA PEINE DE MORT LE 10 MAI 1966 AU PALAIS DE JUSTICE DE PARIS. . .EXPOSÉS DE MM. JEAN ROSTAND. . .ALBERT NAUD. . .ANDRÉ RICHARD. . .JEAN GRAVEN. . . Paris: l'Association, 1967?

Aukrust, Olav O. DODSSTRAFFEN; FORSOK PA EN SAKLIG ORIENTERING. Oslo: A. Gimnes, 1946.

Australia. Senate. STANDING COM. ON CONSTITUTIONAL AND LEGAL AFFAIRS. REPORT ON DEATH PENALTY ABOLITION BILL, 1970. (Parliamentary pa. no. 234–1971). Canberra: Commonwealth Government Printing Office, 1971.

Badinter, Robert. L'EXÉCUTION. Paris: Grasset, 1973.

Barzun, J. "In favor of capital punishment," THE DEATH PENALTY IN AMERICA edited by H. A. Bedau. Chicago: Aldine Pub., 1964. pp. 154-165.

2

—. "In favor of capital punishment," CONTEMPORARY MORAL ISSUES edited by H. K. Girvetz. Belmont: Wadsworth Pub., 1963. pp. 105-112.

Beccaria, Cesare Bonesana. AN ESSAY ON CRIMES AND PUNISHMENTS. With commentary by M. D. Voltaire. Stanford, California: Academic Reprints, 1953.

—. TRATADO DE LOS DELITOS Y DE LAS PENAS (DEI DELITTI E DELLE PENE) TRADUCCION, PROLOGO Y EPILOGO POR CONSTANCIO BERNALDO DE QUIROS. México: J. M. Cajica, Jr., 1957.

Bedau, Hugo A. and Chester M. Pierce, eds. CAPITAL PUNISHMENT IN THE UNITED STATES. New York: AMS Press, 1976.

Bedau, H. A. "Death as a punishment," THE DEATH PENALTY IN AMERICA edited by H. A. Bedau. Chicago: Aldine Pub., 1964. pp. 214-231.

—. THE DEATH PENALTY IN AMERICA; AN ANTHOLOGY. Chicago: Aldine Pub., 1968, 1967.

—. "General introduction," THE DEATH PENALTY IN AMERICA edited by H. A. Bedau. Chicago: Aldine Pub., 1964. pp. 1-32.

—. "Murder, errors of justice, and capital punishment," THE DEATH PENALTY IN AMERICA edited by H. A. Bedau. Chicago: Aldine Pub., 1964. pp. 434-452.

—. "Offenses punishable by death," THE DEATH PENALTY IN AMERICA edited by H. A. Bedau. Chicago: Aldine Pub., 1964. pp. 39-52.

—. "Social science research in the aftermath of Furman vs. Georgia: creating new knowledge about capital punishment in the United States," ISSUES IN CRIMINAL JUSTICE: PLANNING AND EVALUATION. (Riedel), New York: Praeger, 1976. pp. 75-86.

—. "The struggle over capital punishment in New Jersey," THE DEATH PENALTY IN AMERICA edited by H. A. Bedau. Chicago: Aldine Pub., 1964. pp. 374-395.

3

Bellemare, Guret. PLAN GENERAL DE ORGANIZACION JUDICIAL PARA BUENOS AIRES. REEDICION FASIMIL (1829). Noticia preliminar de Ricardo Levene: Buenos Aires, 1949.

Berlit, Jan-Wolfgang. TODESSTRAFE, IM NAMEN DES VOLKES? Diessen/Ammersee: W. Frhr. v. Tucher, 1964.

Bishop, George Victor. EXECUTIONS, THE LEGAL WAYS OF DEATH. Los Angeles: Sherbourne Press, 1965.

Bisiach, Gianni. COSI SI MUORE. Genova: Immordino, 1968.

Black, Charles Lund. CAPITAL PUNISHMENT, THE INEVITABILITY OF CAPRICE AND MISTAKE. New York: Norton, 1974.

Bleackey, Horace. HANGMEN OF ENGLAND: HOW THEY HANGED AND WHOM THEY HANGED. Montclair, New Jersey: Patterson Smith, Pub., 1974.

✳ Block, Eugene B. AND MAY GOD HAVE MERCY; THE CASE AGAINST CAPITAL PUNISHMENT. San Francisco: Fearon Pub., 1962.

Blom-Cooper, Louis Jacques. THE HANGING QUESTION: ESSAYS ON THE DEATH PENALTY. London: Published on behalf of the Howard League for Penal Reform by Duckworth, 1969.

Board of Christian Service of the General Conference Mennonite Church. CHURCH, THE CASE AND THE OFFENDER. Newton: Faith and Life Press, 1963.

Boiter, Albert. THE DEATH PENALTY IS NOT WITHERING AWAY: A RATION LIBERTY ANALYSIS. New York: Radio Liberty, 1964.

Botti, Ferruccio. LA FORCA D.BRETTA. STORIA DEL BANDITO BERRETTA E CENNI SUI CONDANNATI A MORTE IN PARMA DAL 1560 AL 1860. Parma: Scuola tipografica benedettina, 1967.

Bowers, William J. EXECUTIONS IN AMERICA. Lexington: Lexington Books, 1974.

Bresler, Fenton S. REPRIEVE; A STUDY OF A SYSTEM. London:

Harrap, 1965. p. 324.

British Information Service. SELECT BIBLIOGRAPHY ON CAPITAL PUNISHMENT IN BRITAIN. 1956.

Brown, Edmund G. STATEMENT OF GOVERNOR EDMUND G. BROWN ON CAPITAL PUNISHMENT. Sacramento: Office of the Governor, 1963.

Büchert, Herbert. DIE TODESSTRAFE; GESCHICHTLICH, RELIGIÖS UND RECHTLICH BETRACHTET. Berlin: H. Luchterhand, 1956.

Burns, Creighton. THE TAIT CASE. Parkville, Victoria: Melbourne University Press, 1962.

Cahn, E. N. "Fact skepticism and Fundamental Law," CONFRONTING JUSTICE. (Cahn). Boston: Little, Brown, 1966. pp. 292-304.

—. "Reflections on Hanging: Preface for Americans," CONFRONTING JUSTICE. (Cahn). Boston: Little, Brown, 1966. pp. 305-314.

California. Department of Corrections. EXECUTIONS IN CALIFORNIA, 1943 THROUGH 1963. Sacramento, Department of Corrections, Research Division, Administrative Statistics Section, 1965.

California. Governor. STATEMENT OF GOVERNOR EDMUND G. BROWN ON CAPITAL PUNISHMENT, TRANSMITTED TO THE CALIFORNIA LEGISLATURE, THURSDAY, JANUARY 31, 1963. Sacramento: Office of the Governor, 1963.

California. Legislature. Assembly. FACTS AND FIGURES CONCERNING EXECUTIONS IN CALIFORNIA, (1938-1962, by George E. Danielson. Sacramento: Legislative Reference Service, 1963.

California. Legislature. Assembly. Interim Committee on Judicary. REPORT OF THE SUBCOMMITTEE OF THE JUDICIARY COMMITTEE ON CAPITAL PUNISHMENT, PERTAINING TO THE PROBLEMS OF THE DEATH PENALTY AND ITS ADMINISTRATION IN CALIFORNIA. Sacramento: Assembly of the State of California, 1957.

California. Legislature. Senate. Committee on Judiciary. REPORT, MARCH 9, 1960. HEARING, REPORT, AND TESTIMONY ON SENATE BILL NO. 1, 1960, SECOND EXTRAORDINARY SESSION, WHICH PROPOSED TO ABOLISH THE DEATH PENALTY IN CALIFORNIA AND TO SUBSTITUTE LIFE IMPRISONMENT WITHOUT POSSIBILITY OF PAROLE. Sacramento: Senate of the State of California, 1960.

California. State Library, Sacramento. Law Library. CAPITAL PUNISHMENT: A SELECTIVE BIBLIOGRAPHY. Sacramento: 1965.

Calvert, Eric Roy. CAPITAL PUNISHMENT IN THE TWENTIETH CENTURY. Port Washington, New York: Kennikat Press, 1971.

—. CAPITAL PUNISHMENT IN THE TWENTIETH CENTURY, FIFTH EDITION REVISED, 1936 & THE DEATH PENALTY ENQUIRY, FIRST PUBLISHED 1931. Montclair: Patterson Smith, 1973.

Campion. D. R. "Attitudes of state police toward the death penalty," THE DEATH PENALTY IN AMERICA edited by H. A. Bedau. Chicago: Aldine Pub., 1964. pp. 252-258.

—. "Does the death penalty protect state police?" THE DEATH PENALTY IN AMERICA edited by H. A. Bedau. Chicago: Aldine Pub., 1964. pp. 301-315.

Camus, Albert. REFLECTIONS ON THE GUILLOTINE, AN ESSAY ON CAPITAL PUNISHMENT. Michigan City: Fridjob-Karla Pub., 1960, p. 55.

—. RÉFLEXIONS SUR LA PEINE CAPITALE. Paris: Clamann-Lévy, 1957.

Canada. ACT TO AMEND THE CRIMINAL CODE (CAPITAL MURDER). Acts, 1960-1961.

Canada. Department of Justice. CAPITAL PUNISHMENT. Toronto, Ontario: Information Canada, 1965.

—. CAPITAL PUNISHMENT: MATERIAL RELATING TO ITS PURPOSE AND VALUE. Ottawa: Information Canada, 1965.

—. CAPITAL PUNISHMENT; NEW MATERIAL: 1965-1972. Ottawa: Information Canada, 1972.

—. LA PEINE CAPITALE: DOCUMENTATION SUR SON OBJET ET SA VALEUR. Ottawa: Information Canada, 1965.

Canada. Department of the Solicitor General. A STUDY OF THE DETERRENT EFFECT OF CAPITAL PUNISHMENT, WITH SPECIAL REFERENCE TO THE CANADIAN SITUATION. Ottawa: Information Canada, 1972.

Canada. Minister of Justice. CAPITAL PUNISHMENT: MATERIAL RELATING TO ITS PURPOSE AND VALUE. Ottawa: Information Canada, 1965.

Canada. Parliament. Joint Committee on Capital and Corporal Punishment and Lotteries. MINUTES OF PROCEEDINGS AND EVIDENCE. Ottawa: Information Canada, 1954.

Canada. Parliament. Joint Committee of the Senate and House of Commons. CAPITAL PUNISHMENT, CORPORAL PUNISHMENTS, LOTTERIES. REPORTS. Ottawa: Information Canada, 1956. pp. 86-88.

Canadian Association of Chiefs of Police. A BRIEF ON CAPITAL PUNISHMENT; SUBMITTED TO THE FEDERAL GOVERNMENT. Canada: The Association, 1973.

Canadian Criminology and Corrections Association. THE DEATH PENALTY: AN OFFICIAL STATEMENT OF POLICY. Canada: The Association, 1972.

Capistran de la Llata, René. LA PENA DE MUERTE. México, 1949.

CAPITAL PUNISHMENT: NINETEENTH-CENTURY ARGUMENTS. New York: Arno Press, 1974.

CAPITAL PUNISHMENT. PART I. REPORT, 1960; PART 2. DEVELOPMENTS, 1961 to 1965. (Sales No. E.76.4.15). New York: United Nations Sales Sec. Room, 1968.

CAPITAL PUNISHMENT. (United Nations Publication 62.4.2). New York: United Nations Sales Sec. Room, 1962.

Carter, Robert M. CAPITAL PUNISHMENT IN CALIFORNIA: 1938-1953. Berkeley: The University of California, Graduate School, 1953.

Ceylon. REPORT OF THE COMMISSION OF INQUIRY ON CAPITAL PUNISHMENT. Colombo, Ceylon: The Government Press, 1959.

Charpentier, Jacques. POUR LA PEINE DE MORT, PAR LE BÂTONNIER JACQUES CHARPENTIER. CONTRE LA PEINE DE MORT, PAR M. ALBERT NAUD... Nancy: Berger-Levrault, 1967.

Christoph, James Bernard. CAPITAL PUNISHMENT AND BRITISH POLITICS; THE BRITISH MOVEMENT TO ABOLISH THE DEALTH PENALTY, 1945-57. Chicago: University of Chicago Press, 1962; London: Allen & Urwin, 1622.

Citizens against legalized murder, Inc. CAPITAL PUNISHMENT: A SELECTED BIBLIOGRAPHY. New York, 1973.

Cobin, H. L. "Abolition and restoration of the death penalty in Delaware," THE DEATH PENALTY IN AMERICA edited by H. A. Bedau. Chicago: Aldine Pub., 1964. pp. 359-373.

Cocteau, J. "On the Death Penalty," HAND OF A STRANGER (Cocteau). New York: Horizon Press, 1959. pp. 48-56.

Cohen, Bernard Lande. LAW WITHOUT ORDER; CAPITAL PUNISHMENT AND THE LIBERALS. New Rochelle: Arlington House, 1970.

Colloque sur la peine de mort, Athens. COLLOQUE SUR LA PEINE DE MORT, TENU A ATHENES, DU 4 au 8 AVRIL 1960, SOUS LES AUSPICES DE L'ÉTOLE DES SCIENCES POLITIQUES "PANTIOS." Athènes: École des sciences politiques "Pantios," 196-.

Commonwealth Club of California. SHOULD WE ABOLISH CAPITAL PUNISHMENT? (Commonwealth 39 (45) part 2). San Francisco: The Club, 1963.

Connecticut. ACT CONCERNING THE DEATH PENALTY. Public acts

1972-1973.

CONTROVERSY OVER CAPITAL PUNISHMENT: PRO AND CON. (Congressional digest. 52:1). Washington, D.C.: Government Printing Office, 1973.

Cooper, David D. THE LESSON OF THE SCAFFOLD: THE PUBLIC EXECUTION CONTROVERSY IN VICTORIAN ENGLAND. Athens: Ohio University Press, 1974.

Corniero Suarez, Alejandro. LA PENA DE MUERTE. TEXTO: ALEJANDRO CORNIERO. PORTADO: MA. ROSA VELA. ILUS.: SERRA. Barcelona,: Ediciones G. P.; Difundido por Plaza & Janés, 1962.

Costello, Mary. DEATH PENALTY REVIVAL. Washington, D.C.: Editorial Research Reports, 1973.

Council of Europe. European Committee on Crime Problems. THE DEATH PENALTY IN EUROPEAN COUNTRIES. Strasbourg: Council of Europe, 1962.

Cova Garcia, Luis. PROYECTO DE LEY DE RÉGIMEN DE EJECUCION DE LA PENA. ES O NO ES EFICAZ LA PENA DE MUERTE PARA LA EXTINCTION DEL DELITO? (DISCURSO PARA MI INGRESO COMO MIEMBRO DE LA ACADEMIA MEJICANA DE CIENCIAS PENALES). Caracas: Tip. Americana, 1949.

Csatsko, Imre. BUNTETÉSJOGI ELMÉLETEK TEKINTETTEL A BUNTETÉSFAJAIRA, KULONOSEN HALALBUNTETÉSRE; MIKÉP GYAKOROLTATOTT EZ RÉGI S UJABB NÉPEKNÉL. Bécsben, Stassno és Sommer betuivel, 1843.

Dalman, Gustav Albert. SVERIGES SISTE SKARPRATTARE A. G. DALMAN; FOREGANGARE OCH FORRATTNINGAR, AV C. A. DALMAN OCH G. O. Gunne. Stockholm: Special-förlaget, 1946.

Danielson, George E. FACT AND FIGURES CONCERNING EXECUTIONS IN CALIFORNIA, 1938-1962. PREPARED WITH THE ASSISTANCE OF THE ASSEMBLY LEGISLATIVE REFERENCE SERVICE. Sacramento, 1963.

Dann, R. H. "Abolition and restoration of the death penalty in Oregon,"

THE DEATH PENALTY IN AMERICA edited by H. A. Bedau. Chicago: Aldine Pub., 1964. pp. 343-351.

Darrow, C. S. "The futility of the death penalty," VERDICTS OUT OF COURT by C. S. Darrow. New York: Quadrangle Books, 1963. pp. 225-232.

Delcombre, André. AU NOM DE VOS LOIS; ESSAI SUR LE PEINE DE MORT. Paris: Presses du temps présent, 1964.

—. ÉLOGE DE LA GUILLOTINE. . . Éditions de la Crique, 3, rue Lecoq, 1971.

De Marcus, J. P. CAPITAL PUNISHMENT. (Informational Bulletin, No. 40). Frankfort: Kentucky Legislative Research Committee, 1965.

Diepenhorst, J. A. HETVRAAGSTUK VAN DE DOODSTRAF. Verslag van de bijeenkomst op 2 Maart 1946 te Amsterdam. Amsterdam: F. van Rossen, 1946.

DiSalle, Michael Vincent and Lawrence G. Blochman. THE POWER OF LIFE OR DEATH. New York: Random House, 1965.

DiSalle, M. V. and Louis Wyman. SHOULD WE ABOLISH CAPITAL PUNISHMENT. (American Forum, 23, 16). Washington, D.C.: Merkle Press, 1960.

Dokumentation über die Todesstrafe. MIT EINER RECHTSVERGLEI-CHENDEN DARSTELLUNG DES PROBLEMS DER TODESSTRAFE IN ALLER WELT, VON ARMAND MERGEN. Darmstadt: N. Stoytscheff, 1963.

Duff, Charles. A HANDBOOK ON HANGING; being a short introduction to the fine art of execution, containing much useful information on neck-breaking, throttling, strangling, asphyxiation, decapitation and electrocution; data and wrinkles on hangmanship. Yorkshire, England: EP Publishing; Totowa: Rowman & Littlefield, 1974.

Düsing, Bernhard. DIE GESCHICHTE DER ABSCHAFFUNG DER TODESSTRAFE IN DER BUNDESREPUBLIK DEUTSCHLAND. Mit einem Vorwort des des Bundesministers der Justiz Thomas Dehler. Offenbach: Main, Bollwerk-Verland, 1952.

10

Ebbinghaus, Julius. DIE STRAFEN FUR TOTUNG EINES MENSCHEN NACH PRINZIPIEN EINER RECHTSPHILOSOPHIE DER FREI-HEIT. Bonn: H. Bouvier, 1968.

Egen, Jean. L'ABATTOIR SOLENNEL. Paris: G. Authier, 1973.

Ehrmann, H. B. "The death penalty and the administration of justice," THE DEATH PENALTY IN AMERICA edited by H. A. Bedau. Chicago: Aldine Pub., 1964. pp. 415-434.

Ehrmann, Herbert B. THE UNTRIED CASE: THE SACCO-VANZETTI CASE AND THE MORELLI GANG. New York: Vanguard Press, 1960.

Ehrmann, S. R. "The human side of capital punishment," THE DEATH PENALTY IN AMERICA; an anthology edited by H. A. Bedau. Chicago: Aldine Pub., 1964.

Eshelman, Byron E. DEATH ROW CHAPLAIN. Englewood Cliffs: Prentice-Hall, 1962.

ESSAYS ON CAPITAL PUNISHMENTS. (Republished from *Paulson's Daily Advertiser*). Philadelphia: Brown and Merritt, 1811.

Feiertag, Erwin L. CAPITAL PUNISHMENT IN NEW JERSEY: 1664-1950. New York: Columbia University. The Graduate School, 1951.

Feucht, Dieter. GRUBE UND PFAHL. EIN BEITRAG ZUR GESCHI-CHTE DER DEUTSCHEN HINRICHTUNGSBRAUCHE. Tübingen: Mohr, 1967.

Filota, Fila. BRANIO SAM NA SMRT OSUDENE. Beograd: Prosveta, 1970.

Finland. Lainvalmistelukunta. EHDOTUS HALLITUKSEN ESITYKSEKSI EDUSKUNNALLE KUOLEMANRANGAISTUSTA KOSKEVAN LA-INSAADANNON UUDISTAMISESTA. Helsinki, Jakaja: Valtion painatuskeskus, 1968.

—. FORSLAG TILL REGERINGENS PROPOSITION TILL RIKSDAGEN ANGAENDE REVISION AV LAGSTIFTNINGEN RORANDE DODS-STRAFFET. Helsingfors, Distr.: Statens trychericentral, 1968.

11

Florida. Governor's Committee to Study Capital Punishment. REPORT. Tallahassee, 1972.

Florida. Special Commission for the Study of Abolition of Death Penalty in Capital Cases. REPORT, 1963-1965. Tallahassee, 1965.

Folgerm, Robert M. CAPITAL PUNISHMENT: NINETEENTH-CENTURY ARGUMENTS. New York: Arno Press, 1974.

Frankfurter, F. "Problems of Capital Punishment," OF LAW AND MEN. (Frankfurter). New York: Harcourt, 1956. pp. 77-102.

Frescaroli, Antonio. HISTORIA DE LA TORTURA A TRAVÉS DE LOS SIGLOS. Barcelona: De Vecchi, 1972.

—. LA TORTURA ATTRAVERSO I SECOLI. Milano: G. De Vecchi, 1970.

Freud, S. "Freud's View on Capital Punishment," COMPULSION TO CONFESS. (Reik). New York: Farrar, Straus, 1959. pp. 469-474.

✕ Friends Committee on Legislation. SAN FRANCISCO. CAPITAL PUNISHMENT: A SELECTED BIBLIOGRAPHY. San Francisco: The Committee, 1966.

—. SAN FRANCISCO. CAPITAL PUNISHMENT: A SELECTED BIBLIOGRAPHY. San Francisco: The Committee, 1969.

—. THIS LIFE WE TAKE: THE CASE AGAINST CAPITAL PUNISHMENT. San Francisco: The Committee, 1959.

Garcia Cervantes, Fernando. LA PENA DE MUERTE; SU JUSTIFICACION EN LA LEGISLACION PENAL MILITAR Y EL PROBLEMA DE SU REIMPLANTACION EN LA LEGISLACION PENAL COMUN. México, 1951.

Garcia Valdés, Carlos. LA PENA DU MUERTE. Madrid: Cuadernos para el Dialogo, 1973.

Gardiner, Gerald. CAPITAL PUNISHMENT AS A DETERRENT, AND THE ALTERNATIVE. London: V. Gollancz, 1956.

General Conference Mennonite Church. Peace and Social Concerns Committee. THE CHURCH, THE STATE, AND THE OFFENDER. Newton, Kan.: Faith and Life Press, 1963.

Georgia. General Assembly. Senate. Capital Punishment Committee. REPORT. Atlanta, 1966.

Glenzdorf, Johann Caspar and Fritz Treichel. HENKER, SCHINDER UND ARME SUNDER. n.p.: Rost, 1970.

Gloege, Gerhard. DIE TODESSTRAFE ALS THEOLOGISCHES PROBLEM. Köln u. Opladen: Westdeutscher Verlag, 1966.

Gollancz, Victor. CAPITAL PUNISHMENT: THE HEART OF THE MATTER. London, 1955.

Gottlieb, Gerald H. GERALD H. GOTTLIEB ON CAPITAL PUNISHMENT; followed by a discussion. Santa Barbara: Center for the Study of Democratic Institutions, 1967.

—. "Is the death penalty unconstitutional?" THE DEATH PENALTY IN AMERICA edited by H. A. Bedau. Chicago: Aldine Pub., 1964. pp. 194-213.

Goulard, Roger. UN LIGNÉE D'EXÉCUTEURS DES JUGEMENTS CRIMINELS, LES SANSON, 1688-1847. Melun: Archambault, 1968.

Gowers, Sir Ernest Arthur. A LIFE FOR A LIFE? THE PROBLEM OF CAPITAL PUNISHMENT. London: Chatto and Windus, 1956.

Grajewski, Henryk. KARA SMIERCI W PRAWIE POLSKIM DO POLOWY XIV WIEKU. Warszawa, Wydawn: Prawnicze, 1956.

Gram Jensen, Sv. STUDIER OVER LOVENS STRENGESTE STRAF I DANMARK 1858-1957. Sv. Gram Jensen: Kobenhavn, Ejlers, 1974.

Graves, W. F. "The deterrent effect of capital punishment in California," THE DEATH PENALTY IN AMERICA edited by H. A. Bedau. Chicago: Aldine Pub., 1964. pp. 322-332.

Great Britain. Home Office. THE CASE OF TIMOTHY JOHN EVANS; report of an inquiry by the Hon. Mr. Justice Brabin. British Information Services, 1966.

Great Britain. MURDER (ABOLITION OF DEATH PENALTY) ACT 1965; ACT TO ABOLISH CAPITAL PUNISHMENT IN THE CASE OF PERSONS CONVICTED IN GREAT BRITAIN OF MURDER OR CONVICTED OF MURDER OR A CORRESPONDING OFFENCE BY COURT-MARTIAL AND, IN CONNECTION THEREWITH, TO MAKE FURTHER PROVISION FOR THE PUNISHMENT OF PERSONS SO CONVICTED. Public General Acts, 1965.

Great Britain. Royal Commission on Capital Punishment. MEMORANDA AND REPLIES TO A QUESTIONNAIRE RECEIVED FROM FOREIGN AND COMMONWEALTH COUNTRIES. London: H. M. Stationery Office, 1951-1953.

—. MINUTES OF EVIDENCE. London: H. M. Stationery Office, 1949-1951.

—. REPORT. London: H. M. Stationery Office, 1953.

Greinwald, Sigisbert. DIE TODESSTRAFE. Westheim bei Augsburg: G. Rost, 1948.

Grenier, Bernard. LA PEINE DE MORT; DONNÉES NOUVELLES, 1965-1972. Ottawa: Information Canada, 1972.

Guillot, E. E. "Abolition and restoration of the death penalty in Missouri," THE DEATH PENALTY IN AMERICA edited by H. A. Bedau. Chicago: Aldine Pub., 1964.

Guizot, François Pierre Guillaume. GIUSTIZIA E POLITICA. A CURA DI ANTONINO REPACI. Torino: Chiantore, 1945.

Gysin, Kurt. TODESSTRAFE UND TODESWURDIGE VERBRECHEN IM SCHWEIZERISCHEN MILITARSTRAFRECHT. Aaru: H. R. Sauerländer, 1953.

Hale, Leslie. HANGED IN ERROR. Harmondsworth, England: Penguin Books, 1961.

Han, Bing Siong. TJARA MELAKSANAKAN HUKUMAN MATI, PADA WAKTU SEKARANG DAN PADA WAKTU JANG LAMPAU. Djakarta: Dimar Sondang, 1960.

Heline, Theodore. CAPITAL PUNISHMENT, HISTORICAL TRENDS TOWARD ITS ABOLISHMENT. Lost Angeles: New Age Press, 1965.

Hentig, Hans von. VOM URSPRUNG DER HENKERSMAHLZEIT. Tübingen: Mohr, 1958.

Hoenigsberg, Julio. ANTE LE PENA DE MUERTE; HOMENAJE A COLOMBIA EN EL CINCUENTENARIO DE HABERSE EXPEDIDO EL ACTO LEGISLATIVO NO. 3 DE 1910, REFORMATORIO DE LA CONSTITUCION NACIONAL DE 1.886, POR EL CUAL SE SUPRIMIO LA PENA CAPITAL. Barranquilla, Columbia: Impr. Departamental, 1962.

Hoffmann, Eduard Hermann. DER RUF NACH DEM SCHARFRICHTER. KRIMINOLOGISCHE ARGUMENTE FUR AND GEGEN DIE TODESSTRAFE. Hamburg: Kriminalistik-Verlag, 1967.

Hollis, Christopher. THE HOMICIDE ACT. London: V. Gollancz, 1964.

Hook, S. "The death sentence," THE DEATH PENALTY IN AMERICA edited by H. A. Bedau. Chicago: Aldine Pub., 1964. pp. 146-154.

Hoover, J. E. "Statements in favor of the death penalty," THE DEATH PENALTY IN AMERICA; an anthology edited by H. A. Bedau. Chicago: Aldine Pub., 1964. pp. 130-135.

Horwitz, Elinor Lander. CAPITAL PUNISHMENT, U.S.A. Philadelphia: Lippincott, 1973.

Huertax Berro, Fermin I. LA PENA DE MUERTE. Montevideo, 1961.

Hugo, Victor Marie. THE LAST DAYS OF A CONDEMNED; CLAUDE GOEUX. (The Novels, complete and Unabridged of Victor Hugo, v. 28). Philadelphia: George Barrie & Son, 1894.

Illinois Commission to Abolish Capital Punishment. DEATH PENALTY. Chicago: The Commission, 1960.

Imbert, Jean. LA PEINE DE MORT. Paris: Presses universitaires de France, 1972.

—. LA PEINE DE MORT, HISTOIRE, ACTUALITÉ. Paris: A. Colin, 1967.

AN INDEX TO ESSAYS ON CAPITAL PUNISHMENT. Philadelphia: Merritt, 1812.

India (Republic). Law Commission. CAPITAL PUNISHMENT, SEPTEMBER, 1967. Delhi: Manager of Publications, 1971.

Ingram, Tolbert Robert. ESSAYS ON THE DEATH PENALTY. Houston: St. Thomas Press, 1963.

Innerst, J. Stewart. IS CAPITAL PUNISHMENT THE ANSWER? Richmond, Indiana: Board of Peace and Social Concern, The Five Years Meeting of Friends, 1959.

Inns of court conservative and unionist society. MURDER: SOME SUGGESTIONS FOR THE REFORM OF THE LAW RELATING TO MURDER IN ENGLAND. London: The Society, 1956.

Italy. Ministero della giustizia e degli affari del culto. NOTIZIE STATISTICHE SULLE CONDANNE ALLA PENA DI MORTE IN ITALIA NEL DECENNIO 1867-1876. Pub. per cura del ministro di grazia e giustizia. Roma: Tipografia Elzerviriana nel Ministero delle finanze, 1878.

Jadhav, Uttamrao Keshavrao. IS CAPITAL PUNISHMENT NECESSARY? Bombay: Anand Pub., 1973.

Johnsen, Julia Emily. CAPITAL PUNISHMENT. (The Reference Shelf. V.13, No. 1). New York: The H. W. Wilson Company, 1939.

Johnson, E. H. "Executions and commutations in North Carolina," THE DEATH PENALTY IN AMERICA edited by H. A. Bedau. Chicago: Aldine Pub., 1964. pp. 452-463.

Jones, Barry O. THE PENALTY IS DEATH; CAPITAL PUNISHMENT IN THE TWENTIETH CENTURY, RETENTIONIST AND ABOLITIONIST ARGUMENTS WITH SPECIAL REFERENCE TO AUSTRALIA. Melbourne: Sun Books in association with the Anti-Hanging Council of Victoria, 1968.

Joyce, James Avery. CAPITAL PUNISHMENT, A WORLD VIEW. New York: T. Nelson, 1961.

—. THE RIGHT TO LIFE; A WORLD VIEW OF CAPITAL PUNISHMENT. London: Gollancz, 1962.

Jungblut, Tony. DAS HENKERBUCH. Luxemburg: Verlag des "Tageblatt," 1953.

Kazis, I. J. "Judaism and the death penalty," THE DEATH PENALTY IN AMERICA edited by H. A. Bedau. Chicago: Aldine Pub., 1964. pp. 171-174.

Keller, Albrecht. DER SCHARFRICHTER IN DER DEUTSCHEN KULTURGESCHICHTE. MIT EINEM VORWORT VON CHRISTIAN HELFER. Hildesheim: G. Olms, 1968.

Keller, Dieter. DIE TODESSTRAFE IN KRITISCHER SICHT. Berlin: De. Gruyter, 1968.

Kentucky. Legislative Research Commission. CAPITAL PUNISHMENT. Frankfort: The Commission, 1965.

Kevorkian, Jack. MEDICAL RESEARCH AND THE DEATH PENALTY; A DIALOGUE. New York: Vantage Press, 1960.

Klare, Hugh J. NOTES ON CAPITAL PUNISHMENT. London: Howard League for Penal Reform, 1963.

Koestler, Arthur. HANGED BY THE NECK; AN EXPOSURE OF CAPITAL PUNISHMENT IN ENGLAND. Baltimore: Penguin Books, 1961.

—. REFLECTIONS ON HANGING. London: Gollancz, 1956, 1957.

—. REFLECTIONS ON HANGING. New York: Macmillan, 1957.

—. THE TRAIL OF THE DINOSAUR AND REFLECTIONS ON HANGING. London: Hutchinson, 1970.

Krimpen, Hendrik van. DOODSTRAF EN CASSATIE IN DE BIJZONDERE RECHTSPLEGING. Leiden: E. J. Brill, 1947.

Kuebler, Jeanne. PUNISHMENT BY DEATH. (Editorial Research Reports, v. 2, No. 3). Washington, D.C.: Government Printing Office, 1963.

Kunstler, William M. BEYOND REASONABLE DOUBT? THE ORIGINAL TRIAL OF CARYL CHESSMAN. New York: William Morrow, 1961.

Lawes, Lewis Edward. MAN'S JUDGMENT OF DEATH; AN ANALYSIS OF THE OPERATION AND EFFECT OF CAPITAL PUNISHMENT BASED ON FACTS, NOT ON SENTIMENT. Montclair: Patterson Smith, 1969.

Legislative Council Committee on Capital Punishment. REPORT OF THE LEGISLATIVE COUNCIL COMMITTEE ON CAPITAL PUNISH-MENT. Baltimore: The Council, 1962.

Leigh, Ruth. MAN'S RIGHT TO LIFE. (Issues of Conscience 3). New York: Committee on Social Action of Reform Judaism, 1959.

Leopold, Nathan F. LIFE PLUS 99 YEARS. New York: Doubleday, 1961.

Lewis, C. S., et al. ESSAYS ON THE DEATH PENALTY. Houston: St. Thomas, 1971.

Lippens, Louis. FACE A LA PEINE DE MORT. GRAVURES ORIGIN-ALS INÉDITES DE DIDIER RAYNAL. Linselles: Nor "Élan poétique et littéraire," 1968.

Lira, Jorge Buarque. A PENA DE MORTE; OU, "UMA LAGRIMA NO OLHO DE LEI" (DE TALIAO A CHESSMAN) Prefacio de Roberto Lyra: Niteroi, 1961.

Lunden, Walter A. THE DEATH PENALTY, AN ANALYSIS OF CHAPI-TAL PUNISHMENT AND FACTORS RELATED TO MURDER. Anamosa: Iowa State Reformatory Printing Department, 1960.

Lunden, Walter A. THE DEATH PENALTY, AN ANALYSIS OF CAPI-PENALTY? Ames: Iowa Art Press, 1969.

Lutheran Church of America. CAPITAL PUNISHMENT. (Study Report No. 5, April, 1966). New York: Lutheran Church of America Board of Social Ministry, 1966.

McCafferty, James A. CAPITAL PUNISHMENT. Chicago, Aldine-Atherton, 1972.

—. CAPITAL PUNISHMENT IN THE UNITED STATES: 1930-1952. Columbus: Ohio State University. The Graduate School, 1954.

—. "The death sentence, 1960," THE DEATH PENALTY IN AMERICA edited by H. A. Bedau. Chicago: Aldine Pub., 1964. pp. 90-103.

McClellan, Grant S. CAPITAL PUNISHMENT. New York: Wilson, 1961.

McGehee, Edward G. THE DEATH PENALTY: A LITERARY AND HISTORICAL APPROACH. Boston: Heath, 1964.

McGrath, W. T. SHOULD CANADA ABOLISH THE GALLOWS AND THE LASH? Winnipeg: Stovel, 1956.

Machlin, Milton. NINTH LIFE. New York: G. P. Putnam's Sons, 1961.

Mackey, Philip E. VOICES AGAINST DEATH: CLASSIC APPEALS AGAINST THE DEATH PENALTY IN AMERICA 1787-1974. Philadelphia: B. Franklin, 1976.

✳ MacNamara, D.E.J. "Statement against capital punishment," THE DEATH PENALTY IN AMERICA edited by H. A. Bedau. Chicago: Aldine Pub., 1964. pp. 182-194.

Maddocks, Charles Prentiss. THE ETHICAL JUSTIFICATION OF CAPITAL PUNISHMENT: A METAMORPHOSIS. (Louisiana. University of Southwestern Louisiana, Lafayette. Master's theses). Lafayette, Louisiana: University of Southwestern Louisiana, 1976.

Marchesan, Marco. LA PENA DI MORTE DAI PUNTI DI VISTA PSICOLOGICO E TEOLOGICO. Milano: Istituto di indagini psicologiche, 1965.

Marcus, Michael H. THE DEATH PENALTY CASES. Berkeley: School of Law, University of California, 1968. pp. 1268-1490.

Maryland. Legislative Council. Committee on Capital Punishment. REPORT. Baltimore, 1962.

Mas Godayol, José. HISTORIA DE LA PENA DE MUERTE. Barcelona: Editorial Trimer, 1961.

Mas, J. LA PENA DE MUERTE. Barcelona: Bruguera, 1971.

Massachusetts. Special Commission Relative to the Abolition of the Death Penalty in Capital Cases. REPORT AND RECOMMENDATIONS. Boston: Wright & Potter Print. Co., 1959.

Mattick, Hans W. THE UNEXAMINED DEATH. Chicago: John Howard Association, 1963.

Meador, Roy. CAPITAL REVENGE: FIFTY-FOUR VOTES AGAINST LIFE. Ardmore: Dorrance, 1975.

Meisl, Rudolf. DIE RECHTMASSIGKEIT DER TODESSTRAFE. Horn: Berger, 1966.

Meltsner, Michael. CRUEL AND UNUSUAL; THE SUPREME COURT AND CAPITAL PUNISHMENT. New York: Random House, 1973; paper edition New York: W. Morrow, 1974.

Mencker, August. BY THE NECK; A BOOK OF HANGINGS, SELECTED FROM CONTEMPORARY ACCOUNTS. New York: Hastings House, 1942.

Milligan, C. S. "A Protestant's view of the death penalty," THE DEATH PENALTY IN AMERICA edited by H. A. Bedau. Chicago: Aldine Pub., 1964. pp. 175-182.

Montarron, Marcel. LA VEUVE; OU, L'HISTOIRE DES CHATIMENTS. Paris: Plon, 1973.

Munoz Leon, José. LA PENA CAPITAL; SU JUSTIFICACION Y LA NECESIDAD DE SU APLICACION EN MÉXICO. México, 1954.

Naud, Albert Léopold. L'AGONIE DE LA PEINE DE MORT? Paris: La Table ronde, 1972.

—. TU NE TUERAS PAS. Paris: Morgan, 1960; Paris: La Table ronde, 1963.

New Jersey. Assembly. Judiciary Committee. SECOND PUBLIC HEAR-
ING ON ASSEMBLY BILLS NOS. 33 AND 34 (abolition of capital
punishment), held, Trenton, New Jersey, June 19, 1958. Trenton:
The Assembly, 1958.

New Jersey. Capital Punishment Study Commission. REPORT TO GOV-
ERNOR WILLIAM T. CAHILL, FINAL REPORT. Trenton: The Commission, 1973.

New Jersey. Commission to Study Capital Punishment. BIBLIOGRAPHY.
Trenton: The Commission, 1964.

New Jersey. COMMISSION APPOINTED TO STUDY CAPITAL PUNISH-
MENT PURSUANT TO SENATE JOINT RES. NO. 3. PUBLIC HEAR-
ING, JULY 10, 1964. Trenton: The Commission, 1964.

New Jersey. COMMISSION APPOINTED TO STUDY CAPITAL PUN-
ISHMENT. PUBLIC HEARING, HELD JULY 24, 1964, ASSEMBLY
CHAMBER, STATE HOUSE. Trenton: The Commission, 1964.

New Jersey. Commission to Study Capital Punishment. REPORT. Trenton: The Commission, 1964.

New Jersey. Legislature. General Assembly. Committee on Institutions,
Public Health and Welfare. PUBLIC HEARING ON ASSEMBLY
BILLS NOS. 19 AND 21 (concerning abolition of capital punishment
and providing for sentences of imprisonment for life). Trenton: The
Committee, 1957.

New Jersey. Legislature. General Assembly. Judiciary Committee. PUB-
LIC HEARING ON ASSEMBLY BILLS NOS. 33 AND 34 (abolition of
capital punishment). Trenton: The Committee, 1958.

—. PUBLIC HEARING ON ASSEMBLY BILL NO. 90 (Abolish the death
penalty in New Jersey). Trenton: The Committee, 1970.

—. PUBLIC HEARING BEFORE ASSEMBLY JUDICIARY COMMITTEE
ON SENATE BILL NO. 799 AND ASSEMBLY BILLS 556 AND
1318 (death penalty). Trenton: The Committee, 1972.

—. PUBLIC HEARING BEFORE ASSEMBLY JUDICIARY COMMITTEE
ON PROPOSED AMENDMENTS TO SENATE BILL NO. 799 (Death

penalty bill). Trenton: The Committee, 1973.

New York State. ACT TO AMEND THE PENAL LAW AND THE CODE OF CRIMINAL PROCEDURE, IN RELATION TO ABOLISHING CAPITAL PUNISHMENT. Laws, 1965.

New York State. Legislature. Assembly. Selected Committee on Capital Punishment. REPORT IN FAVOR OF THE ABOLITION OF THE PUNISHMENT OF DEATH BY LAW by John L. O'Sullivan. New York: Arno Press, 1974.

New York State. TEMPORARY COMMITTEE ON REVISION OF THE PENAL LAW AND CRIMINAL CODE. FOURTH INTERIM REPORT. Albany, 1965.

The New York Times. "Juveniles and capital punishment," THE DEATH PENALTY IN AMERICA edited by H. A. Bedau. Chicago: Aldine Pub., 1964. pp. 52-56.

Nunez, David. LA PENA DE MUERTE, FRENTE A LA IGLESIA Y AL ESTADO. Buenos Aires: Organizacion San José, 1970.

O'Donnell, Bernard. SHOULD WOMEN HANG? London: W. H. Allen, 1956.

Ohio. Legislative Service Commission. CAPITAL PUNISHEMNT; LEGIS-LATIVE IMPLICATIONS OF U.S. SUPREME COURT DECISION IN FURMAN v. GEORGIA. Columbus: The Commission, 1972.

—. CAPITAL PUNISHMENT; REPORT. Columbus: The Commission, 1961.

ON CAPITAL PUNISHMENT: IS IT TORTURE? Santa Barbara: Center for the Study of Democratic Institutions, 1969.

ON CAPITAL PUNISHMENT: WHO PAYS FOR THE DEATH PENAL-TY? Santa Barbara: Center for the Study of Democratic Institutions, 1969.

O'Sullivan, John L. REPORT IN FAVOR OF THE ABOLITION OF THE PUNISHMENT OF DEATH BY LAW, MADE TO LEGISLATURE OF THE STATE OF NEW YORK APRIL 14, 1841. New York: Arno,

1974.

Pennsylvania. General Assembly. Joint Legislative Committee on Capital Punishment. REPORT. Harrisburg: The Committee, 1961.

Pennsylvania. Governor's Study Commission on Capital Punishment. REPORT. Harrisburg: The Commission, 1973.

Phillipson, Coleman. THREE CRIMINAL LAW REFORMERS: BECCARIA, BENTHAM, ROMILLY. Montclair: P. Smith, 1970.

Playfair, Giles. THE OFFENDERS; THE CASE AGAINST LEGAL VENGEANCE. New York: Simon and Schuster, 1957.

—. THE OFFENDERS; SOCIETY AND THE ATROCIOUS CRIME. London: Secker & Warburg, 1957.

Poenaru, Iulian. CONTRIBUTII LA STUDIUL PEDEPSEI CAPITALE/ IULIAN POENARU. Bucuresti: Editura Academiei Republicii Socialiste Romania, 1974.

Poland. Laws, statutes, etc. ARTYKULY PRAWA MAJDEBURSKIEGO. POSTEPEK SADOW OKOLO KARANIA NA GARDLE. USTAWA PLACEJ U SADOW. RED. ORAZ WSTEP I OBJASNIENIA KAROLA KORANYIEGO; PRZEKLAD TEKSTOW LACINKICH JAKUBA SAWICKIEGO. Warszawa, Wydawn. Prawnicze, 1954.

Polsby, D. P. "The death of capital punishment? Furman vs. Georgia," THE SUPREME COURT REVIEW. 1972. Chicago: University of Chicago Press, 1974. pp. 1-40.

Potter, John Deane. THE ART OF HANGING. South Brunswick: A. S. Barnes, 1969.

—. THE FATAL GALLOWS TREE. London: Elek, 1965.

Prettyman, Barrett. DEATH AND THE SUPREME COURT. New York: Harcourt, Brace & World, 1961.

PRISON JOURNAL FOR OCTOBER 1958, IS ENTITLED, CAPITAL PUNISHMENT. PARTIAL CONTENTS ARE: SURVEY OF THE DEBATE ON CAPITAL PUNISHMENT IN CANADA, ENGLAND, AND

THE UNITED STATES. 1948-1958, by Hugo Adam Bedau; A brief history of capital punishement in Pennsylvania by Leonard D. Savitz; Pennsylvania criminal homicide and execution statistics.

Pritchard, John Laurence. A HISTORY OF CAPITAL PUNISHMENT, WITH SPECIAL REFERENCE TO CAPITAL PUNISHMENT IN GREAT BRITAIN. Port Washington: Kennikat Press, 1971.

Quiroz Cuaron, Alfonso. LA PENA DE MUERTE EN MÉXICO. México: Ediciones Botas, 1962.

Randall, Peter. THE DEATH PENALTY AND THE CHURCH IN SOUTH AFRICA; A STUDY DOCUMENT FOR SOUTH AFRICAN CHRISTIANS. Braamfontein: South African Council of Churches, 1970.

Reid, Don. EYEWITNESS. Houston: Cordovan Press, 1973.

REPORT OF NEW JERSEY COMMISSION TO STUDY CAPITAL PUNISHMENT. Trenton: New Jersey State Library. Department of Education, 1964.

Rosal, Juan del. 4 (i.e. Cuatro) PENAS DE MUERTE, 4. Madrid: Instituto de Criminologia, 1973.

Rossa, Kurt. TODESSTRAFEN. IHRE WIRKLICHKEIT IN DREI JAHRTAUSENDEN. Oldenburg und Hamburg: Staling, 1966.

Roucek, Joseph S. CAPITAL PUNISHMENT. (Topics of our Times, No. 15). Charlottesville: Samhar Press, 1975.

—. CAPITAL PUNISHMENT IN ITS LEGAL AND SOCIAL ASPECTS. Bridgeport: The Author, 1971.

—. CAPITAL PUNISHMENT IN THE USSR. Bridgeport: The Author, 1974.

Ruler, Arnold Albert van. VISIE EN VAART. Amsterdam: Holland Uitgeversmaatschappij, 1947.

Russell, Francis. TRAGEDY IN DEDHAM: THE STORY OF THE SACCO-VANZETTI CASE. New York: McGraw-Hill, 1962.

24

St. John-Stevas, Norman. THE RIGHT TO LIFE. New York: Holt, Rinehart and Winston, 1964; London: Hodder and Stoughton, 1963.

Saleh, Roeslan. MAS'ALAH PIDANA MATI. Jogjakarta: Public Relations Badan Koordinasi, 1959.

Savey-Casard, Paul. LA PEINE DE MORT. ESQUISSE HISTORIQUE ET JURIDIQUE. PRÉFACE DE FRANÇOIS PERROUX. Genève: Droz, 1968.

Savitz, L. D. "The deterrent effect of capital punishment in Philadelphia," THE DEATH PENALTY IN AMERICA edited by H. A. Bedau. Chicago: Aldine Pub., 1964. pp. 315-322.

Scher, J. M. "Death—the Giver of Life," THE INTERPRETATION OF DEATH. (Ruitenbeek). New York: J' Aronson, 1973. pp. 96-105.

Schierbeck, Ole. DODSDOMT. Kobenhavn: Bogan: eksp. DEK, 1974.

Schreiber, Hermann. GOTTERSPRUCH UND HENKERHAND. DIE TODESSTRAFEN IN DER GESCHICHTE DER MENSCHHEIT. Von Ludwig Barring. (Bergisch-Gladbach) Lübbe, 1967.

Schultz, Hermann. DAS TODESRECHT IM ALTEN TESTAMENT. STUDIEN Z. RECHTSFORM D. MOT-JUMAT-SATZE. Berlin: Töpelmann, 1969.

✗ Scott, George Ryley. THE HISTORY OF CAPITAL PUNISHMENT, INCLUDING AN EXAMINATION OF THE CASE FOR AND AGAINST THE DEATH PENALTY. London: Torchstream Books, 1950.

Sellin, Johan Thorsten. CAPITAL PUNISHMENT. New York: Harper & Row, 1969.

—. "Death and imprisonment as deterrents to murder," DEATH PENALTY IN AMERICA edited by H. A. Bedau. Chicago: Aldine Pub., 1964. pp. 274-284.

—. THE DEATH PENALTY; A REPORT FOR THE MODEL PENAL CODE PROJECT OF THE AMERICAN LAW INSTITUTE. Philadelphia: Executive Office, American Law Institute, 1959.

25

—. "Does the death penalty protect municipal police? " THE DEATH PENALTY IN AMERICA edited by H. A. Bedau. Chicago: Aldine Pub., 1964.

—. "Effect of repeal and reintroduction of the death penalty on homicide rates," THE DEATH PENALTY IN AMERICA edited by H. A. Bedau. Chicago: Aldine Pub., 1964.

Sewing, Johanna. STUDIEN ZUR TODESSTRAFE IM NATURRECHT. Bonn: Röhrscheid, 1966.

Sharp, Malcom P. WAS JUSTICE DONE? THE ROSENBERG-SOBELL CASE. New York: Monthly Review Press, 1956.

Shelly, P. B. "Essay on the punishment of death,.. SHELLEY'S PROSE; OR THE TRUMPET OF A PROPHECY edited by David Lee Clark. Alberquerque: University of New Mexico Press, 1954. pp. 154-158.

Smith, Charles L. CAPITAL PUNISHMENT. A SELECTED BIBLIOGRAPHY. Berkeley: Friends Committee on Legislation, 1969.

Sonnenfels, Josef von. UEBER DIE ABSCHAFFUNG DER TORTUR. Zürich: Orell, Gessner Fuesslin und Co., 1775.

Ström, Folke. ON THE SACRAL ORIGIN OF GERMANIC DEATH PENALTIES. Stockholm: Wahlström & Widstrand, 1942.

Strub, Bettina. DER EINFLUSS DER AUFKLARUNG AUF DIE TODESSTRAFE. Zürich: Juris-Verlag, 1973.

Sturm, Friedrich. SYMBOLISCHE TODESSTRAFEN. Hamburg: Kriminalistik Verlag, 1962.

Suarez Ramirez, Jeronimo. LA PENA DE MUERTE EN EL FUERO DE GUERRA. México, 1959.

Subramanyam, Karattoluvu Ganapati. CAN THE STATE KILL ITS CITIZEN? Madras: Madras Law Journal Office, 1969.

Sueiro, Daniel. EL ARTE DE MATAR. Madrid: Alfaguara, 1968.

—. LA PENA DE MUERTE: CEREMONIAL, HISTORIA, PROCEDI-

MIENTOS. Madrid: Alianza Editorial, 1974.

Teeters, Negley King. SCAFFOLD AND CHAIR; A COMPILATION OF THEIR USE IN PENNSYLVANIA, 1682-1962. Philadelphia, 1963.

Templewood, Samuel John Gurney Hoare. THE SHADOW OF THE GALLOWS. London: Gollancz, 1951.

Thomas, P. A. "Attitudes of wardens toward the death penalty," THE DEATH PENALTY IN AMERICA edited by H. A. Bedau. Chicago: Aldine Pub., 1964. pp. 242-252.

Thomas, Trevor. THIS LIFE WE TAKE; A CASE AGAINST THE DEATH PENALTY. San Francisco: Friends Committee on Legislation, 1970.

Tidmarsh, Mannes. CAPITAL PUNISHMENT: A CASE FOR ABOLITION. London, New York: Sheed and Ward, 1963.

Todesstrafe? THEOLOGISCHE UND JURISTISCHE ARGUMENTE. MIT BEITRAGEN VON MARTIN DORFMULLER. Stuttgard: Kreuz-Verlag, 1960.

Tuttle, Elizabeth Ann (Orman). THE CRUSADE AGAINST CAPITAL PUNISHMENT IN GREAT BRITAIN. London, Stevens; Chicago: Quadrangle Books, 1961.

United Nations. Department of Economic and Social Affairs. CAPITAL PUNISHMENT. New York, 1962.

—. CAPITAL PUNISHMENT: DEVELOPMENT 1961-1965. New York: 1965.

United Nations. Economic and Social Council. CAPITAL PUNISHMENT: NOTE BY THE SECRETARY-GENERAL. New York: United Nations, 1971.

United Nations. Economic and Social Council. Social Committee. CAPITAL PUNISHMENT; REPORT. New York, 1971.

U. S. Army. Judge Advocate General. International Affairs Division. CAPITAL PUNISHMENT IN THE SOVIET UNION by Foreign Law Branch, International Affairs Division, Office of the Judge Advocate

General, Department of the Army. Washington, 1963.

U. S. Bureau of Prisons. "Executions 1962," THE DEATH PENALTY IN AMERICA edited by H. A. Bedau. Chicago: Aldine Pub., 1964. pp. 103-119.

—. NATIONAL PRISONER STATISTICS: CAPITAL PUNISHMENT. Washington.

—. LIBRARY. CAPITAL PUNISHMENT: A BIBLIOGRAPHY. Washington, D.C.: The Library, 1970.

U. S. Congress. House of Representatives. AMENDING SECTION 801, OF ACT TO ESTABLISH CODE OF LAW FOR DISTRICT OF COLUMBIA APPROVED MARCH 3, 1901. REPORT TO THE COMMITTEE ON DISTRICT OF COLUMBIA TO ACCOMPANY H. R. 12483, HOUSE REPORT ON PUBLIC BILLS, 86th CONGRESS. Washington: GPO, June 15, 1960.

—. AMENDING SECTION 801 OF ACT ESTABLISHING CODE OF LAW FOR DISTRICT OF COLUMBIA. REPORT FROM COMMITTEE ON DISTRICT OF COLUMBIA TO ACCOMPANY H. R. 5143, JUNE 29, 1961. (RELATES TO MANDATORY DEATH PENALTY FOR 1st DEGREE MURDER. INCLUDES MINORITY VIEW.) Washington: GPO, 1961.

—. PUBLIC LAWS H. R. 5143, ACT TO AMEND SECTION 801 OF ACT ENTITLED ACT TO ESTABLISH CODE OF LAW FOR DISTRICT OF COLUMBIA, APPROVED MARCH 3, 1901, APPROVED MARCH 22, 1962. Washington: GPO, 1962.

U. S. Congress. House. Committee on the Judiciary. ABOLITION OF CAPITAL PUNISHMENT. HEARING BEFORE SUBCOMMITTEE NO. 2 ON H. R. 870, TO ABOLISH THE DEATH PENALTY UNDER ALL LAWS OF THE UNITED STATES EXCEPT THE UNIFORM CODE OF MILITARY JUSTICE, AND AUTHORIZE THE IMPOSITION OF LIFE IMPRISONMENT IN LIEU THEREOF. MAY 25, 1960. Washington: GPO, 1960.

—. SUBCOMMITTEE NO. 2. ABOLITION OF CAPITAL PUNISHMENT: HEARING MAY 25, 1960, ON H. R. 870 TO ABOLISH THE DEATH PENALTY UNDER ALL LAWS OF THE UNITED STATES EXCEPT

THE UNIFORM CODE OF MILITARY JUSTICE, AND AUTHORIZE THE IMPOSITION OF LIFE IMPRISONMENT IN LIEU THEREOF. Washington: GPO, 1960.

U. S. Congress. House. Committee on the Judiciary. Subcommittee No. 3. CAPITAL PUNISHMENT. HEARINGS, NINETY-SECOND CONGRESS, SECOND SESSION. Washington: GPO, 1972.

U. S. Congress. House of Representatives. Judiciary Committee. ABOLITION OF CAPITAL PUNISHMENT, HEARINGS BEFORE THE SUBCOMMITTEE. NO. 2. 86th CONGRESS, 2d SESSION. Washington: GPO, 1961.

U. S. Congress. Senate. AMENDING SECTION 801 OF ACT TO ESTABLISH CODE OF LAW FOR DISTRICT OF COLUMBIA, APPROVED MARCH 3, 1961. REPORT FROM COMMITTEE ON DISTRICT OF COLUMBIA, TO ACCOMPANY 5. 1380. Washington: GPO, June 14, 1961.

U. S. Congress. Senate. Committee on the Judiciary. Subcommittee on Criminal Laws and Procedures. IMPOSITION OF CAPITAL PUNISHMENT. HEARING, NINETY-THIRD CONGRESS, FIRST SESSION, ON S. 1, S. 1400, and S. 1401. Washington: GPO, 1973.

—. TO ABOLISH THE DEATH PENALTY. HEARINGS, NINETIETH CONGRESS, SECOND SESSION, ON S. 1760. MARCH 20, 21, AND JULY 2, 1968. Washington: GPO, 1970.

U. S. Federal Bureau of Prisons. NATIONAL PRISONER STATISTICS: EXECUTIONS, 1956. Washington: GPO, 1957.

U. S. Justice Department. Prisons Bureau. CAPITAL PUNISHMENT. A BIBLIOGRAPHY. Washington: GPO, 1971.

—. NATIONAL PRISONER STATISTICS, NPS BULLETIN, CAPITAL PUNISHMENT, 1930-1968. Washington: GPO, 1969.

—. NATIONAL PRISON STATISTICS. EXECUTIONS, 1961. Washington: GPO, 1962.

—. NATIONAL PRISONER STATISTICS, NPS BULLETIN. EXECUTIONS, 1930-1966. Washington: GPO, 1967.

29

—. NATIONAL PRISONER STATISTICS, NPS BULLETIN. EXECU-
TIONS, 1930-1967. Washington: GPO, 1967.

University of Chicago Law Review Staff. CRIMINAL JUSTICE IN EX-
TREMIS: ADMINISTRATION OF JUSTICE DURING THE APRIL
1968 CHICAGO DISORDER. Chicago: American Bar Forum, 1969.

Vellenga, J. J. "Christianity and the death penalty," THE DEATH PEN-
ALTY IN AMERICA edited by H. A. Bedau. Chicago: Aldine Pub.,
1965. pp. 123-130.

Villegas Angel, Camilo. LA PENA DE MUERTE. Cartagena: Colombia,
1965.

Volandt, Erich. CHRISTLICHER GLAUBE UND TODESSTRAFE. Glad-
beck/Westf.: Schriftenmissions-Verlag, 1966.

Weihofen, Henry. THE URGE TO PUNISH; NEW APPROACHES TO THE
PROBLEM OF MENTAL IRRESPONSIBILITY FOR CRIME. New
York: Farrar, Straus, and Cudahy, 1956; London: V. Gollancz, 1957.

Weittstein, Erich. DIE GESCHICHTE DER TODESSTRAFE IM KANTON
ZURICH. Winterthur: H. Schellenberg, 1958.

Wexley, John. THE JUDGMENT OF JULIUS AND ETHEL ROSENBERG.
New York: Cameron and Rahn, 1955.

Williams, Brad. DUE PROCESS: THE FABULOUS STORY OF CRIMI-
NAL LAWYER GEORGE T. DAVIS AND HIS THIRTY-YEAR BAT-
TLE AGAINST CAPITAL PUNISHMENT. Caldwell: Morrow, 1960.

Wisconcon. Legislative Reference Bureau. THE DEATH PENALTY:
LEGAL STATUS SINCE FURMAN. Madison: The Reference Bureau,
1973.

Wolf, Ernst. NATURRECHT ODER CHRISTUSRECHT; TODESSTRAFE.
Berlin: Vog, 1960.

Wolfe, Burton H. PILEUP ON DEATH ROW. Garden City, New York:
Doubleday, 1973.

Wright, Elizur. PERFORATIONS IN THE "LATTER-DAY PAMPHLETS,"

BY ONE OF THE EIGHTEEN MILLIONS OF BORES. Freeport:
Books for Libraries Press, 1972.

Yallop, David A. TO ENCOURAGE THE OTHERS. New York: St. Martin's, 1974.

Yoder, John Howard. THE CHRISTIAN AND CAPITAL PUNISHMENT.
Newton: Faith and Life Press, 1961.

SUBJECT INDEX TO PERIODICAL LITERATURE

ABBOTT, B. W.
see: Executions and Executioners

ADOLESCENTS AND CAPITAL PUNISHMENT
Australian adolescents to crime and punishment, by D. Watkins, et al. AUSTRALIAN AND NEW ZEALAND JOURNAL OF SOCIOL-OGY 11(2):62-64, June, 1975.

British cry murder as a boy is hanged. LIFE 34:22-23, February 9, 1953.

Capital punishment in the case of women and adolescents. JUSTICE OF THE PEACE 117:669, October 17, 1953.

Two boys and the death penalty. TIME 91:64-65, February 2, 1968.

NEWSPAPER ARTICLES

Causes of crime go deeper. CHRISTIAN SCIENCE MONITOR 21:2, March 17, 1966, (Eastern Edition); 15:1, March 17, 1966 (Western and Midwestern Edition).

Joey Kagebien is 16 and on death row in DeWitt, Ark., for the slaying of a hunter. THE NATIONAL OBSERVER 11/13-6, 1971.

R. Reed comments on Cummins (Ark.) Prison Farm inmate J. N. Kagebien, youngest person in U.S. under death sentence, and his waiting for U.S. Supreme Court ruling on capital punishment. NEW YORK TIMES 14:4, January 22, 1972.

What about Ruby? CHRISTIAN SCIENCE MONITOR 17:1, March

13, 1964, (Eastern Edition); 15:1, March 13, 1964, (Western Edition); 19:1, March 13, 1964, (Midwestern Edition).

ALGERIA

NEWSPAPER ARTICLES

Algerian President Boumedienne, on July 4, reprieves all Algerian prisoners condemned to death, changes their sentences to prison terms. NEW YORK TIMES 37:2, July 5, 1972.

Death penalty set for serious economic crimes. NEW YORK TIMES 13:1, July 17, 1966.

AMERICAN CIVIL LIBERTIES UNION
A.C.L.U. attacks capital punishment. CHRISTIAN CENTURY 82: 1150, September 22, 1965.

NEWSPAPER ARTICLES

ACLU, New Jersey State Association on Correction and Coalition on Penal Reform attack plan for public hearing on death penalty proposal, saying it is politically motivated because it comes in midst of gubernatorial and legislative election campaign; hearing is set for September 13. NEW YORK TIMES 74:2, September 10, 1973.

ACLU of Northern California and NAACP challenge capital punishment in California Supreme Court, Anderson and Saterfield cases; claim Death Row inmates are denied right to counsel after State Supreme Court review of their sentences, that so-called 'scrupled' jurors, those opposed to death penalty, are excluded from hearing capital cases, and that juries in such cases are without standards or guidelines in reaching decision. NEW YORK TIMES 67:1, June 9, 1968.

ACLU Southern California chapter voices doubt about construction of voter-approved measure to restore death penalty in state for certain crimes, but does not plan to file suit against it at this time; death penalty issue was placed on ballot by California Prison Guards Association after US Supreme Court outlawed state's death penalty as unconstructive; guards association measure establishes mandatory death penalty for killing prison guard, train wrecking with injuries, perjury resulting in death of innocent person and treason against California. NEW YORK TIMES 38:2, November 12, 1972.

American civil liberties union opposes. CHRISTIAN SCIENCE MONITOR 2:5, June 22, 1965, (Eastern Edition); 2:3, June 22, 1965, (Midwestern Edition).

California Superior Court rules California death penalty is constitutional even in cases where murder has not been committed, ACLU suit; holds penalty does not constitute cruel and unusual punishment. NEW YORK TIMES 43:8, November 28, 1967.

U.S. Appeals Court refuses Attorney General Lynch request that it set aside stays; NAACP Legal Defense Fund and ACLU aides hail move. NEW YORK TIMES 20:1, July 11, 1967.

AMERICAN LEAGUE TO ABOLISH CAPITAL PUNISHMENT
Comment on movement in U.S. to abolish penalty; December, 1964 letter from late Justice Frankfurter to Mrs. S. Ehrmann, executive director of American League to Abolish Capital Punishment, hailing British Commons vote to abolish penalty quoted. NEW YORK TIMES IV,10:1, February 28, 1965.

ANGOLA
Execution of Daniel Gearhart in Angola; statements, July 9-10, 1976, by R. H. Nessen, et al. DEPARTMENT OF STATE BULLETIN 75:163, August 2, 1976.

ARGENTINA
NEWSPAPER ARTICLES

Argentina President Lanusse abolishes death penalty in nation on December 30; capital punishment had been reintroduced in June, 1970. NEW YORK TIMES 36:4, December 31, 1972.

AS DETERRENCE
Capital punishment and deterrence: some considerations in dialogue form, by D. A. Conway. PHILOSOPHY AND PUBLIC AFFAIRS

3:431-443, Summer, 1974.

Capital punishment and its deterrent effect, by G. Schedler. SOCIAL THEORY AND PRACTICE 4:47-56, Fall, 1976.

Capital punishment: does it deter or degrade? [with a list entitled], "Where the states stand on capital punishment—two years after U.S. Supreme court decision." CONGRESSIONAL QUARTERLY WEEKLY REPORT 32:1419-1422, June 1, 1974.

Capital punishment: does it prevent crime?, by F. J. Cook. NATION 182:194-198, March 10, 1956; Discussion, 182:363-364, April 28, 1956; inside cover, May 5, 1956.

Capital punishment; effects of abolition. ECONOMIST 213:950+, November 28, 1964.

Capital punishment; effects of the death penalty; data and deliberations from the social sciences; symposium, edited by H. Bedau. AMERICAN JOURNAL OF ORTHOPSYCHIATRY 45:580-726, July, 1975.

Crime and punishment, by J. V. Barry. AUSTRALIAN LAW JOURNAL 30:119, July, 1956.

Death penalty as a deterrent: argument and evidence, by H. A. Bedau. ETHICS 80:205-217, April, 1970; Reply with rejoinder by E. van den Haag, 81:74-76, October, 1970.

The death penalty in the United States. ANNALS OF THE AMERICAN ACADEMY OF POLITICAL AND SOCIAL SCIENCE pp. 45-100, November, 1952.

Deterrence and the death penalty: a reconsideration, by H. A. Bedau. JOURNAL OF CRIMINAL LAW AND CRIMINOLOGY 61:539, December, 1970.

Deterrence: certainty, severity, and skyjacking [does the additional severity of capital punishment over life imprisonment serve to deter potential criminals, specifically skyjackers?], by R. Chauncey. CRIMINOLOGY 12:447-473, February, 1975.

Deterrent effect of capital punishment: a question of life and death, by I. Ehrlich. AMERICAN ECONOMIC REVIEW 65:397-417, June, 1975.

Deterrent effect of the death penalty: facts v. faiths, by H. Zeisel. SUPREME COURT REVIEW 1976:317-343, 1976.

Deterrent effect of the death penalty: a statistical test, by P. Passell. STANFORD LAW REVIEW 28:61-80, November, 1975.

Deterrent effect of punishment, by F. Brooker. CRIMINOLOGY 9:469, February, 1972.

Deterrent to the deterrent argument; death penalty. CHRISTIAN CENTURY 94:132-133, February 16, 1977.

Does punishment deter crime?, by J. Andenaes. CRIMINAL LAW QUARTERLY 11:76, November, 1968.

Nixon administration and the deterrent effect of the death penalty, by H. A. Bedau. UNIVERSITY OF PITTSBURGH LAW REVIEW 34:557-566, Summer, 1973.

On deterrence and the death penalty, by E. van den Haag. ETHICS 78:280-288, July, 1968.

—. JOURNAL OF CRIMINAL LAW AND CRIMINOLOGY 60:141, June, 1969.

Prosecutors may no longer tell juries capital punishment is a known deterrent: historic California Supreme court decision. CALIFORNIAN 3:5, February, 1962.

Royal Commission on Capital Punishment—death and deterrence, by G. H. L. Fridman. SOLICITOR 22:80-82, March, 1955.

Statistical evidence on the deterrent effect of capital punishment—A comparison of the work of Thorsten Sellin and Isaac Ehrlich on the deterrent effect of capital punishment, by D. C. Baldus, et al. YALE LAW JOURNAL 85:164-227, December, 1975.

NEWSPAPER ARTICLES

A. Lewis discusses issue under study in GB and US; holds death penalty has not proved to be an effective deterrent, serves mainly to satisfy obsessive public emotions. NEW YORK TIMES 32:6, December 22, 1969.

Article reviews efforts to eliminate death penalty in Western civilization during past 200 years; results of contemporary studies on effect of death penalty's abolition on crime rate noted. NEW YORK TIMES 14:1, June 30, 1972.

Attorney General-designate Edward H. Levi believes death penalty, if enforced, would be deterrent to crime, and that imposition ought to be left to individual states, Senate Judiciary hearings on his confirmation; suggests it be applied for skyjacking, murder of police officers and murder in prisons by persons already sentenced for crimes (S). NEW YORK TIMES 17:3, January 28, 1975.

Capital punishment for children selling. CHRISTIAN SCIENCE MONITOR 14:2, April 18, 1973, (Eastern Edition); 5:1, April 18, 1973, (Midwestern Edition); 8:2, April 18, 1973, (London and Overseas Edition).

Capital punishment—no deterrent. CHRISTIAN SCIENCE MONITOR 4:5, January 13, 1968, (Eastern Edition); 4:5, January 13, 1968, (London and Overseas Edition).

Columns it Edwin A. Roberts, Jr., says the first step in decreasing crime is to be sure the criminal will get appropriate punishment. THE NATIONAL OBSERVER p. 15, March 24, 1973.

Comment on growth of crime rate in Hong Kong resulting in strong popular demand for renewed death penalty, still on statute books but not enforced since 1966. NEW YORK TIMES 7:1, August 5, 1975.

Correction Cong decries death penalty worth as crime deterrent; ex-San Quentin warden C. T. Duffy opposes penalty. NEW YORK TIMES 15:6, August 29, 1956.

ECOSOC urges governments to study value of death penalty as crime deterrent. NEW YORK TIMES 19:6, April 10, 1963.

E. De Luca lr. maintains that death penalty is deterrent to crime; holds that NYS Appeals Court decision declaring death penalty unconst is unjust. NEW YORK TIMES 38:4, June 19, 1973.

Economists are submitting new evidence that capital punishment is indeed a deterrent to crime. THE NATIONAL OBSERVER p. 1, June 19, 1976.

El Salvador President Lemus to ask Cong establish use to check recent crime rise. NEW YORK TIMES 78:4, November 1, 1956.

FBI acting director L. P. Gray 3d on January 25 says he has been 'unable to uncover any statistics that prove that the death penalty does not deter crime,' National Conference on Criminal Justice; says he studied June, 1972 Supreme Court decision that rendered unconstitutional death penalty as it is now imposed and had not found 'any absolute prohibitions' that would keep states from passing properly worded and properly enforced capital punishment statutes. NEW YORK TIMES 7:1, January 26, 1973.

H. N. Furber lr., commenting on J. P. Young's September 3 lr., holds that existence of death penalty makes no difference in person's decision to kill or not to kill. NEW YORK TIMES IV,10:5, September 17, 1972.

James Q. Wilson, a professor of government at Harvard University and an expert on crime, has written a book, Thinking About Crime, which tells why most crime cures don't work. THE NATIONAL OBSERVER p. 9, June 14, 1975.

Kings County Asst. Dist. Attorney J. M. Rsenberg lr. comments on D. A. Windsor's March 19 lr. on death penalty as deterrent on crime; maintains that death penalty does not serve as deterrent. NEW

YORK TIMES 46:4, March 29, 1973.

M. V. DiSalle, Dr. H. A. Bedau and Dr. L. J. West urge medical and legal profession unite in campaign to abolish death penalty, ss, American Psychiatric Association convention; hold capital punishment fails as deterrent to crime. NEW YORK TIMES 123:1, May 15, 1966.

Mexico weighs restoring death peanlty in Fed. Dist. in effort to curb capital crime; penalty abolished in Dist. in '29 but is used in 20 of 28 states; Judicial Studies Coll. confs. find strong support for restoration; criminal attorneys minimize move; leading attorney V. Velasquez holds Mexicans contempt for death makes penalty no deterrent. NEW YORK TIMES 36:2, August 12, 1956.

NYS Commander McHugh favors 5-year moratorium to test likely effects on crime rate, TV interview. NEW YORK TIMES 24:6, September 30, 1957.

NYS Governor Carey, in response to question concerning legislature proposals for extending death penalty, says 'certainty of punishment' is greater factor than degree of punishment in deterring crime; declines further comment while issue is before US Supreme Court (S). NEW YORK TIMES 94:2, March 19, 1975.

Number of murders has dropped, England and Wales, since November 1965 abolition of capital punishment. NEW YORK TIMES 23:8, July 20, 1967.

Oklahoma Governor D. Hall on May 17 signs death penalty bill into law, hailing it as deterrent to crime. NEW YORK TIMES 75:4, May 18, 1973.

R. Hammer article The Case That Could End Capital Punishment sees forthcoming US Supreme Court ruling on W. Maxwell's appeal from death sentence having major impact on future policy in US and on about 500 inmates on death rows. NEW YORK TIMES VI:46, October 12, 1969.

Retired New Jersey Supreme Court Justice H. Proctor believes death penalty is useful as deterrent to murder, int; says execution should be reserved for cold-blooded or premeditated murders; illus.: his career detailed; was born in 1903. NEW YORK TIMES 54:4, July 22, 1973.

UAR weighs using penalty to deal with narcotics smugglers. NEW YORK TIMES 2:1, May 30, 1966.

UN ECOSOC asks Secretary General Hammarskjold study effect of death penalty on crime. NEW YORK TIMES 11:8, April 7, 1960.

US Assistant Attorney General H. E. Petersen, testifying before H. R. Judiciary Subcommittee hearings on const. of capital punishment, defends use of capital punishment as deterrent value, even though he personally abhors it; testimony detailed; other testimony noted. NEW YORK TIMES. 16:4, March 10, 1972.

ASSASSINATIONS

Question of value; death penalty in case of assassination of president or vice president. TIME 86:16-17, July 2, 1965.

NEWSPAPER ARTICLES

Senator Byrd, on May 18, asks death penalty for persons who assassinate Presidential candidates, s, Sen. NEW YORK TIMES 34:3, May 19, 1972.

ATTITUDES TOWARD CAPITAL PUNISHMENT

Attitude toward capital punishment: scale validation [Thurstone's scale], by M. Moore. PSYCHOLOGICAL REPORTS 37:21-22, August, 1975.

Attitudes to taking human life, by D. G. Beswick. AUSTRALIAN AND NEW ZEALAND JOURNAL OF SOCIOLOGY 6:120-130, October, 1970.

Attitudes toward war and capital punishment as to size of community, by M. Smith. SCHOOL AND SOCIETY 58:220-222, September 18, 1943.

Australian adolescents to crime and punishment, by D. Watkins, et al. AUSTRALIAN AND NEW ZEALAND JOURNAL OF SOCIOLOGY 11(2):62-64, June, 1975.

Capital punishment: a reaction from a member of the clergy, by L. Kinsolving. AMERICAN BAR ASSOCIATION JOURNAL 42: 850-852, September, 1956.

Concordance in change of attitude with reference to war and capital punishment, by M. Smith. JOURNAL OF SOCIAL PSYCHOLOGY 12:379-386, 1940.

Helping behavior and attitude congruence toward capital punishment, by S. A. Karabenick. JOURNAL OF SOCIAL PSYCHOLOGY 96(2):295-296, August, 1975.

Offender's attitude toward punishment, by M. Schmideberg. JOURNAL OF CRIMINAL LAW AND CRIMINOLOGY 51:328, September-October, 1960.

Parliament's agony over capital punishment: an inside view of an MP, his conscience and some rather disturbing mail [Canada], by P. Reilly. SATURDAY NIGHT 88:15-17, March, 1973.

The poor and capital punishment: some notes on a social attitude, by M. Riedel. PRISON JOURNAL 45:24-28, Spring-Summer, 1965.

Public opinion and the death penalty [examination of public opinion polls and other social science studies on public attitudes toward capital punishment], by N. Vidmar, et al. STANFORD LAW REVIEW 26:1245-1270, June, 1974.

The relationship between attitudes toward capital punishment and assignment of the death penalty, by G. Stricker, et al. JOURNAL OF PSYCHIATRY AND LAW 2(4):415-422, Winter, 1974.

Retributive and utilitarian motives and other correlates of Canadian attitudes toward the death penalty, by N. Vidmar. CANADIAN PSYCHOLOGIST 15(4):337-356, October, 1974.

ATTITUDES TOWARD CAPITAL PUNISHMENT

Scaling technique for measuring social attitudes toward capital punishment, by J. K. Balogh, et al. SOCIOLOGY AND SOCIAL RESEARCH 45:24-26, October, 1960.

A sociological perspective on public support for capital punishment, by C. W. Thomas. AMERICAN JOURNAL OF ORTHO-PSYCHIATRY 45(4):641-657, July, 1975.

Spontaneous change of attitude toward capital punishment, by M. Smith. SCHOOL AND SOCIETY 47:318-319, March 5, 1938.

AUSTRALIA
Australian adolescents to crime and punishment, by D. Watkins, et al. AUSTRALIAN AND NEW ZEALAND JOURNAL OF SOCIOLOGY 11(2):62-64, June, 1975.

Corporal punishment in South Australia. ADELAIDE LAW REVIEW 2:83, June, 1963.

Crime and punishment, by J. V. Barry. AUSTRALIAN LAW JOURNAL 30:119, July, 1956.

AUSTRIA
NEWSPAPER ARTICLES

AUSTRIA: death penalty ends. NEW YORK TIMES 19:2, May 25, 1950.

BAGHDAD
Carnival in Baghdad; public hangings of Iraqi Jews in Baghdad. NEWSWEEK 73:31-32, February 10, 1969.

Death diplomacy and diminishing peace; political executions in Baghdad. TIME 93:22-23, February 7, 1969.

BALCOMBE STREET SIEGE
see: Great Britain

BARZUN, JACQUES
Mr. Barzun and capital punishment: comments on Jacques Barzun's

BARZUN, JACQUES

article, "In favor of capital punishment," in the Spring Scholar, by J. Nathanson, et al. AMERICAN SCHOLAR 31:436-437, Summer, 1962.

BECCARE, CESARE

Pioneer for the abolition of capital punishment: Cesare Beccare, by M. Maestro. JOURNAL OF THE HISTORY OF IDEAS 34:463-468, July, 1973.

BELL, MIKE

see: Cases Involving Capital Punishment

BENTLEY, DEREK

see: Cases Involving Capital Punishment

BIBLIOGRAPHY

Bibliography on capital punishment and related topics, 1948-1958. PRISON JOURNAL 38:41-45, October, 1958.

Capital punishment: a selected bibliography, 1940-1968, by A. Dikijian. CRIME AND DELINQUENCY 15:162-164, January, 1969.

Capital punishment—a selected bibliography, by D. B. Lyons. CRIMINAL LAW BULLETIN 8:783-802, November, 1972.

A survey of recent literature on capital punishment, by D. E. J. Mac-Namara. AMERICAN JOURNAL OF CORRECTION 24:16-19, March-April, 1962.

BOLIVIA

NEWSPAPER ARTICLES

Bolivia drops death penalty. NEW YORK TIMES 20:4, February 5, 1967.

Penalty ended in Bolivia under new Constitution. NEW YORK TIMES 26:1, August 13, 1961.

BOOK REVIEWS

A review of Cruel and unusual by M. Meltsner, by D. B. Maskowitz.

BUSINESS WEEK pp. 29-30, September 15, 1973.

A review of Cruel and unusual: the Supreme court and capital punishment by M. Meltsner, by J. W. Bishop, Jr. REVIEW COMMENTARY 57:82+, February, 1974; Reply with rejoinder by M. Meltsner, 57:17-18, May, 1974.

A review of Execution of Private Slovik by W. B. Huie. NEWSWEEK 43:107, April 26, 1954.

A review of Executions in America by W. J. Bowers, by E. Z. Friedenberg. SOCIETY 12:88-90, September, 1975.

A review of New handbook on hanging by C. Duff. TIME 65:86, February 7, 1955; a Discussion by C. Duff. TIME 65:4, February 28, 1955.

A review of Offenders by G. Playfair, et al, by C. Curran. NEW REPUBLIC 137:19-20, November 18, 1957.

—, by G. Hughes. NATION 185:413-414, November 30, 1957.

—, by W. M. Kunstler. SATURDAY REVIEW 41:20+, March 15, 1958.

A review of Power of life and death by M. V. DiSalle, by J. F. Fixx. SATURDAY REVIEW 49:29-30, January 1, 1966.

A review of Reflections on hanging by A. Koestler, by R. Campion. AMERICA 97:446+, July 27, 1957.

—, by H. Weihofen. SATURDAY REVIEW 40:32, July 20, 1957.

—, by R. Hatch. NATION 185:54, August 3, 1957.

—, by R. Niebuhr. NEW REPUBLIC 137:18, August 26, 1957.

NEWSPAPER ARTICLES

A. Koestler book on British history reviewed. NEW YORK TIMES

VII,6:1, June 30, 1957.

B. Prettyman Jr. book Death and the Supreme Court reviewed. NEW YORK TIMES VII:5, October 1, 1961.

B. F. Davis book opposing penalty reviewed. NEW YORK TIMES VII:14, June 4, 1961.

Book Capital Punishment. The Inevitability of Caprice and Mistake by C. L. Black, Jr., reviewed by M. E. Gale. NEW YORK TIMES VII:1, January 5, 1975.

M. DiSalle-L. G. Blochmann book The Power of Life or Death reviewed. NEW YORK TIMES VII:3, November 7, 1965.

BURNING TO DEATH
New light on the fiery furnace, by J. B. Alexander. JOURNAL OF BIBLICAL LITERATURE 69:375-376, December, 1950.

CALLAGHAN
Mr. Callaghan's nettle. ECONOMIST 233:24, December 13, 1969.

CAMUS, ALBERT
see: The Morality of Capital Punishment
Philosophy

CANADA
Capital punishment—a practical viewpoint, by D. E. W. Tisdale. CANADIAN BAR JOURNAL 2:255, August, 1959.

The death penalty in other countries. ANNALS OF THE AMERICAN ACADEMY OF POLITICAL AND SOCIAL SCIENCE pp. 137-166, November, 1952.

Hangman stays; vote in Canada. TIME 87:40, April 15, 1966.

Limitation death penalty; Canada, by J. R. Mutchmor. CHRISTIAN CENTURY 85:120+, January 24, 1968.

Retributive and utilitarian motives and other correlates of Canadian attitudes toward the death penalty, by N. Vidmar. CANADIAN PSYCHOLOGIST 15(4):337-356, October, 1974.

Time lapse between sentence and execution: the United States and Canada compared, by W. A. Lunden. AMERICAN BAR ASSOCI-ATION JOURNAL 48:1043-1045, November, 1962.

NEWSPAPER ARTICLES

Canada set to end death penalty. CHRISTIAN SCIENCE MONITOR 5:1, July 12, 1976, (All Editions).

Canadian Commons, 143-112, retains hanging for those convicted of murder despite death penalty opposition by Liberal, Conservative and New Dem party leaders; Prime Minister Pearson assailed her laxity on issue. NEW YORK TIMES 22:1, April 6, 1966.

Canadian Government's official executioner criticizes recent Canadian Government decision to abolish death penalty except in certain cases, telephone int. NEW YORK TIMES 31:7, January 12, 1968.

Canadian House of Commons decides on October 24 that for 5 more years capital punishment should be limited to killers of on-duty policemen and prison guards; Prime Minister Trudeau wanted to ban all capital punishment but finally agreed to concentrate on renewing earlier limitation. NEW YORK TIMES 29:7, October 25, 1973.

Canadian Minister Turner sees reintroduction of capital punishment possible following slaying of Minister Laporte by Quebec separat-ists. NEW YORK TIMES 2:5, October 20, 1970.

Canadian mouse. NATION 183:50, July 21, 1956.

Canadian Parliamentary commons urge retaining death penalty, but abolishing hanging. NEW YORK TIMES 3:4, June 28, 1956.

Canadian Senator and Commons joint com weighs revising legislature. NEW YORK TIMES 7:2, March 4, 1956.

Canadian Sen. on November 22 approves extension of partial ban on hanging for 5 more years; ban limits death penalty to killers of policemen on duty and prison guards. NEW YORK TIMES 13:1, November 23, 1973.

Government statistics show that abolition of death penalty in Canada on December 29, 1967, failed to bring any major increase in number of murders; figures show fairly even increases in years since 1961, in years both before and after death penalty was abolished. NEW YORK TIMES 16:1, January 21, 1973.

House of Commons. CHRISTIAN SCIENCE MONITOR 2:3, April 7, 1966, (Eastern and Midwestern Editions); 2:1, April 7, 1966, (Western Edition).

House of Commons approves. CHRISTIAN SCIENCE MONITOR 19:5, November 25, 1967, (Eastern Edition); 2:3, November 27, 1967, (Western Edition); 17:5, November 25, 1967, (London and Overseas Edition).

Issue of capital punishment in Canada is not yet settled despite bill introduced January 4 by Prime Minister Trudeau's Solicitor General W. Alimond to keep moratorium in effect until 1977; concern over increased crime is pushing public opinion away from humanitarian sentiments, vote in Parliament uncertain. NEW YORK TIMES 22:3, February 11, 1973.

Liberals push to abolish capital punishment. CHRISTIAN SCIENCE MONITOR p. 9 c. 3, March 2, 1976, (All Editions).

MP H. Winch offers bill, Canada, limiting death penalty to those convicted of treason, levying war or piracy. NEW YORK TIMES 7:6, December 20, 1957.

Minister Fulton holds most Canadians oppose abolition, Commons debate on limiting application. NEW YORK TIMES 15:1, May 24, 1961.

Move to bar heavily opposed. CHRISTIAN SCIENCE MONITOR p. 4 c. 1, July 21, 1975, (All Editions).

CANADA

Opposition, party filibuster seeks to block Canadian House of Commons approval of bill to end death penalty for murder for 5-year trial period, except in slaying of policemen and prison guards. NEW YORK TIMES 16:5, November 17, 1967.

Penalty backed by Canada's official executioner J. Ellis. NEW YORK TIMES 4:5, Feburary 1, 1965.

Recent outbreak of killings in Canada spurs call by police officers, Parliment members and citizens groups for restoration of death penalty; meeting of Maritime police officers in Moncton urges death for all murders unless jury recommends clemency; 1967 law abolished capital punishment except for murder of ptl. and prison guards on duty; Justice Minister Otto Lang and Solicitor General Warren Allmand caution against irrational response to recent surge of criminal violence; outburst of criticism followed stay of execution granted by Cabinet to Rene Vaillancourt, convicted of killing Toronto ptl. in February 1973 bank robbery (M). NEW YORK TIMES 18:1, February 16, 1975.

To abolish—close vote in Canadian House of Commons. CHRISTIAN SCIENCE MONITOR 2:4, June 24, 1976, (All Editions).

2,700 delegates from Canada's governing Liberal party approve resolution asking Parliament to repeal death penalty (S). NEW YORK TIMES 20:5, November 10, 1975.

CAPITAL PUNISHMENT—AGAINST

A.C.L.U. attacks capital punishment. CHRISTIAN CENTURY 82: 1150, September 22, 1965.

Abolish the penalty of death, by R. R. Start, et al. PENNSYLVANIA BAR ASSOCIATION QUARTERLY 31:408, June, 1960.

Abolition and after, by C. H. Rolph. NEW STATESMAN 51:267-268, March 24, 1956.

Abolition of capital punishment—a symposium, by Feinberg, et al. CANADIAN BAR REVIEW 32:485-519, May, 1954.

Abolition of the death penalty in California, by C. Blease. LAWYERS GUILD REVIEW 19:58, Summer, 1958.

Bastard or legitimate child of Furman (Furman v. Georgia, 92 Sup. Ct. 2726)? An analysis of Wyoming's new capital punishment law. LAND AND WATER REVIEW 9:209-236, 1974.

Bill to abolish capital punishment in Pennsylvania, by F. Worley. DICKINSON LAW REVIEW 60:167, January, 1956.

Bishops v. the death penalty. SENIOR SCHOLASTIC 78:10-11, May 17, 1961.

Britian abolishes the hangman's job. U. S. NEWS AND WORLD REPORT 59:16, November 8, 1965.

Britain faces end of death penalty. CHRISTIAN CENTURY 73:259, February 29, 1956.

British constitution and the capital punishment abolition controversy, by H. S. Albinski. JOURNAL OF PUBLIC LAW 12:193, 1963.

Capital punishment, absolute penalty or obsolete remedy? pro and con discussion. SENIOR SCHOLASTIC 71:6-7+, September 20, 1957.

Capital punishment and life imprisonment in North Carolina, 1946 to 1968: implications for abolition of the death penalty, by C. H. Patrick. WAKE FOREST INTERNATIONAL LAW REVIEW 6:417, May, 1970.

Capital punishment: ban proposed. NEW REPUBLIC 148:5, June 8, 1963.

Capital punishment: defense against crime or legalized murder? pro and con discussion. SENIOR SCHOLASTIC 76:8-9+, March 9, 1960.

Capital punishment is legalized murder, by A. Kohn. SEVENTEEN 32:248, August, 1973.

Capital punishment is murder!, by D. Dressler. CORONET 47:135-140, January, 1960.

Capital punishment is not the answer, by E. Havemann. READER'S DIGEST 76:114-119, May, 1960.

Capital punishment is on the way out, by D. M. Berman. PROGRESSIVE 24:33-34, April, 1960.

Capital punishment—the issues and the evidence [excerpt from the majority report to the Massachusetts legislature of the Special commission to investigate the abolition of the death penalty; recommends abolition] ; The right of the state to inflict capital punishment, by T. J. Riley. CATHOLIC LAWYER 6:269-278+, 279-285, Autumn, 1960.

Capital punishment; pro and con, by H. H. Punke. THE CLEARING HOUSE 35:103-107, October, 1960.

Capital punishment: a sharp medicine reconsidered; historical background and the arguments pro and con, by E. J. Younger. AMERICAN BAR ASSOCIATION JOURNAL 42:113-116+, February, 1956.

Capital punishment [trend in sentiment against capital punishment in various countries] , by L. F. Hatfield. CANADIAN FORUM 33:54-56, June, 1953.

Case against capital punishment, by A. Fortas. NEW YORK TIMES MAGAZINE pp. 8-9+, January 23, 1977.

✳ The case against capital punishment, by D. E. MacNamara; Capital punishment: a Christian approach, by C. S. Milligan; Vengeance and the law, by B. E. Eshelman. SOCIAL ACTION 27:4-26, April, 1961.

The case against the death penalty, by H. A. Bedau. NEW LEADER 42:19-21, August 17-24, 1959.

Case for the abolition of capital punishment. LOUISIANA LAW RE-

VIEW 29:396, February, 1969.

Cases for and against capital punishment. The case for the death penalty, by D. S. Smith; The case against capital punishment, by R. Kingsley. LOS ANGELES BAR BULLETIN 32:195, May, 1957.

Challenge to abolitionists, by G. Playfair, et al. NEW STATESMAN 52:63-64, July 21, 1956; Discussion, 52:104, 136, 162, 187, 215, 244, July 28-September 1, 1956.

Competency of jurors who have conscientious scruples against capital punishment. WASHBURN LAW JOURNAL 8:352, Spring, 1969.

Constitutional law—challenge for cause on the ground of conscientious scruples against capital punishment. ARKANSAS LAW REVIEW 23:108, Spring, 1969.

Controversy over capital punishment: pro & con. CONGRESSIONAL DIGEST 52:1-32, January, 1973.

De facto abolition of the death penalty in Louisiana?, by W. H. Forman, Jr. LOUISIANA BAR JOURNAL 18:199, December, 1970.

Death penalty abolished; action in Iowa, by P. B. Mather. CHRISTIAN CENTURY 82:382, March 24, 1965.

Death penalty: bill to abolish execution. NEWSWEEK 72:28, July 15, 1968.

Death penalty must go. CHRISTIAN CENTURY 74:412-413, April 3, 1957.

Death sentence: its pros. cons, by H. Wechsler. LIFE 48:46-48, May 9, 1960.

Dismantling the cross: a case against capital punishment, by L. M. Jendrzejczyk. CHRISTIAN CENTURY 94:296-297, March 30, 1977.

Effects of abolition. ECONOMIST 213:950+, November 28, 1964.

End to all death sentences? U. S. NEWS AND WORLD REPORT 64: 15, June 7, 1968.

Gallows must go in Great Britain. TIME 67:29-30, February 27, 1956.

Hanging; abolition's progress. ECONOMIST 215:283, April 17, 1965.

Hanging on [moves to abolish death penalty]. ECONOMIST 177:639, November 19, 1955.

Hanging's no answer, by C. H. Rolph. NEW STATESMAN 61:578, April 14, 1961.

Horror of death at Eastertime; with views of M. Dees, by J. M. Wall. CHRISTIAN CENTURY 94:315-316, April 6, 1977.

Issues on abolition of capital punishment, by S. K. Bhattacharyya. SOCIAL DEFENSE 10(37):16-23, July, 1974.

Killing the death penalty. TIME 90:47-48, July 7, 1967.

Law of murder: the prospects of abolishing capital punishment are not necessarily being improved by the tactics of some abolitionists [Great Britain]. ECONOMIST 198:436-437, February 4, 1961.

Let's abolish capital punishment; interview edited by J. Robbins and J. Robbins, by E. G. Brown. GOOD HOUSEKEEPING 151:57+, August, 1960.

The lords who said "no" [characteristics of the British peers who voted on the Death penalty (abolition) bill, House of lords, July 9-10, 1956]. LABOUR RESEARCH 45:113-114, August, 1956.

Mass public executions in Iraq deplored by United States; text of letter to the president of the Security council, January 29, 1969, by C. W. Yost. DEPARTMENT OF STATE BULLETIN 60:145-146, February 17, 1969.

A matter of conviction, by E. G. Brown. FELLOWSHIP 26:14-16, July 1, 1960.

Movement to abolish capital punishment in America, 1787-1861, by D. B. Davis. AMERICAN HISTORICAL REVIEW 63:23-46, October, 1957.

Murderers' reminiscences [abolition of capital punishment will end demand for such articles], by C. Hollis. SPECTATOR 195:37-39, July 8, 1955.

Negating the absolute; backing for abolition of federal death penalty. TIME 92:17, July 12, 1968.

New attempts under way to abolish death penalty; What a poll shows. U. S. NEWS AND WORLD REPORT 58:13, April 5, 1965.

New York abolishes death. TIME 85:61, June 11, 1965.

New York Senate would curtail capital punishment. CHRISTIAN CENTURY 82:669, May 26, 1965.

Nigeria; time to stop [public executions]. ECONOMIST 244:37, July 29, 1972.

Now a new fight over the death penalty [campaign against capital punishment is now developing in the United States]. U. S. NEWS AND WORLD REPORT 48:52, March 7, 1960.

On the way out. NATION 199:367, November 23, 1964.

161 trips to the room to watch men die [Don Reid, Jr. battles capital punishment], by R. Friedman. EDITOR AND PUBLISHER 93: 72-73, May 7, 1960.

Pioneer for the abolition of capital punishment: Cesare Beccare, by M. Maestro. JOURNAL OF THE HISTORY OF IDEAS 31:463-468, July, 1973.

Plea in mitigation, by H. Hargrove. SOLICITOR 25:270, October, 1958.

Protest—Julian Grimau's death sentence, by P. Robinson. CONTEM-

PORARY REVIEW 203:287-288, June, 1963.

Psychiatrists condemn capital punishment. SCIENCE NEWS 89:386, May 21, 1966.

Quality of mercy. SPECTATOR 204:648, May 6, 1960.

Quality of mercy [in California and Illinois]. ECONOMIST 204:525, August 11, 1962.

Retreat to barbarism. PROGRESSIVE 38:11-12, May, 1974.

Road up from barbarism. SOCIAL SERVICE REVIEW 46:431-432, September, 1972.

Sacking the hangman; Great Britain. TIME 94:15-16, December 26, 1969.

Should Ohio abolish capital punishment? CLEVELAND-MARSHALL LAW REVIEW 10:365, May, 1961.

Should we abolish capital punishment in California? TRANSACTIONS OF THE COMMONWEALTH CLUB OF CALIFORNIA 58:17-37, November 11, 1963.

The strength of sin is the law [opposes capital punishment], by A. Burdett. LIBERATION: AN INDEPENDENT MONTHLY 5:17-18, November, 1960.

Tactics of abolition, by C. Hollis. SPECTATOR 195:706-707, November 25, 1955.

Thou shalt not kill, by L. Woolf. NEW STATESMAN 50:608+, November 12, 1955.

Toward abolition of capital punishment. SOCIAL SERVICE REVIEW 43:92, March, 1969.

Toward a more humane society; abolishing the death penalty. CHRISTIAN CENTURY 82:261, March 3, 1965.

Trend against hanging. AMERICA 108:213, February 16, 1963.

Trends in the abolition of capital punishment, by M. V. DiSalle. UNIVERSITY OF TOLEDO LAW REVIEW 1969:1, Winter, 1969.

Two-front attack on the death penalty, by R. A. Woodley. LIFE 64:108, June 7, 1968.

NEWSPAPER ARTICLES

A. Lewis article discusses US Supreme Court decision to abolish capital punishment; states Court has a history of overturning and reinterpreting 'traditional' practices and laws; discusses role of Supreme Court in society. NEW YORK TIMES 21:1, July 1, 1972.

ACLU to open nationwide drive to abolish capital punishment. NEW YORK TIMES 23:6, June 21, 1965.

'Abolish,' Attorney General R. Clark. CHRISTIAN SCIENCE MONITOR E:3, July 12, 1968, (All Editions).

Abolished. CHRISTIAN SCIENCE MONITOR. 2:2, July 3, 1965, (Eastern Edition); 2:4, July 3, 1965, (Western Edition); 2:1, July 3, 1965, (Midwestern Edition).

Abolition bill assured of floor action in NYS Legislator. NEW YORK TIMES 23:1, April 21, 1965.

Abolition urged, pub. meeting, Yonkers, called by 3 NYS legislators. NEW YORK TIMES 86:4, April 4, 1965.

Acting US Attorney General Clark opposes penalty. NEW YORK TIMES 24:6, March 1, 1967.

Adm. asks Congress to abolish death penalty for all Federal crimes, including President assassinations, and to reduce to life imprisonment sentences of Federal prisoners on Death Row; Attorney General Clark, in reversal of his previous position, urges US join the over 70 nations that have abandoned capital punishment, Sen com. hearings on Senator Hart bill; holds studies show death penalty does not deter crime; notes 2,066 Negroes and 1,751 whites have been executed since Justice Department began keeping records; Federal crimes now punishable by death listed. NEW YORK TIMES 1:2, July 3, 1968.

American Civil Liberties Union opposes. CHRISTIAN SCIENCE MONITOR 2:5, June 22, 1965, (Eastern Edition); 2:3, June 22, 1965; (Midwestern Edition).

Approval to abolish. CHRISTIAN SCIENCE MONITOR 2:4, July 15, 1965, (Eastern Edition); 2:2, July 15, 1965, (Western Edition); 2:5, July 15, 1965, (Midwestern Edition).

Arguments against capital punishment discussed. NEW YORK TIMES IV,12:4, July 7, 1968.

Assemblyman Podell offers bill to abolish death penalty in NYS; cites G. Whitmore case. NEW YORK TIMES 1:2, February 17, 1965.

Bill to abolish death penalty passes 3d and final reading, Brit. Commons. NEW YORK TIMES 12:3, June 29, 1956.

Brit. Commons gets bill to abolish death penalty for murder. NEW YORK TIMES 10:3, December 5, 1964.

Brown pessimistic on abolition prospects. NEW YORK TIMES 20:6, March 2, 1960.

Capital punishment—attacked. CHRISTIAN SCIENCE MONITOR 2:5, March 16, 1964, (Eastern Edition).

Chief Justice Warren opposes capital punishment but believes its abolition should be left to the states, int. NEW YORK TIMES 42:1, July 6, 1968.

Codes Coms. of Legis. open public hearings on abolition, Albany; abolition urged by Professor Redlich, opposed by R. H. Kuh, NYS Police Supt. Cornelius and Judge Hofstadter. NEW YORK TIMES 25:1, March 26, 1965.

Colorado voters reject proposal. NEW YORK TIMES 36:1, November 10, 1966.

Comment on curbs on death penalty already imposed by most nations. NEW YORK TIMES 28:3, December 21, 1969.

Death penalty opposed by Dr. F. Wertham and Professor S. Hook, backed by Judge Leibowitz, debate, NYS District Attorneys Association forum. NEW YORK TIMES 6:3, January 28, 1961.

Death penalty opposed by Governor DiSalle, defended by New Hampshire Attorney General Wyman, TV debate. NEW YORK TIMES 3:6, April 25, 1968.

Death penalty; pro and con arguments, by J. Q. Wilson. NEW YORK TIMES MAGAZINE pp. 26-27, October 28, 1973.

District Attorney O'Connor backs abolition; says death penalty has not deterred crime; urges moratorium on executions pending legislator decision. NEW YORK TIMES 28:1, March 22, 1965.

Donald Soper speaks out against capital punishment, by D. Soper. THE OBSERVER pp. 11-12, June 1, 1958.

Dr. W. G. Katz urges abolishing death penalty in NYS. NEW YORK TIMES 14:5, October 11, 1961.

Editorial backs death penalty abolition. NEW YORK TIMES 30:2, February 25, 1965.

Editorial deploring sentencing of assassin S. B. Sirhan to death calls for abolition of death penalty in US. NEW YORK TIMES 46:2, April 24, 1969.

Editorial hails abolition proposal by NYC Bar Association com. NEW YORK TIMES 36:1, April 13, 1965.

Editorial on hearing favors outright abolition. NEW YORK TIMES 6:2, December 12, 1962.

Editorial praises US Supreme Court decision abolishing capital punishment; urges states to take Chief Justice Burger's suggestion to review question, but instead of reviving penalty as Burger suggests, to abolish it once and for all. NEW YORK TIMES 16:1, July 3, 1972.

Editorial urges abolition. NEW YORK TIMES 32:1, March 22, 1965.

Editorial urges eliminating exceptions from bill to abolish death penalty. NEW YORK TIMES 34:2, May 17, 1965.

Editorial urges NYS abolish it. NEW YORK TIMES 22:2, June 6, 1964.

Editorial urges nationwide abolition. NEW YORK TIMES 6:2, February 2, 1963.

Editorial urges universal abolition. NEW YORK TIMES 26:2, August 22, 1963.

Eleventh state to bar. CHRISTIAN SCIENCE MONITOR 10:1, March 30, 1965, (Eastern Edition).

Ex-Governor G. M. Williams calls for abolition of death penalty, US Senate subcommittee. NEW YORK TIMES 12:1, March 22, 1968.

Ex-Governor Meyner, Democratic candidate for New Jersey Governor says he would welcome 'public discussion' on abolishing death penalty, position paper. NEW YORK TIMES 29:2, August 27, 1969.

G. Ace lr. in response to K. Macleod's September 5 lr. advocating restoration of capital punishment; disregarding morality, he holds Con. Ed. cannot even provide enough electricity to keep air conditioners going in Queens, let alone supply current for electric chairs. NEW YORK TIMES 34:5, September 10, 1973.

Governor Cargo signs bill banning death penalty in New Mexico except in 2 situations; bill commutes to life imprisonment sentences of 3 men now on Death Row. NEW YORK TIMES 38:2, April 1, 1969.

Governor McKeldin, testifying in favor of 2 bills to abolish capital punishment in Maryland, says he is ashamed he let 4 prisoners be executed during his term. NEW YORK TIMES 35:1, February 15, 1968.

Governor Peabody hails Massachusetts Senate approval of to abolish penalty. NEW YORK TIMES 22:1, April 19, 1963.

Herkimer County (NY) District Attorney H. D. Blumberg Ir. on T. Wicker's December 9 column says Wicker is wrong to suggest abandonment of death penalty; holds it should be expanded to include persons who commit repeated acts of violence resulting in serious physical injury to others; cites death of A. DeSalvo and assault on J. V. Corona in prisons as examples of deficiencies in incarceration. NEW YORK TIMES IV,20:5, December 23, 1973.

Illinois Senate committee rejects bill for 6-year moratorium. NEW YORK TIMES 36:6, June 16, 1965.

Indiana Governor Branigan vetoes bill, says abolition should be decided by referendum; Governor has been under pressure to veto bill since recent shooting of state trooper. NEW YORK TIMES 74:3, March 14, 1965.

Indiana Senate approves bill to abolish it. NEW YORK TIMES 19:6, February 23, 1965.

Indiana Senate approves 2 bills abolishing penalty for 1st-degree murder and 4 other crimes. NEW YORK TIMES 14:3, February 10, 1965.

Iowa Legis. abolishes penalty. NEW YORK TIMES 21:1, February 19, 1965.

Ital Penal Law Association President G. Persico urges elimination of death penalty, International Congress of Penal Law. NEW YORK TIMES 13:4, September 28, 1953.

Justice Clark opposes death penalty, doubts it deters crime. NEW YORK TIMES 64:1, March 12, 1961.

Kentucky House considers legis. to abolish death penalty; defeats move to kill bill, 40-38; hears Tennessee convict who escaped electric chair. NEW YORK TIMES 17:4, February 16, 1966.

L. Orland article, noting recent US Supreme Court decision abolishing capital punishment, warns against mandating life sentences for crimes which may have been punishable by death before decision; notes murderers with life sentences who may eventually be paroled are most adaptable of prisoners and have lowest recidivism rate of any major felony offender; argues that mandatory life sentences defeat purpose of rehabilitation and destroy any hope prisoner may have. NEW YORK TIMES 25:6, July 8, 1972.

Legislative opposes abolition. NEW YORK TIMES 30:6, April 5, 1965.

Legislative opposes penalty. NEW YORK TIMES 20:6, June 29, 1953.

Legislative scores abolition of penalty in NYS. NEW YORK TIMES 26:6, February 19, 1966; Correction, 38:6, February 23, 1966.

Legislative urges abolition in NYS. NEW YORK TIMES 32:4, March 1, 1960.

Legislative urges NYS abolish death penalty. NEW YORK TIMES IV,8:5, November 22, 1964.

Lutheran Church in America urges abolition; discounts 5th Commandment as basis for move; denies it repudiates power of state to take life. NEW YORK TIMES 26:3, June 30, 1966.

Lyons, David—a vote for life. CHRISTIAN SCIENCE MONITOR 15:4, July 13, 1970, (Eastern and London and Overseas Editions); 13:4, July 13, 1970, (Western Edition); 11:4, July 13, 1970, (Midwestern Edition).

M. E. Travis opposes death penalty, reply to Hook April 6, lr. NEW YORK TIMES 42:5, April 19, 1973.

Massachusetts Senate, 26-14, sustains Governor Michael S. Dukakis' veto of bill providing death penalth for 9 types of murder; state House had earlier voted to override veto (S). NEW YORK TIMES 23:1, May 2, 1975.

Move to restore death penalty in New Jersey has apparently been laid aside in Assembly, partly on advice of Governor's Study Comm. on Capital Punishment; Assembly Judiciary Com. voted to consider 3 capital-punishment proposals before it, despite comm's recommendation, but no bill restoring penalty has emerged from com; proposals detailed. NEW YORK TIMES 86:4, April 29, 1973.

NAACP Legal Defense and Education Fund, which along with ACLU filed suit that was basis for California Supreme Court's decision declaring that capital punishment is unconstitutional, praises ruling; says that campaign to abolish capital punishment will be carried on to other states. NEW YORK TIMES 28:4, February 19, 1972.

NYC Correction Comr. Malcolm and Bronx District Attorney Roberts on April 24 join 45 civil groups, news conference, in vehement protest agianst bill before NYS Assembly that would reinstate death penalty for homicides; call capital punishment immoral, racist and counter-productive; send message to Legis. warning against augmenting 'drift toward violence' by restoring capital punishment to state's statute books. NEW YORK TIMES 40:2, April 25, 1972.

NYC ex-Comr. MacCormick urges abolition, lr. NEW YORK TIMES 36:5, March 25, 1965.

NYC group opens drive to prevent NYS Legislator from restoring death penalty; Assemblyman Passannante advises members. NEW YORK TIMES 36:4, March 18, 1968.

NYS bill abolishing death penalty signed; provisions, exceptions outlined; Rockefeller to commute to life terms sentences ot 17 men awaiting execution; will review cases of 3 others whose crimes were covered by exceptions. NEW YORK TIMES 1:1, June 2, 1965.

NYS Comm. on Revision of Penal Law urges abolition, report to Legislator; panel split, 8-4; minority urges further study; Professor Wechsler drafted majority report. NEW YORK TIMES 1:6, March 20, 1965.

NYS Council of Chs. backs 5 pending bills for abolition. NEW YORK TIMES 25:1, January 14, 1960.

NYS Government Dem. aspirant Goldberg, in article written with Harvard Professor A. Dershowitz for current Harvard Law Review, says that he believes that capital punishment is unconstitutional. NEW YORK TIMES 68:4, June 21, 1970.

NYS Senator Duffy and ACLU NY chap. reverse stands, urge death penalty abolition. NEW YORK TIMES 22:4, March 12, 1965.

NYS Senate, 47-9, approves bill to abolish death penalty for murder, kidnapping and treason and to substitute life imprisonment; would retain death sentence for murder of peace officer acting in line of duty and murder by life-term convict in course of escape; Senator Zaretzki and Assemblyman Bartlett hail vote; Governor Rockefeller stand uncertain; he terms measure a curtailment rather than abolition bill. NEW YORK TIMES 1:5, May 13, 1965; Roll-call, 28:3, May 13, 1965.

NYS Senator majority leader Anderson on February 26 says that he does not know if reimposition of death penalty will reach floor for debate, but that if it does he will oppose it. NEW YORK TIMES 44:2, February 27, 1973.

National Campaign for Abolition of Capital Punishment sends petition signed by 2,500 prominent persons to Min. Eden. NEW YORK TIMES. 11:1, October 22, 1956.

National Council of Churches urges abolition of capital punishment, policy statement. NEW YORK TIMES 37:1, September 14, 1968.

National District Attorneys Association urges abolition. NEW YORK TIMES 24:1, March 18, 1965.

National Lawyers Congress, Spain, adopts resolution to end death penalty. NEW YORK TIMES 17:1, June 21, 1970.

National Urban League calls for abolition of death penalty throughout US; holds it discriminates against Negroes and poor. NEW YORK TIMES 19:1, March 4, 1969.

New Jersey Capital Punishment Study Comm. on March 22 recommends that legislative action on restoring death penalty be put off until US Supreme Court makes final decision on its constitution; Legislator is reportedly ready to take up bill, sponsored by Senator Azzolina, to restore capital punishment, despite comm's report; report notes legal experts agree Court's June, 1972 ruling do not say whether capital punishment can ever be constitution permissible; Governor Cahill, who established comm. in October 1971, declines to comment on its report, except to say that it will be reviewed by his Adm. and that he will await reactions of members of Legis; will be forced to take stand on issue should Azzolina bill pass the Assembly. NEW YORK TIMES 79:1, March 23, 1973.

New Jersey Senate on May 3 rejects move to restore capital punishment in state; Senator J. Azzolina, principal sponsor of bill, says that he will seek to bring it to vote in future. NEW YORK TIMES 1:1, May 5, 1972.

New Mexico HR passes bill to abolish capital punishment for almost all crimes. NEW YORK TIMES 91:4, March 18, 1969.

Newly re-elected Utah Attorney General V. Romney says on November 9 that he will push for reinstitution of death peanlty at next session of state legislator, proposing a carefully framed statute that might meet US Supreme Court tests. NEW YORK TIMES 7:1, November 11, 1972.

North Carolina General Assembly abolishes death penalty for total duel. NEW YORK TIMES 18:6, May 21, 1965.

Opponents of penalty demand reopening of issue, GB. NEW YORK TIMES 15:1, June 28, 1953.

Oregon sets referendum on abolition. NEW YORK TIMES 14:8, May 29, 1963.

Oregon voters approve abolition of death penalty. NEW YORK TIMES 18:3, November 5, 1964.

PE Church opens drive for abolition; sends to all dioceses compilation of theological and other arguments published by National Council; scores Dir. Hoover stand; views of other Protestant Churches, RC Church and Jewish authorities on death penalty noted. NEW YORK TIMES 1:2, March 20, 1961.

Penalty abolished, Monacao. NEW YORK TIMES 2:3, June 20, 1964.

Philippines Press Inst. opposes bill to impose death penalty for killing newsmen on grounds it would violate equal protection clause of Constitution. NEW YORK TIMES 18:3, April 3, 1967.

Readers write. Reader opposes ruling. CHRISTIAN SCIENCE MONI-TOR E:5, June 4, 1971, (Western and Midwestern Editions); E:5, June 3, 1971, (Eastern and London and Overseas Editions).

Referendum calling for end to penalty set, Colorado. NEW YORK TIMES 28:7, October 25, 1966.

Representative Drinan introduces bill on March 14 that would abolish death penalty under Federal law; says that President Nixon is exploiting people's fear of crime; contends that capital punishment is ineffective as deterrent to crime. NEW YORK TIMES 25:7, March 15, 1973.

Representative Kastenmeier offers bill to abolish penalty for Federal crimes. NEW YORK TIMES 36:5, June 10, 1966.

San Francisco Mayor Christopher urges abolition. NEW YORK TIMES 4:6, February 20, 1960.

Senator Hart bill would abolish penalty, US. NEW YORK TIMES 21:7, July 26, 1966.

Senator Hatfield offers bill to abolish death penalty for military personnel. NEW YORK TIMES 8:8, August 6, 1970.

Special comm. urges abolition, Massachusetts. NEW YORK TIMES 74:6, December 31, 1958.

Ten states have abolished. CHRISTIAN SCIENCE MONITOR 1:1, March 4, 1965, (Eastern, Western, and Midwestern Editions).

Tennessee Governor Clement in effect abolishes capital punishment for remaining 2 years of term by commuting 5 death sentences, news conference after House rejects his abolition plea. NEW YORK TIMES 1:7, March 20, 1965.

20 leaders of Boston church and civic groups meet with Massachusetts Governor F. W. Sargent on December 6 to urge him not to sign death penalty bill that awaits decision by December 10. NEW YORK TIMES 55:6, December 7, 1973.

2 pacifists protest California law, Sacramento. NEW YORK TIMES 16:8, January 3, 1961.

Urban League reporter M. S. Isaacs charges that NYS laws tend to make Negroes and Puerto Ricans main victims of death penalty, NYS Penal Law Revision Comm. hearing; Justice Breitel, most other witnesses urge abolishing death penalty; Justices Rand and Leibowitz and Assistant District Attorney Uviller defend it. NEW YORK TIMES 25:5, December 8, 1962.

US Supreme Court, 5 to 4, abolishes on June 29 death penalty as it is imposed under present statutes, ruling it is 'cruel and unusual'; decision will save 600 persons now on death rows in US; Justices Douglas, Brennan and Marshall hold that death penalty is in itself cruel and unusual; 'swing men' Potter Stewart and White, voting with majority, reason that present legal system operates in cruel and unusual way because it gives judges and juries discretion to decree life or death; maintain that they impose it erratically, mostly against poor and blacks; 4 Nixon appointees dissent; Chief Justice Burger notes that states could retain capital punishment by altering laws to conform with Court's ruling; illus. of prisoner.

CAPITAL PUNISHMENT—AGAINST

NEW YORK TIMES 1:8, June 30, 1972.

US Supreme Court, rejecting request by California Attorney General Younger, refuses to block from taking effect California Supreme Court decision abolishing death penalty in that state. NEW YORK TIMES 25:1, March 21, 1972.

V. Silber lr. scores July 31 lr. in favor of repeal of death peanlty. NEW YORK TIMES 34:3, August 15, 1972.

Vermont House approves abolition bill. NEW YORK TIMES 32:2, April 14, 1965.

Vermont House approves bill to abolish death penalty except in murder convictions for 2d offense unrelated to 1st slaying. NEW YORK TIMES 11:2, March 6, 1965.

Washington State Supreme Court on September 28 strikes down state laws allowing capital punishment, following recent US Supreme Court ruling that death penalty is unconstitutional. NEW YORK TIMES 29:1, September 29, 1972.

West Virginia Legislature approves abolition bill. NEW YORK TIMES 8:8, March 13, 1965.

West Virginia, New York, Kentucky, Illinois, Vermont and Indiana legislatures weigh ending death penalty; Kentucky General Assembly stays 9 executions pending decision; NYS Trail Lawyers Association backs abolition. NEW YORK TIMES 23:4, March 8, 1965.

YS should discard? CHRISTIAN SCIENCE MONITOR 11:1, July 13, 1964, (Western and Midwestern Editions); 13:1, July 13, 1964, (Eastern Edition).

CAPITAL PUNISHMENT—FOR
Bring back the chair; warden and deputy murdered in Holmesburg prison. NEWSWEEK 81:30+, June 11, 1973.

The campaign to extend the death penalty [Russia], by Y. P. Mironenko. INSTITUTE FOR THE STUDY OF THE USSR. BULLETIN 6:25-30, January, 1959.

Capital punishment, absolute penalty or obsolete remedy? pro and con discussion. SENIOR SCHOLASTIC 71:6-7+, September 20, 1957.

Capital punishment: defense against crime or legalized murder? pro and con discussion. SENIOR SCHOLASTIC 76:8-9+, March 9, 1960.

Capital punishment is necessary, by J. Rawitsch. SEVENTEEN 32: 248, August, 1973.

Capital punishment: pro and con, by H. H. Punke. THE CLEARING HOUSE 35:103-107, October, 1960.

Capital punishment: a sharp medicine reconsidered; historical background and the arguments pro and con, by E. J. Younger. AMERICAN BAR ASSOCIATION JOURNAL 42:113-116+, February, 1956.

Capital punishment should be retained, by W. B. Hagarty. CANADIAN BAR JOURNAL 3:42, February, 1960.

A case for capital punishment [for Arab terrorism in Israel], by G. Weller; A case against capital punishment, by L. Sheleif (Shaskolsky); A new high in ethnocentrism [commenting on the article by G. Weller], by D. Amit. NEW OUTLOOK 17:46-58, October, 1974.

The case for capital punishment (sanctioned by Constitution and by majority of Americans), by M. S. Evans. HUMAN EVENTS 37: 8+, February 12, 1977.

✳ Cases for and against capital punishment. The case for the death penalty, by D. S. Smith; The case against capital punishment, by R. Kingsley. LOS ANGELES BAR BULLETIN 32:195, May, 1957.

Controversy over capital punishment: pro & con. CONGRESSIONAL DIGEST 52:1-32, January, 1973.

Crusading for death; J. F. Britt, district attorney of Lumberton, N.C., by J. K. Footlick, et al. NEWSWEEK 86:31, July 21, 1975.

The death penalty gets a big push [United States]. U. S. NEWS AND WORLD REPORT 74:70, March 26, 1973.

Death penalty; pro and con arguments, by J. Q. Wilson. NEW YORK TIMES MAGAZINE pp. 26-27+, October 28, 1973.

Death sentence: its pros. cons., by H. Wechsler. LIFE 48:46-48, May 9, 1960.

Family experience and public support of the death penalty, by R. J. Gelles. AMERICAN JOURNAL OF ORTHOPSYCHIATRY 45(4):596-613, July, 1975.

For the death penalty, by L. D. Summerfield. NEVADA STATE BAR JOURNAL 25:105, July, 1960.

Getting tough: more death sentences are imposed as backers push for restoration, by W. E. Green. WALL STREET JOURNAL 182:1+, September 18, 1973.

Hangman stays: vote in Canada. TIME 87:40, April 15, 1966.

House bill 200: the legislative attempt to reinstate capital punishment in Texas. HOUSTON LAW REVIEW 11:410-423, January, 1974.

In defense of capital punishment. KENTUCKY LAW JOURNAL 54: 742, Summer, 1966.

—, by B. L. Cohen. DALHOUSIE REVIEW 44:442-451, Winter, 1964-1965.

—, by R. R. Kinney. KENTUCKY LAW JOURNAL 54:742-756, Summer, 1966.

In favor of capital punishment, by J. Barzun. AMERICAN SCHOLAR 31:181-191, Spring, 1962; Discussion, 31:436-447, 659, Summer-Autumn, 1962; also in CRIME & DELINQUENCY 15:21, January, 1969.

Keep capital punishment, by R. W. Childs. PENNSYLVANIA BAR ASSOCIATION QUARTERLY 31:337, March, 1960.

Moves to restore the death penalty. U. S. NEWS AND WORLD REPORT 73:60, December 4, 1972.

On capital punishment [favoring its retention], by S. B. S. Devi. MODERN REVIEW. INDIA AND PAKISTAN 108:384-388, November, 1960.

Resounding vote for the death penalty. NATION'S BUSINESS 61: 20-21, April, 1973.

Should the death penalty be restored selectively? "Yes", by R. L. Hruska; "No", by R. F. Drinan. AMERICAN LEGION MONTHLY 98:14-15, June, 1975.

Should the death penalty be retained? "Yes", by N. Galifianakis; "No", by R. V. Dellums. AMERICAN LEGION MONTHLY 93:16-17, November, 1972.

Vote for death. ECONOMIST 245:40, November 11, 1972.

NEWSPAPER ARTICLES

California Governor Reagan demands reinstatement of capital punishment, which was recently declared unconstitutional by California Supreme Court; says that he does not consider death penalty cruel and unusual punishment, but rather as a deterrent. NEW YORK TIMES 46:7, March 1, 1972.

California voters will have opporutnity in November to vote for reintroduction of death penalty for state; Governor Reagan leads battle to put referendum on ballot. NEW YORK TIMES 37:3, June 26, 1972.

Capital punishment, abortion, and war are forms of legitimized killing and should be appraised as such. Editorial. THE NATIONAL OBSERVER p. 12, January 22, 1972.

Capital punishment should not be abolished but limited to a specific list of crimes and executed without public fanfare. THE NATIONAL OBSERVER p. 11, January 8, 1972.

Capital punishment states resist anti bids. CHRISTIAN SCIENCE MONITOR 4:5, August 9, 1963, (Eastern Edition); 5:1, August 20, 1963, (Western Edition); 4:4, August 6, 1963, (Midwestern Edition).

'Causes' YS right to be active. CHRISTIAN SCIENCE MONITOR 13:1, July 25, 1964, (Eastern Edition and Western Edition); 11:1, July 25, 1964, (Midwestern Edition).

Comment on campaign to restore death penalty in NYS; notes Assemblyman R. F. Kelly bill would make death penalty mandatory for all convicted murderers unless jury recommends life sentence. NEW YORK TIMES IV,3:6, April 23, 1972.

Comment on considerable sentiment in New Jersey State Legislature, despite legal obstacles, rereinstate capital punishment in state; obstacles include January order by State Supreme Court abolishing death penalty in state and US Supreme Court ruling in June that death penalty as it now exists is unconstitutional; New Jersey State Senators and Assemblymen comment. NEW YORK TIMES 160:4, December 10, 1972.

Comment on New Jersey State Senate passing Senator Azzolina's bill to reinstate death penalty in New Jersey; opposition to restoration of death penalty noted. NEW YORK TIMES IV,3:6, May 14, 1972.

Editorial urges Rockefeller signature. NEW YORK TIMES 42:2, May 20, 1965.

Focus: pressure for return. CHRISTIAN SCIENCE MONITOR 1:1, August 3, 1969, (All Editions).

Former NYC HRA speech writer Nettie Leaf comments on her reasons for changing her stand against capital punishment; illustrations of Carl Chessman. NEW YORK TIMES 33:2, July 2, 1975.

Georgia State Senate on February 22 votes, 47 to 7, to restore capital punishment in state; Governor Carter is expected to sign bill into law. NEW YORK TIMES 15:7, February 23, 1973.

Governor Rockefeller says he will sign bill. NEW YORK TIMES 36:1, March 11, 1966.

Incoming Attorney General Mitchell says he is not opposed to capital punishment, news conference. NEW YORK TIMES 28:6, January 22, 1969.

J. P. Young advocates reinstatement of death penalty. NEW YORK TIMES IV,12:4, September 3, 1972.

K. Macleod lr. decries crime, corruption and amorality in US; calls for taking law into our own hands as only recourse left; supports capital punishment in face of cruel, decadent and corrupt times. NEW YORK TIMES 40:5, September 5, 1973.

Louisiana Governor G. W. Edwards on June 20 signs bill restoring death penalty in state, saying that he has serious reservations as to whether Supreme Court would hold any bill constitutional which provides for capital punishment. NEW YORK TIMES 36:6, June 21, 1973.

Mexico weighs restoring death penalty in Federal District in effort to curb capital crime; penalty abolished in District in 1929 but is used in 20 of 28 states; Judicial Studies Coll confs. find strong support for restoration; criminal attorneys minimize move; leading attorney V. Velasquez holds Mexicans contempt for death makes penalty no deterrent. NEW YORK TIMES 36:2, August 12, 1956.

National Association of Attorneys General on December 6 approves, 32 to 1, resolution recommending death penalty for certain crimes, meeting, Coronado, California; says that US Supreme Court, which recently outlawed death penalty in its present form, did not specifically preclude rights of Congress and state legislatures for death penalty as the sanction for commission of certain crimes. NEW YORK TIMES 30:4, December 7, 1972.

New Jersey Association of Chiefs of Police passes resolution urging reinstatement of capital punishment and asking that public be allowed to vote to amend state and Federal Constitutions for that purpose. NEW YORK TIMES 72:2, June 30, 1973.

New Jersey gubernational candidate C. W. Sandman, Jr. on September 13 tells Assembly Judiciary Com. that he supports pending legis. to restore death penalty in state; Democratic candidate B. T. Byrne sends com. statement saying proposed legis. would be pointless until US Supreme Court completes its review of similar state laws; com. is considering several amendments to bill; Public Defender S. Van Ness says bill is unconstitutional and discriminates against blacks and minorities; Senator J. Azzolina says he would favor public executions and death by hanging if it would stop crime. NEW YORK TIMES 83:1, September 14, 1973.

New Jersey gubernatorial candidates Representative C. W. Sandman, Jr. and B. T. Byrne debate major issues of campaign, New York Times, October 21; Sandman says he supports reinstatement of death penalty; says he intends to ask for judicial conference in January on street crime and propose that muggers receive mandtory prison sentence; says court system should be streamlined to reduce time between apprehension and conviction; Byrne says death penalty is not solution to crime and holds it is not a deterrent; says key to law enforcement policy has to do with sureness of law-enforcement process, detection, arrest, conviction, punishment and rehabilitation; criticizes delay by Governor in filling judicial vacancies. NEW YORK TIMES 35:4, October 22, 1973.

New Jersey League of Women Voters, attending convention in Morristown, reject resolution opposing reinstitution of death penalty. NEW YORK TIMES 67:7, April 14, 1975.

New Jersey Prosecutors Association, meeting in Atlantic City, urges that death penalty be reinstated for crimes that have traditionally been subject to capital penalty in the state (S). NEW YORK

TIMES 63:8, March 17, 1975.

New Jersey Senator on May 11 approves, 22-10, measure that would restore capital punishment in state; move to reinstate capital punishment in New Jersey comes 4 months after New Jersey Supreme Court struck down death penalty and 1 day after capital punishment study comm. appointed by Governor Cahill opened series of public hearings; bill's sponsor Senator Azzolina comments on its chances of passage in Assembly. NEW YORK TIMES 14:1, May 12, 1972.

New York judge wants back. CHRISTIAN SCIENCE MONITOR 10:3, October 19, 1972, (Eastern Edition); 4:3, October 19, 1972, (London and Overseas Editions).

New York State Assembly Codes Com. holds public hearing in World Trade Center, NYC, December 8, on possible restoration of death penalty for killing of police or correctional officers; law enforcement, civic, religious, education and political groups advance arguments for and against restoration; Lindsay adm. spokesman opposes any restoration; backed by ACLU NY Chapter; com chairman D. DiCarlo favors restoration; Governor Rockefeller has indicated that he would sign bill for mandatory execution for killing of peace officers. NEW YORK TIMES 35:1, December 9, 1973.

New York State Assembly votes to restore death penalty for murder of firemen. NEW YORK TIMES 95:1, March 28, 1968.

New York State Conservative party urges NYS restore penalty. NEW YORK TIMES 32:2, January 25, 1967.

New York State Governor Rockefeller on June 20 promises to try to restore state's death penalty for murders of policemen and prison guards, saying that punishment is vital as deterrent to such crimes; Appeals Court decision is expected to be appealed to Supreme Court; if Court does not reverse Appeals Court, Rockefeller will introduce legislature next year to restore penalty. NEW YORK TIMES 13:1, June 21, 1973.

New York State Senate (Speno) Com. on Codes opens hearings on recommending restoration of death penalty, NYC; hears conflicting views from law enforcement officials , churchmen, lawyers and others; B. B. Roberts, Acting Bronx District Attorney, opposes death penalty; PBA President J. Cassese sends statement backing it; Senator Speno says many legislators have received heavy mail urging its restoration. NEW YORK TIMES 21:1, October 4, 1968.

New York State Trial Lawyers Association and Methodist Church Northern New York Conference urge Rockefeller to sign bill. NEW YORK TIMES 76:1, May 23, 1965.

100 Hamburg, Germany, taxi drivers demonstrate for reintroduction of penalty; 180 drivers have been slain in West Germany since World War II. NEW YORK TIMES 68:1, August 30, 1964.

Philadelphia District Attorney Crumlish says his office will continue to seek death penalty where warranted despite Governor Lawrence order freezing execution until State Legislature rules. NEW YORK TIMES 28:5, March 28, 1961.

Professor H. Paolucci article defends capital punishment as necessary. NEW YORK TIMES 29:1, May 27, 1972.

Referendum on restoration of death penalty is approved by California voters by large margin in November 7 California election. NEW YORK TIMES 28:1, November 8, 1972.

S. Hughes Ir. supports death penalty. NEW YORK TIMES 30:3, March 17, 1973.

State of California asks US Supreme Court on March 31 to nullify California Supreme Court ruling that outlawed death penalty; California Attorney General Younger argues that state court's ruling had illegally assumed legislature role by abolishing death penalty when public support to retain it was high. NEW YORK TIMES 48:8, April 1, 1972.

13 states have enacted laws to bring back death penalty; measures reinstating capital punishment are awaiting action by Governors of 2 other states, and issue is pending in 16 states; measures to restore

penalty have been defeated in 8 states; issue has not been considered in 8 states; bill was passed and veoted in Mississippi because of unclear language; states that have restored death penalty are Arkansas, Colorado, Connecticut, Florida, Georgia, Indiana, Montana, Nebraska, Nevada, New Mexico, Ohio, Utah and Wyoming; measures are waiting gubernatorial action in Arizona and Tennessee. NEW YORK TIMES 18:1, May 10, 1973.

US Attorney General Levi, in TV interview, says he thinks death penalty would be considered constitutional if 1 concedes it is going to be equitably used and there are proper standards (S). NEW YORK TIMES 40:5, December 22, 1975.

Union of South Africa proposes death penalty for wide range of crimes classified as sabotage. NEW YORK TIMES 19:1, May 13, 1962.

United Nations security chief Lt. Col. H. Trimble, in November 9 radio broadcast from London, advocates worldwide return to institution of capital punishment. NEW YORK TIMES 36:6, November 10, 1972.

W. E. Farrell comments on NYS Assembly Codes Com's action in bringing to Assembly floor bill that would restore death penalty in most homicide cases; opposition noted. NEW YORK TIMES 35:6, April 29, 1972.

We think it would be a mistake to abandon the death penalty altogether. Editorial. THE NATIONAL OBSERVER p. 12, November 16, 1970.

Wicker article discusses restoration of death penalty in California by voters in November 7 election. NEW YORK TIMES IV,11:6, November 12, 1972.

Wicker, noting California Attorney General Younger's opposition to State Cupreme Court's ruling that declared capital punishment unconstitutional, comments on his efforts to draft constitutional amendment re-establishing capital punishment that would be put to referendum vote in November. NEW YORK TIMES 41:1, March 9, 1972.

CAPITAL PUNISHMENT–GENERAL

Abolition or retention? ANNALS OF THE AMERICAN ACADEMY OF POLITICAL AND SOCIAL SCIENCE pp. 101-136, November, 1952.

Again the issue of capital punishment, by W. Wyatt. NEW YORK TIMES MAGAZINE p. 17+, January 8, 1956.

Assessment of capital punishment, by W. H. Dempsey, Jr. COMMON-WEAL 75:496-497, February 2, 1962.

Bitter battle over capital punishment, by J. Star. LOOK 27:23-28, May 7, 1963.

Books; matter of life and death, by R. H. Rovere. NEW YORKER 33:164+, September 14, 1957.

Bring back the death penalty? pro and con views, by E. van den Haag, et al. U. S. NEWS AND WORLD REPORT 80:37-38, April, 1976.

Capital punishment. IRISH LAW TIMES 92:149, 1955, June 14-21, 1958+.

—. NEW STATESMAN AND NATION 39:87, January 28, 1950+; Discussion, 39:132, 161, February 4-11, 1950.

—. SOUTH AFRICAN LAW JOURNAL 73:344, August, 1956.

—, by G. H. Gottlieb. CRIME AND DELINQUENCY 15:1, January, 1969.

—, by J. F. Coakley. AMERICAN CRIMINAL LAW QUARTERLY 1:27, May, 1963.

—, by M. Meltsner. NEW REPUBLIC 169:12-13, July 21, 1973.

—, by M. Wright. NEW SOUTH 19:3-8, October, 1964.

—, by T. Sellin; A moderate view of capital punishment, by R. G. Murdey; Major trends in the use of capital punishment, by J. A.

McCafferty. FEDERAL PROBATION 25:3-21, September, 1961.

—, by W. Lester. AMERICA 112:484-486, April 10, 1965; Discussion, 112:831-833, June 5, 1965.

Capital punishment: cementing a fragile victory, by S. Caswell; A TRIAL interview: Hugo Adam Bedau, by S. Caswell. TRIAL 10:47-49+, May-June, 1974.

Capital punishment controversy, by W. O. Hochkammer, Jr. JOURNAL OF CRIMINAL LAW AND CRIMINOLOGY 60:360, September, 1969.

Capital punishment: the debate continues. NATION 182:190-191, March 10, 1956.

Capital punishment? debate-of-the-month, by J. B. S. Edwards, et al. ROTARIAN 94:10-13, May, 1959.

Capital punishment; decline in the imposition. REPORTER 36:14+, January 12, 1967.

Capital punishment: a fading practice. TIME 75:19, March 21, 1960.

Capital punishment—the latest round, by W. J. Bolt. JUSTICE OF THE PEACE 120:673, October 27, 1956.

Capital punishment: a model for reform. KENTUCKY LAW JOURNAL 57:508, 1968-1969.

Capital punishment: some reflections, by J. K. Balogh, et al. FEDERAL PROBATION 30:24, December, 1966.

Case for total abolition. ECONOMIST 191:609, May 16, 1959.

The case of capital punishment, by C. B. Vedder. POLICE 6:78-81, September-October, 1961.

Casuistry of capital punishment, by C. Hollis. DUBLIN REVIEW 230(471):33-40, 1956.

Comments on capital punishment and clemency, by M. V. DiSalle. OHIO STATE LAW JOURNAL 25:71, Winter, 1964.

Counsel for the doomed. NEWSWEEK 61:36-37, March 25, 1963.

Count down for death, by A. L. Smith, et al. CRIME AND DELINQUENCY 15:77, January, 1969.

Crime and punishment. JUSTICE OF THE PEACE 123:428, August 22, 1959.

Crime on everyones lips. TIME 79:31-32, March 16, 1962.

The crisis in capital punishment [based on address], by C. L. Black, Jr. MARYLAND LAW REVIEW 31:289-311, November 4, 1971.

Dangling man, by K. Menninger. HARPER'S MAGAZINE 219:20, December, 1959.

Death as cover-up?, by T. E. Gaddis. NATION 222:37-38, January 17, 1976.

Death for the death penalty? TIME 85:62-63, April 2, 1965.

Death house beat. TIME 73:60, June 8, 1950.

Death in two chapters, by F. S. Ball, Jr. ALABAMA LAWYER 23:385, October, 1962.

Death penalty. NATIONAL REVIEW 28:437-438, April 30, 1976.

—. NEW REPUBLIC 168:16, February 3, 1973.

—, by C. M. Craven. NEW STATESMAN AND NATION 37:470, May 7, 1949.

—, by C. W. Keeton. SOLICITOR 23:88, April, 1956.

—, by H. H. Jewell. JOURNAL OF THE STATE BAR OF CALIFORNIA 36:228, March-April, 1961.

—, by R. Hovda. COMMONWEAL 70:367-368, July 17, 1959.

Death penalty and fair trial, by W. E. Oberer. NATION 198:342-344, April 6, 1964.

Death penalty—issue that won't go away. U. S. NEWS AND WORLD REPORT 82:47, January 31, 1977.

Death penalty litigation, by A. M. Bickel. NEW REPUBLIC 157:13-14, August 19, 1967.

Death penalty [reprint] , by A. Temple. SPECTATOR 196:880, June 29, 1956.

Death penalty revival, by M. Costello. EDITORIAL RESEARCH RE-PORTS pp. 23-44, January 10, 1973.

A death penalty we can live with, by R. J. Gerber. NOTRE DAME LAWYER 50:251-272, December, 1974.

Death penalty's comeback. NATION 219:453, November 9, 1974.

Death reprieved. ECONOMIST 239:55, May 8, 1971.

Death revived? ECONOMIST 246:51-52, March 17, 1973.

Death sentence and then what?, by J. A. MacCafferty. CRIME AND DELINQUENCY 7:363, October, 1961.

Death sentence is not dead. ECONOMIST 250:53-54, March 23, 1974.

Durable custom. SCIENTIFIC AMERICAN 229:48, July, 1973.

Dying death penalty. TIME 89:50, February 17, 1967.

Edging away from capital punishment, by S. McBee. NEW REPUBLIC 152:11-12, January 30, 1965.

Edward Livingston on the punishment of death, by P. E. Mackey. TULANE LAW REVIEW 48:25-42, December, 1973.

11:20 was too late. NEWSWEEK 49:35, March 25, 1957.

Encouragement to murder, by C. H. Rolph. NATION 195:116-117, September 8, 1962.

End of death penalty? SENIOR SCHOLASTIC 70:19, April 5, 1957.

End to capital punishment. LIFE 66:36, June 20, 1969.

Exit the death penalty. NATION 200:266, March 15, 1965.

Fiat justitia, by R. H. Cecil. SPECTATOR 183:770, December 2, 1949.

Give 'em death?, by M. Roberts. NEW REPUBLIC 172:17-19, April 19, 1975.

HCN: a matter of life and death, by T. Benfey. CHEMISTRY 47:2, April, 1974.

Heard round the world. NATIONAL REVIEW 29:133-134, February 4, 1977.

In spite of all the talk of restoring death penalty—, by P. R. Oster. U. S. NEWS AND WORLD REPORT 78:52, April 14, 1975.

Indecisions. ECONOMISTS 261:63-64, December 11, 1976.

Is the death penalty dead? BAYLOR LAW REVIEW 26:114-122, Winter, 1974.

Is the death penalty necessary?, by G. Playfair. ATLANTIC 200: 31-35, September, 1957.

Is the death sentence dying? NEWSWEEK 61:31+, February 11, 1963.

Joseph Story on capital punishment, by J. C. Hogan. CALIFORNIA LAW REVIEW 43:76-84, March, 1955.

Killing ground: 1964-1973, by B. Hogan. CRIMINAL LAW REVIEW

1974:387-401, July, 1974.

Killing of the truth. NEW STATESMAN AND NATION 46:304, September 19, 1953.

Let reparation fit the crime. JOURNAL OF CRIMINAL LAW AND CRIMINOLOGY 22:167, April-June, 1958.

Life for a life?, by V. C. Ferkiss. COMMONWEAL 63:11-12, October 7, 1955.

Loophole for vengeance. NATION 200:435, April 26, 1965.

Major trends in the use of capital punishment, by J. A. McCafferty. CRIMINAL LAW QUARTERLY 1:9, February, 1963.

—. FEDERAL PROBATION 25:15, September, 1961.

Matter of life or death. NATION'S BUSINESS 58:23, November, 1970.

Moderate view of capital punishment, by R. G. Murdy. FEDERAL PROBATION 25:11, September, 1961.

More evidence on capital punishment. ECONOMIST 158:69, January 14, 1950.

New death penalty statutes: perpetuating a costly myth, by J. R. Browning. GONZAGA LAW REVIEW 9:651-705, Spring, 1974.

New life for the death penalty, by H. A. Bedau. NATION 223:144-148, August 28, 1976.

Notes from the Temple—to hang or nor to hang? IRISH LAW TIMES 90:49+, February 25, 1956.

Notes and comment. NEW YORKER 49:31, April 14, 1973.

Of death and one man, by N. Cousins. SATURDAY REVIEW 43:26, April 23, 1960; Discussion, 43:25-26, May 14, 1960.

Of many things, by D. R. Campion. AMERICA 128:inside cover, April 7, 1973.

On capital punishment. SOCIAL SERVICE REVIEW 47:426-427, September, 1973.

On the death penalty. NATIONAL REVIEW 17:406, May 18, 1965.

One lives, three die. NEWSWEEK 60:17, August 13, 1962.

Persistence of the executioner, by H. A. Bedau. NATION 194:217-220, March 10, 1962.

Plea for the condemned, by I. De Ment. ALABAMA LAWYER 29:440, October, 1968.

Policy statement on capital punishment. CRIME AND DELINQUEN-CY 10:105, April, 1964.

Power to start and end a life. ECONOMIST 245:45, December 2, 1972.

Primitive relic: death sentence, by E. Gertz. NATION 212:48-50, January 11, 1971.

Problem of capital punishment, by H. A. Bedau. CURRENT HISTORY 71:14-18+, July, 1976.

Pros and cons of capital punishment: a panel discussion (DiSalle, Gerstein, Sellin). AMERICAN BAR ASSOCIATION. SECTION OF CRIMINAL LAW 1959:5, 1959.

Pros, cons of an end to death penalty [United States]. U. S. NEWS AND WORLD REPORT 72:56, January 31, 1972.

Punishment by death, by J. Kuebler. EDITORIAL RESEARCH RE-PORTS pp. 527-544, July 17, 1963.

Punishment for crime, by A. D. Barksdale. FEDERAL PROBATION 19:5, September, 1955.

Race in the death house. TIME 69:25, March 25, 1957.

Reconsidering the death penalty. TIME 107:49, April 12, 1976.

Red coat man, by S. L. Chen. SPECTATOR 185:540, November 24, 1950.

Reflections on capital punishment. AMERICA 90:36, October 10, 1953; Discussion, 90:140, October 31, 1953.

Report on capital punishment, by C. Allen. SPECTATOR 191:347, October 2, 1953.

—, by J. C. Arnold. SOLICITOR 20:263-264, 293-295, November-December, 1953.

Ruling for life. ECONOMIST 244:50, July 8, 1972.

School for criminals, by R. Reynolds. NEW STATESMAN 48:152, August 7, 1954.

Sentence of death. ECONOMIST 168:832-834, September 26, 1953.

—. ECONOMIST 178:607, March 17, 1956.

Sentences: the quantum of the penalty. NEW ZEALAND LAW JOURNAL 34:81, April 1, 1958.

Sentencing powers of quarter sessions, by C. E. S. Horsford. CRIMINAL LAW REVIEW 1958:172, March, 1958.

Should capital punishment be revived?, by G. H. Poll. GOOD HOUSEKEEPING 169:24+, November, 1969.

Should we abolish the death penalty? pro and con discussion. SENIOR SCHOLASTIC 66:7-8, May 4, 1955.

Some recent trends in crime and punishment, by G. Hargrove. SOLICITOR 26:273, November, 1959.

Some reflections on do-it-yourself capital punishment, by R. King. AMERICAN BAR ASSOCIATION JOURNAL 47:668, July, 1961.

Star wormwood, by C. Bok. REVIEW NEWSWEEK 53:104-105, February 23, 1959.

The status of capital punishment: a world perspective, by C. H. Pattick. JOURNAL OF CRIMINAL LAW CRIMINOLOGY AND POLICE SCIENCE 56:397-411, December, 1965.

Study in capital punishment, by L. D. Savitz. JOURNAL OF CRIMINAL LAW AND CRIMINOLOGY 49:333, November-December, 1958.

Survival of the death penalty. BAYLOR LAW REVIEW 23:499, Summer, 1971.

Symposium, on capital punishment. District attorneys' association of the state of New York. Foreword. D. Gutman; Panel discussion (Silver, Weschsler, Playfair, Herman, Kuh, Hook. Wertham, Leibowitz, Casey, Savitz, Schwartz, Kapelman). NEW YORK LAW FORUM 7:247, August, 1961.

Theories of punishment, by M. Privette. UNIVERSITY OF KANSAS CITY LAW REVIEW 29:46, Winter, 1962.

Thoughts on capital punishment, by A. Morris. WASHINGTON LAW REVIEW 35:335, Autumn, 1960.

Time to kill the death penalty? pro and con discussion. SENIOR SCHOLASTIC 88:8-9, April 29, 1966.

Vickers case; Anomalies in penalties. ECONOMIST 184:294+, July 27, 1957.

We cannot be sure; death penalty in B. Hauptman case. NATION 224:420, April 9, 1977.

We, the people. NATION 190:219, March 12, 1960.

What shall we do about capital punishment? symposium. ESQUIRE 70:193-199, October, 1968.

Whatever happened to—capital punishment: it's being reviewed in many states. U. S. NEWS AND WORLD REPORT 76:46, March 4, 1974.

Whose executioner; governor's behavior over capital punishment. ECONOMIST 181:311, October 27, 1956.

Without portfolio, by C. B. Luce. MC CALLS 92:12+, May, 1965.

NEWSPAPER ARTICLES

The ADA's undemocratic move. CHRISTIAN SCIENCE MONITOR E:1, October 17, 1969, (All Editions).

Capital penalties fall. CHRISTIAN SCIENCE MONITOR 2:1, October 30, 1965, (Eastern Edition); 6:4, November 4, 1965, (Western Edition); 7:1, November 2, 1967, (Midwestern Edition).

Capital penalty truce. CHRISTIAN SCIENCE MONITOR 2:3, May 28, 1965, (Eastern Edition); 6:1, May 29, 1965, (Western Edition); 2:3, May 29, 1965, (Midwestern Edition).

Capital punishment. CHRISTIAN SCIENCE MONITOR E:1, March 24, 1965, (Eastern, Western, and Midwestern Editions).

Cartoon on issue. NEW YORK TIMES IV,8:2, March 6, 1960.

Columnist Edwin A. Roberts, Jr., comments on the mysterious disappearance of Sheila and Katherine Lyon from their suburban Maryland home and on the death of a friend, Nancy Knapp. THE NATIONAL OBSERVER p. 6, May 3, 1975.

Comment. NEW YORK TIMES IV,2:4, February 19, 1956.

Comment, cartoon. NEW YORK TIMES IV,6:4, December 21, 1969.

Deals below. CHRISTIAN SCIENCE MONITOR 1:1, December 23,

1964, (Eastern Edition); 2:5, December 26, 1964, (Western Edition); 1:1, December 23, 1964, (Midwestern Edition).

Death Row on trial. CHRISTIAN SCIENCE MONITOR 1:1, May 3, 1971, (Western and Midwestern Editions); 1:1, May 1, 1971, (Eastern and London and Overseas Editions).

Debate reviewed. NEW YORK TIMES IV,7:1, February 28, 1960.

E. M. Synder disputes August 22 edition. NEW YORK TIMES 28:4, August 29, 1963.

Editorial backs Clark stand. NEW YORK TIMES 18:1, July 4, 1968.

Editorial hails signing. NEW YORK TIMES 34:2, June 3, 1965.

Ephraim the Eel is a character used to satirize capital punishment. This is another Zoo's Who by Adelaide Field Cummings. THE NATIONAL OBSERVER p. 12, September 20, 1975.

Issue to be debated. CHRISTIAN SCIENCE MONITOR 5:1, August 7, 1965, (Eastern Edition); 12:4, August 4, 1965, (Western Edition).

L. H. Butterfield on July 4 edition. NEW YORK TIMES IV,11:1, July 14, 1968.

Move defeated. CHRISTIAN SCIENCE MONITOR 5:2, June 7, 1963, (Eastern Edition); 3:5, June 7, 1963, (Midwestern Edition).

New battle due. CHRISTIAN SCIENCE MONITOR 7:2, May 8, 1963, (Eastern Edition); 10:3, May 10, 1963, (Western Edition).

Other punishment favored. CHRISTIAN SCIENCE MONITOR 17:1, (Eastern and Midwestern Editions); 13:1, November 11, 1965, (Western Edition).

Professor J. Q. Wilson article discusses major issues surrounding use of death penalty; examines justice, utility and philosophy of capital punishment; illus. NEW YORK TIMES VI:27, October 28, 1973.

Professor S. Hook (Hoover Inst. on War, Revolution and Peace) decries controversy over re-institution of death penalty; holds that punishment must fit criminal, not crime, and that mandatory sentence is not needed in all cases. NEW YORK TIMES 40:3, April 6, 1973.

Scans capital penalty. CHRISTIAN SCIENCE MONITOR 17:5, March 2, 1963, (Eastern Edition).

Shuns death penalty. CHRISTIAN SCIENCE MONITOR 10:4, October 21, 1972, (Western Edition).

Summarizes arguments for and against abolition; illus. NEW YORK TIMES VI:17, January 8, 1956.

World-wide decline in death penalty discussed; chart showing countries and US staes that have abolished it and year of abolition; Brown urges abolition of death penalty, special California Legislature session; reviews arguments for abolition; abolition bill referred to Senate committee. NEW YORK TIMES 18:4, March 3, 1960.

CAPOTE, TRUMAN
NEWSPAPER ARTICLES

T. Capote at odds with American Broadcasting Company over their failure to schedule TV showing of his documentary Death Row, USA; demands showing before US Supreme Court considers pending case of whether protracted delay in capital cases constitutes cruel or unusual punishment. NEW YORK TIMES 95:2, October 31, 1968.

CASES INVOLVING CAPITAL PUNISHMENT
Aftermath of Benjamin Reid, by W. Styron. ESQUIRE 58:79+, November, 1962.

The aftermath of Furman: the Florida experience [in the light of the Supreme court decision in Furman v. Georgia, June 29, 1972, declaring the death penalty to be "cruel and unusual punishment"] : The future of capital punishment in Florida: analysis and recommendations, by C. W. Ehrhardt, et al.; Florida's legislative response to Furman: an exercise in futility, by C. W. Ehrhardt, et al.

JOURNAL OF CRIMINAL LAW AND CRIMINOLOGY 64:2-21, March, 1973.

Another Chessman case?, by E. Duncan. NEWSWEEK 60:15, July 9, 1962.

Ballad of Gary Gilmore. NATIONAL REVIEW 29:18, January 7, 1977.

Billie Sol Esteschvich, by C. Blackmoore. NEW REPUBLIC 147:13-17, September 24, 1962.

Capital punishment after Furman (Furman v. Georgia, 92 Sup. Ct. 2726). JOURNAL OF CRIMINAL LAW AND CRIMINOLOGY 64:281-289, September, 1973.

Capital punishment and Caryl Chessman, by J. Cogley. COMMON-WEAL 71:671, March 18, 1960.

Capital punishment in the light of constitutional evolution: an analysis of distinctions between Furman and Gregg (Gregg v. Georgia, 96 Sup. Ct. 2909), by J. C. England. NOTRE DAME LAWYER 52:596-610, April, 1977.

Capital punishment statutes in the wake of United States v. Jackson: some unresolved questions [ruling concerning constitutionality of the death penalty provisions of the Federal kidnapping act], by D. A. Poe. GEORGE WASHINGTON LAW REVIEW 37:719-745, May, 1969.

Capital punishment under the UCMJ after Furman, by R. E. Tragolo. AIR FORCE LAW REVIEW 16(4):86-95, Winter, 1974.

Capital sentencing—effect of McGautha (MacGautha v. California 91 Sup. Ct. 1454) and Furman (Furman v. Georgia 92 Sup. Ct. 2726). TEMPLE LAW QUARTERLY 45:619, Summer, 1972.

Case of Derek Bentley. NEW STATESMAN 45:109, January 31, 1953; Discussion, 45:150, 178, February 7-14, 1953.

Case of James Weaver, by W. Teeling. SPECTATOR 195:213-214, August 12, 1955.

Case that could end capital punishment: Maxwell v. Bishop, by R. Hammer. NEW YORK TIMES MAGAZINE pp. 46-47+, October 12, 1969.

Charles-Henri Sanson, exécuteur des arrêts criminels à Paris; sa vie privée et publique 1739-1806, by R. Goulard. MERCURE DE FRANCE 311:254-267, February, 1951.

Chessman case. COMMONWEAL 71:616, March 4, 1960.

—. ECONOMIST 195:535, May 7, 1960.

Chessman case: when justice took 12 years. U. S. NEWS AND WORLD REPORT 48:73+, May 16, 1960.

Condemned accomplices; G. M. Gilmore and R. E. White. NATION 223:643-644, December 18, 1976.

Consequences of Chessman, by R. Bendiner. NEW STATESMAN 59: 351, March 12, 1960.

Constitutional law—capital punishment—Furman v. Georgia (92 Sup. Ct. 2726) and Georgia's statutory response. MERCER LAW REVIEW 24:891, Summer, 1973.

Constitutional law—the remains of the death penalty: Furman v. Georgia (92 Sup. Ct. 2726). DE PAUL LAW REVIEW 22:481, Winter, 1972.

Death for Gilmore?, by W. F. Buckley, Jr. NATIONAL REVIEW 28:1422, December 24, 1976.

A death in the family: the story of Gary Mark Gilmore, by M. Gilmore. ROLLING STONE p. 58+, March 10, 1977.

Death-in-life of Benjamin Reid, by W. Styron. ESQUIRE 57:114+, February, 1962.

Death in Zion, by R. S. Anson. NEW TIMES 8:20+, February 4, 1977.

Death of capital punishment? Furman v. Georgia (92 Sup. Ct. 2726), by D. D. Polsby. SUPREME COURT REVIEW 1972:1, 1972.

Death penalty after Furman (Furman v. Georgia, 92 Sup. Ct. 2726), by C. S. Vance. NOTRE DAME LAWYER 48:850, April, 1973.

—, by L. A. Wollan, Jr. LOYOLA UNIVERSITY LAW JOURNAL 4:339-357, Summer, 1973.

Death penalty—the alternatives left after Furman v. Georgia (92 Sup. Ct. 2726). ALBANY LAW REVIEW 37:344, 1973.

Death penalty cases. CALIFORNIA LAW REVIEW 56:1270, October, 1968.

The death penalty cases [California]. CALIFORNIA LAW REVIEW 56:1268-1490, October, 1968.

Death penalty cases: a preliminary comment, by J. M. Junker. WASHINGTON LAW REVIEW 48:95, November, 1972.

Death-row dramatics; case of G. M. Gilmore. TIME 108:46, November 29, 1976.

Death wish; case of G. M. Gilmore, by P. Goldman, et al. NEWSWEEK 88:26-27+, November 29, 1976.

Delay on the death penalty; case of W. Maxwell. TIMES 95:60, June 15, 1970.

Dialogue of comfort and More's execution: some comments on literary purpose, by L. Miles. MODERN LANGUAGE REVIEW 61:556-560, October, 1966.

Doomed penalty; decision regarding sentence of W. Witherspoon. TIME 91:78, June 14, 1968.

Double jeopardy; black and poor: address, January 12, 1969, by

F. H. Williams. VITAL SPEECHES 35:273-277, February 15, 1969.

Dreadful dilemma: case of E. Walker. NEWSWEEK 57:29-30, March 20, 1961.

Eight years on death row: in the shadow of Chessman—Paul Crump, by W. Friedkin. CALIFORNIA 2:6-15, October, 1961.

Ellis case. ECONOMIST 176:209, July 16, 1955.

Evans or Christie?, by I. Gilmore. SPECTATOR 195:270-272, August 26, 1955; Discussion, 195:331, September 9, 1955.

Execution of Daniel Gearhart in Angola; statements, July 9-10, 1976, by R. H. Nessen, et al. DEPARTMENT OF STATE BULLETIN 75:163, August 2, 1976.

Execution of Ruth Ellis. SPECTATOR 195:81, July 15, 1955; Discussion, 195:110, 120-121, 165, July 22-29, 1955.

Exit Jack Ketch. AMERICA 94:604, March 3, 1956.

Far more than Chessman, by M. Ascoli. REPORTER 22:2+, April 14, 1960.

The fate of Caryl W. Chessman. HUMANIST 20:173-175, May-June, 1960.

Fight for life [Chessman case]. ECONOMIST 194:714+, February 20, 1960.

Footnote to Furman (Furman v. Georgia, 92 Sup. Ct. 2726): failing justification for the capital case exception to the right to bail after abolition of the death penalty. SAN DIEGO LAW REVIEW 10:349, February, 1973.

Furman v. Georgia (92 Sup. Ct. 2726) and Kentucky statutory law, by L. M. T. Reed. KENTUCKY BAR JOURNAL 37:25, January, 1973.

Furman v. Georgia (92 Sup. Ct. 2726): the Burger court looks at judicial review, by D. Victor. LAW AND THE SOCIAL ORDER 1972:393, 1972.

Furman (Furman v. Georgia, 92 Sup. Ct. 2726) Case: what life is left in the death penalty? CATHOLIC UNIVERSITY LAW REVIEW 22:651, Spring, 1973.

Furman v. Georgia (92 Sup. Ct. 2726)—death-knell for capital punishment? ST. JOHN'S LAW REVIEW 47:107, October, 1972.

Furman v. Georgia (92 Sup. Ct. 2726): a postmortem on the death penalty. VILLANOVA LAW REVIEW 18:678, March, 1973.

Furman v. Georgia (92 Sup. Ct. 2726): will the death of capital punishment mean a new life for bail? HOFSTRA LAW REVIEW 2:432-443, Winter, 1974.

Gary Gilmore: death wish, by D. A. Williams, et al. NEWSWEEK 88:35-36, November 22, 1976.

Gilmore's future, by R. Rosenblatt. NEW REPUBLIC 176:32, January 1, 1977.

Governor's dilemma; case of E. Walker. NEWSWEEK 57:61, April 3, 1961.

Jury challenges capital punishment, and Labat v. Bennett (365 F 2d 698): a reconciliation. DUKE LAW JOURNAL 1968:283, April, 1968.

Jury selection and the death penalty: Witherspoon (Witherspoon v. Illinois, 88 Sup. Ct. 1770). UNIVERSITY OF CHICAGO LAW REVIEW 37:759, Summer, 1970.

Killing of Grimau, by J. M. Cohen. SPECTATOR 210:558, May 3, 1963.

Letter from Chessman, by C. H. Rolph. NEW STATESMAN 59:615-616, April 30, 1960.

Life and death of Caryl Chessman. NEW STATESMAN 59:653, May 7, 1960.

Life for Chessman, by C. H. Rolph. NEW STATESMAN 59:280+, February 27, 1960.

Litigating against the death penalty: the strategy behind Furman (Furman v. Georgia, 92 Sup. Ct. 2726), by M. Meltsner. YALE LAW JOURNAL 82:1111, May, 1973.

McGautha v. California, May, 1971: on May 3, 1971, the Supreme Court handed down a far-reaching decision that capital punishment procedures in general use throughout the United States today do not violate the constitution [excerpts from the text of the decision]. CURRENT HISTORY 61:40-42+, July, 1971.

Maimed rites; Gilmore case. NATIONAL REVIEW 28:1335-1336, December 10, 1976.

Man of conviction: Aarom C. Mitchell's execution. NEWSWEEK 69:29, April 24, 1967.

Mandatory death: State v. Waddell [(NC)—S E 2d—]. NORTH CAROLINA CENTRAL LAW JOURNAL 4:292, Spring, 1973.

Mike Bell is waiting; Death row, Colorado state penitentiary, by D. Jackson. LIFE 64:92-98+, June 7, 1968.

Much ado about Gary. TIME 108:85-87, December 13, 1976.

The murder of In Ho Oh, by M. Mannes. THE REPORTER 18:21-25, June 26, 1958.

Must Chessman die? NATION 190:cover, 265, March 26, 1960; Discussion, 190:inside cover, April 9, 1960.

—. NEW REPUBLIC 142:3-4, March 28, 1960; Reply, 142:22-23, April 11, 1960; Discussion, 142:23, April 25, 1960.

New approach to M'Naghten v. Durham, by S. Rubin. JOURNAL

OF THE AMERICAN JUDICATURE SOCIETY 45:133, December, 1961.

No. 77; execution of Luis Jose Monge in Colorado. TIME 89:33, June 9, 1967.

Pittman v. State [(Tex) 434 S W 2d 352] : the death penalty and Texas jurors. SOUTHWESTERN LAW JOURNAL 23:405, May, 1969.

Playboy interview: Gary Gilmore. PLAYBOY 24:69+, April, 1977.

Podola case. ECONOMIST 193:408, October 31, 1959.

Politics and Chessman, by R. Meister. NATION 190:275-277, March 26, 1960.

Prosecutors may no longer tell juries capital punishment is a known deterrent: historic California Supreme court decision. CALIFORNIAN 3:5, February, 1962.

Protest—Julian Grimau's death sentence, by P. Robinson. CONTEMPORARY REVIEW 203:287-288, June, 1963.

Recent changes in California law regarding jury's discretion in selecting first degree murder penalty [People v. Green (Cal.) 302 P 2d 307]. SOUTHERN CALIFORNIA LAW REVIEW 31:200, February, 1958.

Response to Furman (Furman v. Georgia, 92 Sup. Ct. 2726): can legislators breathe life back into death? CLEVELAND STATE LAW REVIEW 23:172-189, Winter, 1974.

Resurrection of the death penalty: the validity of Arizona's response to [the U.S. supreme court's decision, June 29, 1972, in the case of] Furman v. Georgia, by G. Forster. ARIZONA STATE LAW JOURNAL 1974(2):257-296, 1974.

Right to die: case of G. Gilmore, by T. Szasz. NEW REPUBLIC 175: 8-9, December 11, 1976; Reply by H. Schwarzschild, 175:32, December 18, 1976.

Sandys delusion. ECONOMIST 233:13-15, November 8, 1969.

Simcox case [doubly guilty of capital murder]. ECONOMIST 210: 871, March 7, 1964.

Speaking out; I don't want to die; excerpts from Brief against death, by E. H. Smith. SATURDAY EVENING POST 241:10+, September 7, 1968.

State supreme court rules death penalty unconstitutional in California. CALIFORNIA JOURNAL 3:51, February, 1972.

Statistical evidence on the deterrent effect of capital punishment—A comparison of the work of Thorsten Sellin and Isaac Ehrlich on the deterrent effect of capital punishment, by D. C. Baldus, et al.; The illusion of deterrence in Esaac Ehrlich's research on capital punishment, by W. J. Bowers, et al.; Deterrence: evidence and inference, by I. Ehrlich. YALE LAW JOURNAL 85:164-227, December, 1975.

Stay of execution; Supreme court ordering indefinite stay of execution in the G. Gilmore case, by D. A. Williams, et al. NEWSWEEK 88:37, December 13, 1976.

Stirrings on death row: execution of Aaron Mitchell at San Quentin prison. TIME 89:25, April 21, 1967.

Sudden rush for blood; murderer G. M. Gilmore's desire to be executed. TIME 108:56, November 22, 1976.

Supreme Court and capital punishment—from Wilkerson to Witherspoon (Witherspoon v. Illinois, 88 Sup. Ct. 1770). ST. LOUIS UNIVERSITY LAW JOURNAL 14:463, Spring, 1970.

Tennessee v. Walsh Jones: the closing argument for the defense, by J. W. Henry, Jr. AMERICAN BAR ASSOCIATION JOURNAL 46:52, January, 1960.

Thoughts on the Bentley case [brief history of the death penalty in England, and present weaknesses of the system, as shown in the recent execution of Derek Bentley], by H. Klare. SOCIALIST COMMENTARY 17:55-57, March, 1953.

Toward expansion of Witherspoon (Witherspoon v. Illinois, 88 Sup. Ct. 1770): capital scruples jury bias, and use of psychological data to raise presumptions in the law, by F. Goldberg. HARVARD CIVIL RIGHTS. CIVIL LIBERTIES LAW REVIEW 5:53, January, 1970.

Unanimity requirement of a jury's determination and the Witherspoon (Witherspoon v. Illinois, 88 Sup. Ct. 1770) exclusionary rule. TEMPLE LAW QUARTERLY 43:46, Fall, 1969.

Waiting on death row; case of G. Tyler, by B. Cory. PROGRESSIVE 40:30-31, August, 1976.

When and why did Hastings lose his head?, by B. P. Wolffe. ENGLISH HISTORICAL REVIEW 89:835-844, October, 1974; Reply by A. Hanham, 90:821-827, October, 1975.

When a condemned man wants to die; case of G. M. Gilmore. U. S. NEWS AND WORLD REPORT 81:19, November 29, 1976.

Who hates Chessman?, by R. Meister. NATION 190:167-169, February 20, 1960.

Wish granted. ECONOMIST 262:21, January 22, 1977.

Witherspoon revisited: exploring the tension between Witherspoon and Furman, by W. S. White. UNIVERSITY OF CINCINNATI LAW REVIEW 45:19-36, 1976.

World looks at Gilmore's execution. ATLAS WORLD PRESS REVIEW 24:9, March, 1977.

You may kill, but you must promise not to use discretion: Furman v. Georgia (92 Sup. Ct. 2726). LOYOLA UNIVERSITY LAW REVIEW 6:526-555, September, 1973.

NEWSPAPER ARTICLES

Absent to stand trial. CHRISTIAN SCIENCE MONITOR 1:1, March 16, 1967, (All Editions).

All-white Oklahoma City jury, ignoring recent US Supreme Court ruling virtually outlawing death penalty, goes beyond a prosecutor's request for million-year prison term and sentences on November 17 *Negro L. Breedlove*, 20, to die in electric chair for murder and armed robbery in connection with slaying of H. Siler family on August 4 in Oklahoma City store; co-defendants W. T. Glover and R. C. Carolina are still awaiting trial; 4th defendant W. Draper, 20, has been sentenced to life. NEW YORK TIMES 74:6, November 18, 1972.

American Bar Foundation finds long delays in carrying out death penalty weaken public confidence in law, study begun at request of American Bar Association Governments Board after C. Chessman execution, 1960; does not debate death penalty merits; urges uniform post-conviction procedures. NEW YORK TIMES 60:1, January 29, 1961.

Amsterdam, representing E. J. Aikens, Negro sentenced to death for murder in California in 1966, and W. H. Furman, convicted of murder in Georgia in 1968, argues that death penalty has been used less and less frequently and therefore is cruel and unusual punishment; NAACP Legal Defense and Education Fund counsel J. Greenberg, representing L. Jackson, Negro convicted of rape in Georgia in 1968, argues that rape is punished capitally in Southern states only; cases detailed. NEW YORK TIMES 15:1, January 18, 1972.

Article on re-erection of gallows used to hang triple slayer A. LeBlanc .in Morristown, New Jersey, in 1833; restoration is accomplished at request of local historian who wishes to take photographs for book on LeBlanc case; gallows illus. NEW YORK TIMES 63:5, January 29, 1973.

Boston, Massachusetts, court sentences L. Johnson to death for murder of J. W. Christian. NEW YORK TIMES 30:4, June 4, 1972.

Brown holds California Constitution bars his granting Chessman clemency, statement as demands for clemency mount. NEW YORK TIMES 41:3, April 27, 1960.

California Superior Court Judge Arnason, allowing black militant A. Davis to be released in $102,500 bail, rules that state law prohibiting bail in 'capital cases' had been invalidated by State Supreme Court decision eliminating death penalty in California. NEW YORK TIMES 1:2, February 24, 1972.

Capital punishment on trial in Cline case. CHRISTIAN SCIENCE MONITOR 36:5, November 29, 1974, (Eastern Edition).

Chessman asks his case be kept separate from abolition debate, lr. to Brown; Brown to press fight for abolition. NEW YORK TIMES 17:1, February 24, 1960.

Chessman urges California Legis. map bill abolishing death penalty so as to exclude him, lr. to Governor Brown; Virginia House of Delegates com. rejects proposal to abolish penalty. NEW YORK TIMES 19:4, 5, March 1, 1960.

Comment on Jesse T. Fowler, sentenced to death for murder in North Carolina, following Supreme Court postponing its decision on his capital punishment case; illus (M). NEW YORK TIMES 1:1, June 24, 1975.

Comment on US Supreme Court hearing death penalty case involving Jesse T. Fowler, sentenced on death in North Carolina for murder; case seen as having affect on constitution of death penalty in other states (S). NEW YORK TIMES IV,6:2, April 27, 1975.

Connecticut State Supreme Court on December 19 reduces death sentence of convicted murderer L. Cofone to life imprisonment, in keeping with state court's understanding of US Supreme Court's ruling on capital punishment on June 29; Cofone had been sentenced to die in electric chair for 1970 murder of C. Diack; ruling leaves open prospect that Governor Meskill will carry out his intention to propose new legis. that would impose death penalty for certain crimes and not to allow courts option of specifying life imprisonment instead. NEW YORK TIMES 59:1, December 20, 1972.

Edgar Smith, the longest inhabitant of death row in the United States says he admitted guilt only to win his freedom. THE NATIONAL OBSERVER p. 6, December 18, 1971.

Effects of Chessman case on efforts to end death penalty discussed; cartoon. NEW YORK TIMES IV,6:2, May 1, 1960.

Excerpts from convicted murder Gary Gilmore's remarks to an Oregon judge after a 1973 attempted robbery are published. THE NATIONAL OBSERVER p. 4, November 20, 1976.

Former NYC HRA speech writer Nettie Leif comments on her reasons for changing her stand against capital punishment; illustrations of Carl Chessman. NEW YORK TIMES 33:2, July 2, 1975.

Freddie Lee Pitts and Wilbert Lee have been convicted for the second time of murdering two men in a service station in 1963. THE NATIONAL OBSERVER p. 14, March 25, 1972.

Freddie Pitts and Wilbert Lee are still trying to get an acquittal for their conviction for a 1963 murder. THE NATIONAL OBSERVER p. 15, August 12, 1972.

G. C. Chalwell is hanged June 28 in British Virgin Islands; it is 1st execution in country in 35 years; Chalwell was convicted October 1971 for murdering his 19-year-old girlfriend, J. Thomas, with a knife. NEW YORK TIMES 4:3, June 29, 1972.

Illinois Supreme Court orders new hearing and sentence for R. Speck, convicted murderer of 8 nurses and student nurses in Chicago in 1966 who was sentenced to death; court is acting in accord with recent US Supreme Court decision banning capital punishment; case reviewed. NEW YORK TIMES 36:3, September 21, 1972.

Issues involved in W. L. Maxwell case, before US Supreme Court discussed; question of procedure in imposing death penalty involved; Maxwell, a Negro, was condemned to death in 1961 for rape,

Arkansas. NEW YORK TIMES IV,11:1, May 10, 1970.

J. Wilson, Alabama Negro, sentenced to die for $1.95 theft; robbery is capital offense in Alabama. NEW YORK TIMES 24:5, August 21, 1958.

Joey Kagebien is 16 and on death row in DeWitt, Arkansas, for the slaying of a hunter. THE NATIONAL OBSERVER p. 6, November 13, 1971.

Judge A. J. Diamond on February 28 sentences 18-year-old R. I. O'Neil to die in electric chair for raping and murdering 57-year-old woman in 1972; sentence, which is mandaotry under Massachusetts law, will automatically be reviewed by State Supreme Court. NEW YORK TIMES 14:5, March 2, 1973.

Major Legis. fight seen; many legislators angered that Brown linked issue to Chessman case; Chessman attorney urges November referendum; Vice President Nixon urges retention in extreme cases. NEW YORK TIMES 45:2, February 21, 1966.

Michael Abdul Malik is hanged on May 16 in Port of Spain, Trinidad, for murder of his cousin Joseph Skerritt; por of Malik (M). NEW YORK TIMES 4:3, May 17, 1975.

New Jersey Supreme Court, 6-0, rules state cannot ask death penalty in retrial of convicted murderer originally sentenced to life term, case of R. Wolf. NEW YORK TIMES 43:1, January 25, 1966.

New York State Supreme Court Justice Joseph A. Martinis, after sentencing convicted murderer Hosie S. Turner to 25 years to life in prison, says existing penalties are ineffectual and urges Legis. to seriously consider reinstituting death penalty (M). NEW YORK TIMES 29:7, February 8, 1975.

New York State Supreme Court, White Plains, jury convicts Joseph Davis for 1974 murder of Yonkers Ptl. Harold Woods during supermarket holdup; Davis thus becomes 1st person in state to face mandatory death sentence under state law revised in 1974 that made death penalty mandatory for killing of police officer; case reviewed (M). NEW YORK TIMES 41:1, November 25, 1975.

News brief—Gilly gets. CHRISTIAN SCIENCE MONITOR 2:1, May 3, 1972 (All Editions).

Pennsylvania Supreme Court overturns on August 24 death sentence given to convicted murderer A. Scoleri, changing his sentence to life imprisonment; Scoleri was convicted in holdup-slaying of a South Philadelphia merchant. NEW YORK TIMES 31:1, August 25, 1972.

Philip Eaton 3d, first person convicted of 1st-degree murder in Delaware since it reinstated capital punishment, is sentenced in Wilmington Superior Court to death by hanging (S). NEW YORK TIMES 47:8, March 26, 1975.

Providence, Rhode Island, Superior Court jury convicts Robert Cline of 1st degree murder for 1974 slaying of Frank A. Pirri; sentence requires death penalty (S). NEW YORK TIMES 35:6, May 1, 1975.

Queens grand jury urges death penalty for C. Butler and L. Hayes, convicted of murdering NYC Ptl. K. Nugent during attempted holdup of Queens luncheonette. NEW YORK TIMES 43:1, April 14, 1972.

Readers write: Ray and Sirhan? CHRISTIAN SCIENCE MONITOR E:5, June 6, 1969, (All Editions).

Reasons for Gary Gilmore's request to be executed are examined. THE NATIONAL OBSERVER p. 4, November 20, 1976.

Ronald Clark O'Bryan, a Pasadena, Texas, optician, was sentenced to die in the electric chair for killing his son, Timothy, 8, last Halloween by giving the boy candy laced with cyanide. Follow-up. THE NATIONAL OBSERVER p. 2, June 14, 1975.

Senator Dirksen's shift from support for Associate Justice Fortas nomination for Chief Justice linked to pressure from Illinois over Supreme Court June ruling on capital punishment in Witherspoon case, in which Fortas voted with majority in a 6-3 ruling. NEW YORK TIMES 30:3, September 28, 1968.

Silverman biography. NEW YORK TIMES 14:3, December 14, 1964.

Texas Criminal Appeals Court, Austin, upholds constitution of death penalty in upholding conviction of R. E. Texeno, who was sentenced to death in December 1969 slaying of O. C. Wright; rules that execution for crime is neither cruel nor unusual punishment as terms are used in US Constitution. NEW YORK TIMES 29:1, March 16, 1972.

Tom Wicker discusses issue of capital punishment in Jesse T. Fowler case now before US Supreme Court; recalls 1972 California Supreme Court decision declaring penalty unconstitutional in state (M). NEW YORK TIMES 35:1, March 11, 1975.

US Appeals Court, 4th Circuit, directs change in procedure for removing from death sentence cases jurors who oppose capital punishment, M. F. Crawford case; says examining judges should inquire whether jurors' opposition will affect their determination of guilt or innocence. NEW YORK TIMES 10:4, April 13, 1968.

US Solicitor General Robert H. Bork requests 15 minutes in oral argument on issue of constitution of capital punishment when case of Jesse T. Fowler, condemned to death in North Carolina for murder, comes before Supreme Court; files friend-of-court brief in case urging Court not to nullify capital punishment statues enacted by 31 states in last 3 years; says Government does not fully support North Carolina in this specific case but is concerned lest Justices seize this occasion to broaden 1972 ruling to make death penalty unconstitutional in all circumstances; holds imposition in particular case should be up to legislators, judges and juries; brief is not addressed to basic issue in North Carolina case but to broader question of whether death penalty always is cruel and unusual punishment; case has not yet been scheduled for argument; case may be postponed because of health of Justice Douglas, who is still hospitalized (M). NEW YORK TIMES 38:4, March 9, 1975.

US Supreme Court begins hearing case of Jesse T. Fowler, convicted murderer sentenced to death in North Carolina; case is 1st involving death penalty that Supreme Court has agreed to consider since June 1972, when it ruled that capital punishment as then practiced in US is unconstitutional under 8th Amendment ban against cruel and unusual punishment; technically question for Court is whether Fowler should be put to death in gas chamber as sentenced, but decision could also affect legis. efforts in other states to reinstate death penalty; opening arguments noted (M). NEW YORK TIMES 21:3, April 22, 1975.

US Supreme Court denies appeal of Negro W. B. Craig, convicted in June 1963 rape of white woman, based on argument that death penalty is instrument of discrimination against Negroes. NEW YORK TIMES 27:3, March 29, 1966.

US Supreme Court sends back to trial court Maxwell case, postpones important ruling on capital punishment expected to produce landmark decision; postponement leaves intact judicial freeze that has halted all executions in US for past 3 years. NEW YORK TIMES 1:4, June 2, 1970.

US Supreme Court sets November 9 as date for its hearing on cases of J. Crampton and D. C. McGautha that challenge procedures for imposing death sentence in US. NEW YORK TIMES 63:6, October 29, 1970.

CENTRAL PRISON
see: The Prisoner and Capital Punishment

CEYLON

NEWSPAPER ARTICLES

Ceylon suspends death penalty for murder for 3-year experimental period. NEW YORK TIMES 4:8, April 23, 1958.

CHESSMAN, CARYL
see: Cases Involving Capital Punishment

CHINA
Death penalty: Chinese style, by C. Douglas. TRIAL 13:44-46,

February, 1977.

Reflections on crime and punishment in China, with appended sentencing documents, by R. Edwards. COLUMBIA JOURNAL OF TRANSNATIONAL LAW 16:45-103, 1977.

NEWSPAPER ARTICLES

Article on legal procedures in People's Republic of China notes that capital punishment is imposed on persons who engage in espionage or who commit murder. NEW YORK TIMES 5:1, November 11, 1973.

Nationalist China to substitute gas chamber or electric chair for firing squad. NEW YORK TIMES 74:5, April 15, 1962.

CHRISTIANS AND CAPITAL PUNISHMENT
see: The Morality of Capital Punishment

CHURCHES
see: The Morality of Capital Punishment

CLEMENCY
Clemency in Arkansas. TIME 97:50, January 11, 1971.

Comments on capital punishment and clemency, by M. V. DiSalle. OHIO STATE LAW JOURNAL 25:71, Winter, 1964.

Commutation of sentences by convening authorities and boards of review, by L. H. Benrubi. JAG JOURNAL 14:91, December, 1960.

Comparison of the executed and the commuted among admissions to death row: is a rational, fair scheme discernible in the commutation of death sentences? or does a selective system appear to operate, differentiating between the executed and commuted upon improper base? [based on a study of] the case records of 439 persons sentenced to death for first degree murder and detained on death row in Pennsylvania between 1914 and 1958, by M. E. Wolfgang, et al. JOURNAL OF CRIMINAL LAW, CRIMINOLOGY, AND POLICE SCIENCE 53:301-311, September, 1962.

Contempt and clemency. TIME 70:15, July 8, 1957.

The dynamics of executive clemency, by S. M. Ringold. AMERICAN BAR ASSOCIATION JOURNAL 52:240-243, March, 1966.

Executive clemency and the death penalty, by W. Rockefeller. CATHOLIC UNIVERSITY LAW REVIEW 21:94, Fall, 1971.

Executive clemency in Wisconsin, by D. Adamany. WISCONSIN BAR BULLETIN 36:54, Ohio, 1963.

Governor's dilemma; case of E. Walker. NEWSWEEK 57:61, April 3, 1961.

Phone call, by C. C. Reid. HARPER'S MAGAZINE 228:164-166, April, 1964.

Stay of execution; Supreme court ordering indefinite stay of execution in the G. Gilmore case, by D. A. Williams, et al. NEWSWEEK 88:37, December 13, 1976.

NEWSPAPER ARTICLES

Arkansas Governor Rockefeller commutes death sentences of all 15 men awaiting execution in state to life imprisonment. NEW YORK TIMES 26:1, December 30, 1970.

Brown commutes sentences of 4 murderers. NEW YORK TIMES 14:5, December 29, 1966.

California Governor Brown weighs clemency for 64; RC Abp McGucken urges move; Governor-elect Reagan appointment of E. Meese 3d as clemency sec noted; they reportedly back penalty. NEW YORK TIMES 7:1, December 24, 1966.

Death sentence of Brooklyn slayer T. Willis commuted to life term, 1st application by court of law abolishing death penalty. NEW YORK TIMES 21:6, June 16, 1965.

Editorial sees recent British Government pardon of T. J. Evans, hanged for murder of daughter, 1950, underlining need for ending penalty. NEW YORK TIMES 42:1, October 20, 1966.

5-member com. rejects former British black power leader Michael Abdul Malik's request for clemency and orders him hanged for murder of Joseph Skerritt, Port of Spain, Trinidad (S). NEW YORK TIMES 2:4, May 16, 1975.

Florida Governor Kirk orders 14 of 51 facing penalty to prepare for final clemency hearings before State Pardon Board; move preludes resumption of penalty, last used in 1964. NEW YORK TIMES 37:1, April 4, 1967.

Government reports sentences of 25 prisoners have been commuted to life imprisonment, that other cases are under study. NEW YORK TIMES 3:1, December 11, 1968.

Governor of Alabama grants reprieve because executions are only allowed at Kilby Prison, which has been abandoned. THE NATIONAL OBSERVER p. 11, August 17, 1970.

Governor Rockefeller commutes death sentences of 2 murderers sentenced before capital punishment law was eased. NEW YORK TIMES 26:3, April 9, 1968.

Governor Rockefeller in October commuted death sentences of 2 holdup men, convicted in 1962 slayings of NYC detectives, under 1965 law abolishing capital punishment except in police or prison guard killings; bill permits death penalty only for premeditated murder; 2 were convicted of felony murder; bill sponsor Assemblyman Corso surprised, says he was unaware of limitation; aides of Governor hold he made it clear when signing bill that all in death row would be given blanket clemency under law, news conference; Corso and Senator Lentol plan study of bill's language. NEW YORK TIMES 1:7, January 28, 1966.

Illinois General Assembly com. approves bill setting 6-year moratorium on penalty; Governor Kerner expected to commute sentences of condemned if bill is passed. NEW YORK TIMES 23:1, April 17, 1967.

Judge sets conviction aside for man on death row for 16 years, but another judge sends him back to prison until it is determined whether he should be allowed bond. THE NATIONAL OBSERVER p. 21, February 8, 1971.

Lameduck Governor Winthrop Rockefeller, with only two weeks left in office, commutes the death sentences of 15 men in Arkansas death row, and critics are fuming. THE NATIONAL OBSERVER p. 18, January 11, 1971.

NYS Governor Rockefeller, acting under policy he announced in 1965, commutes death sentences of 4 convicted murderers. NEW YORK TIMES 45:2, February 29, 1968.

Secretary Lloyd-George seen continuing to recommend reprieves for condemned. NEW YORK TIMES 3:5, July 12, 1956.

Senator Ohrenstein says Governor has power to grant reprieves effective until end of Legis. session. NEW YORK TIMES 32:5, March 3, 1965.

Suffolk Superior Court Judge W. H. McLaughlin reduces death penalty sentence to William M. Gilday, convicted, Boston, of murder in shooting death of policeman during bank holdup, to life imprisonment, thereby denying motion for new trial on grounds that death penalty is unconstitutional in view of recent ruling of US Supreme Court. NEW YORK TIMES 62:1, December 21, 1972.

Tennessee Governor W. Dunn announces on July 18 that he will commute sentences of all 21 prisoners on state's death row to 99 years. NEW YORK TIMES 15:3, July 19, 1972.

US Appeals Court refuses Attorney General Lynch request that it set aside stays; NAACP Legal Defense Fund and ACLU aides hail move. NEW YORK TIMES 20:1, July 11, 1967.

CLINE, ROBERT
see: Cases Involving Capital Punishment

COMMONWEALTH CLUB OF CALIFORNIA
see: United States

COMMUNISM
Capital punishment in the building of communism, by B. A. Ramundo. AMERICAN BAR ASSOCIATION. SECTION OF INTERNATIONAL AND COMPARATIVE LAW BULLETIN 1963:215, 1963.

COMMUTATION OF SENTENCE
see: Clemency

CONSTITUTIONALITY OF CAPITAL PUNISHMENT
see: The Law and Capital Punishment

THE COURTS AND CAPITAL PUNISHMENT
see: The Law and Capital Punishment

CRAMPTON, J.
see: Cases Involving Capital Punishment

CRIME RATE AND CAPITAL PUNISHMENT
see: As Deterrence

CRUCIFIXION
Afterthought [technique of crucifixion], by A. Brien. SPECTATOR 210:822, June 21, 1963.

Does *tlb* in the Temple scroll refer to crucifixion?, by J. M. Baumgarten. JOURNAL OF BIBLICAL LITERATURE 91:472-481, December, 1972.

CRUEL AND UNUSUAL PUNISHMENT
see also: The Law and Capital Punishment
The Morality of Capital Punishment

Capital punishment—cruel and unusual?, by M. S. Enslin. RELIGION IN LIFE 41:254-258, Summer, 1972.

—, by T. A. Long. ETHICS 83:214-223, April, 1973; Reply by

R. S. Gerstein, 85:75-79, October, 1974.

Capital punishment: has it become cruel an unusual?, by A. W. Green. NATIONAL REVIEW 21:384-385+, April 22, 1969.

Constitutional law—Arkansas state penitentiary transgresses constitutional proscription against cruel and unusual punishment. SETON HALL LAW REVIEW 3:159, Fall, 1971.

Constitutional law: capital punishment for rape constitutes cruel and unusual punishment when no life is taken or endangered. MINNESOTA LAW REVIEW 56:95, November, 1971.

Constitutional law—cruel and unusual—capital punishment. NORTH CAROLINA LAW REVIEW 42:909, June, 1964.

Constitutional law—cruel or unusual punishment: the death penalty. SUFFOLK UNIVERSITY LAW REVIEW 6:1045, Summer, 1972.

Constitutional law—cruel and unusual punishments—the imposition and carrying out of the death penalty under current discretionary sentencing statutes constitutes cruel and unusual punishment in violation of the eighth and fourteenth amendments. UNIVERSITY OF CINCINNATI LAW REVIEW 42:172-178, 1973.

Constitutional law—eighth amendment; cruel and unusual punishment; a vehicle for reappraising the application of the criminal law to the individual. CONNECTICUT BAR JOURNAL 40:521, September, 1966.

Constitutional law—eighth amendment—death penalty as currently administered constitutes cruel and unusual punishment. TULANE LAW REVIEW 47:1167-1184, June, 1973.

Constitutional law—eighth amendment—the death penalty as presently administered under discretionary sentencing statues is cruel and unusual. SETON HALL LAW REVIEW 4:244, Fall-Winter, 1972.

Criminal law—capital punishment—the Texas statutes authorizing the death penalty do not violate the eighth amendment's prohibition of cruel and unusual punishment. TEXAS LAW REVIEW 7:170-181, Fall, 1975.

Criminal law—the limited application of the eighth amendment's cruel and unusual punishment clause to the death penalty. WAKE FOREST LAW REVIEW 7:494, June, 1971.

Cruel and unusual by M. Meltsner, a review by D. B. Moskowitz. BUSINESS WEEK pp. 29-30, September 15, 1973.

Cruel and unusual punishment—constitutionality of the death penalty for rape where victim's life neither taken nor endangered. UNIVERSITY OF RICHMOND LAW REVIEW 5:392, Spring, 1971.

Cruel and unusual punishment: of straps and strips cells. CATHOLIC LAWYER 19:200-233, Summer, 1973.

Cruel and unusual punishments. CATHOLIC UNIVERSITY LAW REVIEW 3:117-121, May, 1953.

Cruel punishment proscription: "Evolving standards of decency", by W. H. Forman, Jr. LOYOLA LAW REVIEW 19:81, 1972-1973.

Death killers; cruel and unusual, story behind Supreme court's abolition of the death penalty. TIME 102:94, September 17, 1973.

Death penalty: a cruel and unusual punishment. SOUTHWESTERN LAW JOURNAL 27:298-324, May, 1973.

Death penalty: cruel, unusual, unethical, and futile, by L. H. Dewolf. RELIGION IN LIFE 42:37-41, Spring, 1973.

Effectiveness of the eighth amendment: an appraisal of cruel and unusual punishment. NEW YORK UNIVERSITY LAW REVIEW 36:846, April, 1961.

Mental suffering under sentence of death: a cruel and unusual punishment. IOWA LAW REVIEW 57:814, February, 1972.

Penal institutions and the eighth amendment—a broadened conception of cruel and unusual punishment. LOUISIANA LAW REVIEW 31:395, February, 1971.

Recent judicial concepts of "cruel and unusual punishment", by A. Sultan. VILLANOVA LAW REVIEW 10:271, Winter, 1965.

Revival of the eighth amendment: development of cruel-punishment doctrine by the Supreme Court. STANFORD LAW REVIEW 16:996, July, 1964.

Still cruel and unusual; arguments on capital punishment before the Court, by H. A. Bedau. NATION 220:612-613, May 24, 1975.

NEWSPAPER ARTICLES

California Supreme Court, 4-3 holds death penalty is constitutional; rejects arguments that gas chamber is cruel and unusual punishment, that California laws violate 14th Amendment because they provide no standards by which judges and juries should decide who should receive death sentence; rejects view that juries are 'stacked' because prospective jurors who are opposed to capital punishment are excluded. NEW YORK TIMES 24:4, November 19, 1968.

California Supreme Court refuses to reconsider February 18 decision outlawing death penalty on ground that it constitutes cruel and unusual punishment. NEW YORK TIMES 28:4, March 18, 1972.

California Supreme Court, 6-1, rules that death penalty is illegal on grounds that it constitutes cruel and unusual punishment; orders that in all cases where death penalty had been imposed but not carried out the punishment be changed to life imprisonment; decision, based on suit by NAACP Legal Defense and Education Foundation and ACLU, is based on court's interpretation of state constitution and thus removes any chances for appeal; ruling detailed; among those spared by ruling are Sirhan B. Sirhan, convicted assassin of Senator R. F. Kennedy, and mass murders J. L. Frazier and C. M. Manson; reaction to ruling noted; California Governor Reagan charges that courts had set themselves 'above the people and the legislator'; illus. NEW YORK TIMES 1:8, February 19, 1972.

Connecticut Governor Meskill says on December 1 that he expects Connecticut General Assembly in next 2 years to enact legis. that will widen death penalty to cover rapists and possibly to cover illegal drug traffickers; says that despite June 29 US Supreme Court ruling virtually eliminating death penalty, constitution question of 'cruel and unusual' punishment remains open. NEW YORK TIMES 83:1, December 3, 1972.

Cruel and unusual. CHRISTIAN SCIENCE MONITOR 9:2, October 24, 1973, (All Editions).

Editorial lauds California Supreme Court's action in declaring capital punishment unconstitutional on ground that it constitutes cruel and unusual punishment. NEW YORK TIMES 40:2, February 23, 1972.

Federal Appeals Court in Richmond, Virginia holds that death penalty for rape when victim's life is neither taken nor endangered violates constitutional prohibition against cruel and unusual punishment; ruling upholds appeal of Negro W. Ralph who had been sentenced to death for raping white woman; case reviewed. NEW YORK TIMES 64:1, December 12, 1970.

Florida Governor Askew grants mass stay of execution to 91 prisoners on Florida's death row until July 1, 1973; says he took action because recent court decisions and statistical studies have cast doubt over constitution of capital punishment. NEW YORK TIMES 13:1, February 24, 1972.

Governors and other high state officials comment on impact of June 29 ruling of US Supreme Court that capital punishment is 'cruel and unusual'; officials anticipate revision of capital punishment laws and reduced chance for parole in life sentences for capital offenses. NEW YORK TIMES 1:6, June 30, 1972.

Is it cruel and unusual? CHRISTIAN SCIENCE MONITOR 2:1, January 27, 1972 (All Editions).

Legislators commenting on California Supreme Court decision declaring capital punishment unconstitutional on grounds that it constitutes cruel and unusual punishment. NEW YORK TIMES IV,12:3, February 27, 1972.

Mississippi Supreme Court refuses June 19 to outlaw death penalty as cruel and unusual punishment in suit brought by convicted murderer F. Peterson. NEW YORK TIMES 29:1, June 20, 1972.

Professor A. M. Dershowitz, commenting on California Supreme Court's ruling declaring capital punishment unconstitutional under provision of California Constitution prohibiting cruel and unusual punishment, discusses effect ruling will have on other states; illus. NEW YORK TIMES IV,3:4, February 20, 1972.

Professor L. Pfeffer and B. H. Harris lrs. commenting on California State Supreme Court decision declaring capital punishment unconstitutional on ground that it constitutes cruel and unusual punishment. NEW YORK TIMES IV,10:3, March 12, 1972.

T. Wicker comment on recent US Supreme Court decision abolishing capital punishment; holds court did not rule death penalty per se is cruel and unusual punishment but that infrequency and arbitrariness of death sentences make them cruel and unusual; state legislatures could now reinstate death penalty for specific crimes. NEW YORK TIMES IV,9:2, July 2, 1972.

T. Wicker comments on California Attorney General Younger's attempt to overturn State Supreme Court's ruling that capital punishment is unconstitutional on ground that it constitutes cruel and unusual punishment. NEW YORK TIMES 39:1, March 7, 1972.

US Senator J. L. Buckley, in speech to Federation of Civic Councils of Queens on October 21, says he favors death penalty as 'ultimate deterrent to such crimes as trading in narcotics which destroy human lives'; agrees with US Supreme Court decision that penalty is cruel and unusual punishment because 'it is cruel and inhuman to allow person to linger in prison for long periods of time awaiting death'. NEW YORK TIMES 71:8, October 22, 1972.

US Supreme Court to hear appeal that imposition of death penalty for robbery is 'cruel and inhuman punishment', E. Boykin case. NEW YORK TIMES 32:3, October 15, 1968.

CUBA

Chief executioner; Cuba. TIME 73:46, April 13, 1959.

Fidel's artist, by N. Lewis. NEW STATESMAN 60:964+, December 17, 1960.

Killing in Cuba and a moral issue. LIFE 46:22-23, January 26, 1959.

THE DEATH PENALTY
see: Capital Punishment—Against
Capital Punishment—For
Capital Punishment—General

DEATH ROW
see: The Prisoner and Capital Punishment

DENMARK
A problem of simulation in modern legal history, by G. K. Stürup. ACTA PSYCHIATRICA ET NEUROLOGICA 30:343-350, 1955.

DRUG PEDDLING AND THE DEATH PENALTY
Connecticut Governor Meskill says on December 1 that he expects Connecticut General Assembly in next 2 years to enact legis. that will widen death penalty to cover rapists and possibly to cover illegal drug traffickers; says that despite June 29 US Supreme Court ruling virtually eliminating death penalty, constitution question of 'cruel and unusual' punishment remains open. NEW YORK TIMES 83:1, December 3, 1972.

Georgia Senate, 27-17, defeats bill providing death penalty for drug pushers. NEW YORK TIMES 17:11, January 27, 1972.

EASTON, PHILIP, III
see: Cases Involving Capital Punishment

EDUCATION
   Capital punishment; effects of the death penalty; data and deliberations from the social sciences; symposium, by H. Bedau. AMERICAN JOURNAL OF ORTHOPSYCHIATRY 45:580-726, July, 1975.

   Education and the death penalty. JOURNAL OF EDUCATION (London) 88:85-87, March, 1956.

   Mandatory death sentences, by A. Amsterdam. INTELLECT 103: 281, February, 1975.

NEWSPAPER ARTICLES

   F. T. P. Plimton, S. H. Rifkind, S. I. Roseman, O. H. Schell, Jr., and C. R. Vance lr. tells of role of Legal Defense and Education Foundation in recent US Supreme Court decision to ban capital punishment. NEW YORK TIMES 26:4, July 31, 1972.

EGYPT
   Hemp to Egypt, by D. Stewart. SPECTATOR 207:813, December 1, 1961.

EIGHTH AMENDMENT
   see: The Law and Capital Punishment

THE ELECTRIC CHAIR
   Bring back the chair; warden and deputy murdered in Holmesburg prison. NEWSWEEK 81:30+, June 11, 1973.

   Electricide; first use of the electric chair. SCIENTIFIC AMERICAN 228:45, April, 1973.

   End to the chair. NATION 200:575, May 31, 1965.

   Fifteen dates with the chair: P. Crump, by L. Robinson. EBONY 17:31-34+, July, 1962.

   First electrocution, by A. Beichman. COMMENTARY 35:410-419, May, 1963.

For whom the chair waits, by S. R. Ehrmann. FEDERAL PROBA-
TION 26:14, March, 1962.

Grand success: first legal electrocution was fraught with controversy
which flared between Edison and Westinghouse, by T. Bernstein.
IEEE SPECTRUM 10:54-58, February, 1973.

Is the electric chair condemned?, by Father J. Grant. THE AVE
MARIA 85:8-11, 29, 1957.

Notches on a chair, by C. P. Larrowe. THE NATION 182:291-293,
April 14, 1956.

Two chairs at San Quentin, by R. Meyners. CHRISTIAN CENTURY
77:316, March 16, 1960.

NEWSPAPER ARTICLES

Alabama Governor Wallace, saying 'I hope we'll see some electrocu-
tions in this state', signs into law bill restoring death penalty in
Alabama (S). NEW YORK TIMES 59:8, September 10, 1975.

Comr. McCorkle vetoes New Jersey prison bid for $25,000 electric
chair; holds device used infrequently. NEW YORK TIMES 40:4,
December 24, 1966.

D. McCann, D. A. Windsor and I. Brant lrs. on capital punishment;
illus. of electric chair. NEW YORK TIMES 34:3, March 19, 1973.

Execution by electric chair is a method introduced and perfected at
Sing Sing. THE NATIONAL OBSERVER p. 6, April 6, 1970.

New Jersey Senator J. Azzalina introduces death penalty bill that
would force anyone charged with 1st degree murder to stand
trial and risk death in electric chair. NEW YORK TIMES 85:1,
March 19, 1972.

New York State Assembly Codes Com., in move that surprised and
angered civil liberties groups, votes out bill on April 18 that would
restore death penalty in most homicide cases; under measure,

sponsored by Assemblyman Kelly, any convicted murderer would face electric chair unless jury recommends life imprisonment; opposition to action noted. NEW YORK TIMES 1:2, April 19, 1972.

Pennsylvania Governor-elect M. J. Shapp says he will not send anyone to electric chair during his term. NEW YORK TIMES 32:3, December 27, 1970.

Representative Graves (Michigan), in amendment to bill asking electrocution of 1st-degree murderers, proposes author and backers on any capital punishment bill, must stone condemned. NEW YORK TIMES 70:3, March 8, 1953.

Ronald Clark O'Bryan, a Pasadena, Texas, optician, was sentenced to die in the electric chair for killing his son, Timothy, 8, last Halloween by giving the boy candy laced with cyanide. Follow-up. THE NATIONAL OBSERVER p. 2. June 14, 1975.

ELECTRICIDE
see: The Electric Chair

ENGLISH HOMICIDE ACT OF 1957
see: The Law and Capital Punishment

EPISCOPALIANS
see: The Morality of Capital Punishment

ESTESCHVICH, BILLIE SOL
see: Cases Involving Capital Punishment

ETHICS
see: The Morality of Capital Punishment

EXECUTIONS AND EXECUTIONERS
And the penalty is (sometimes) death [the death penalty and the incidence of actual executions; United States], by R. Slovenko. ANTIOCH REVIEW 24:351-364, Fall, 1964.

Ballad of Gary Gilmore. NATIONAL REVIEW 29:18, January 7, 1977.

British cry murder as a boy is hanged. LIFE 34:22-23, February 9, 1953.

Charles the First in death, by A. A. Mitchell. HISTORY TODAY 16: 149-156, March, 1966.

Chief executioner; Cuba. TIME 73:46, April 13, 1959.

Collector's choice: a first for law & order; execution of J. Forner in San Francisco, by R. Olmsted. AMERICAN WEST 7:11, January, 1970.

Comments on the executions in Iraq [January 27, 1969, on fourteen Iraqi nationals, of the Muslim, Christian dn Jewish faiths, all of whom had been convicted of espionage], by F. Sayegh. ARAB WORLD 15:18-20, January-February, 1969.

Comparison of the executed and the commuted among admissions to death row: is a rational, fair scheme discernible in the commutation of death sentences? or does a selective system appear to operate, differentiating between the executed and commuted upon improper bases? [based on a study of] the case records of 439 persons sentenced to death for first degree murder and detained on death row in Pennsylvania between 1914 and 1958, by M. E. Wolfgang, et al. JOURNAL OF CRIMINAL LAW, CRIMINOLOGY AND POLICE SCIENCE 53:301-311, September, 1962.

Condemned accomplices; G. M. Gilmore and R. E. White. NATION. 223:643-644, December 18, 1976.

Contempt and clemency. TIME 70:15, July 8, 1957.

Crime and punishment [Russia]: Execution: hallmark of "socialist legality", by L. Lipson; The wages of economic sin, by H. Willets. PROBLEMS OF COMMUNISM 11:21-32, September-October, 1962.

Death diplomacy and diminishing peace; political executions in Baghdad. TIME 93:22-23, February 7, 1969.

Death for the assassin; Prince Faisal ibn Musaed. TIME 105:45, June 30, 1975.

Death for Gilmore?, by W. F. Buckley, Jr. NATIONAL REVIEW 28:1422, December 24, 1976.

Death in the afternoon; execution of King Faisal's assassin. NEWS-WEEK 85:31, June 30, 1975.

A death in the family: the story of Gary Mark Gilmore, by M. Gilmore. ROLLING STONE p. 58+, March 10, 1977.

Death in Zion, by R. S. Anson. NEW TIMES 8:20+, February 4, 1977.

Death penalty, by H. B. Shaffer. EDITORIAL RESEARCH REPORTS pp. 573-588, August 14, 1953.

Death-row dramatics; case of G. M. Gilmore. TIME 108:46, November 29, 1976.

Death wish; case of G. M. Gilmore, by P. Goldman, et al. NEWSWEEK 88:26-27+, November 29, 1976.

English treason trials and confessions in the sixteenth century, by L. B. Smith. JOURNAL OF THE HISTORY OF IDEAS 15:471-498, October, 1954.

Execution, by P. Lewis. NEW STATESMAN 61:620+, April 21, 1961.

L'exécution de Louis XVI [par Charles Henri Sanson] (d'après des documents inédits) [excerpt], by R. Goulard. MERCURE DE FRANCE 313:470-481, November, 1951.

Execution eve? NATIONAL REVIEW 28:1167, October 29, 1976.

Execution of Charles I, by C. V. Wedgwood. HORIZON 6:41, Summer, 1964.

Execution of a collaborator, by J. P. Charbonnier. POPULAR PHOTOGRAPHY 47:66-67+, July, 1960.

Execution of Daniel Gearhart in Angola; statements, July 9-10, 1976, by R. H. Nessen, et al. DEPARTMENT OF STATE BULLETIN 75:163, August 2, 1976.

Execution of Michael X, by J. Paine. NEW STATESMAN 89:681, May 23, 1975.

Execution of Private Slovik, a review by W. B. Huie. NEWSWEEK 43:107, April 26, 1954.

Execution of Private Slovik; condensation, by W. B. Huie. LOOK 18: 30-38, May 4, 1954.

Execution of Ruth Ellis. SPECTATOR 195:81, July 15, 1955; Discussion, 195:110, 120-121, 165, July 22-29, 1955.

The executioner: his place in English society, by G. D. Robin. BRITISH JOURNAL OF SOCIOLOGY 15:234-253, September, 1964.

Executions and a rush of protest; Spain; with report by G. Scott. TIME 106:36-37, October 6, 1975.

Fidel's artist, by N. Lewis. NEW STATESMAN 60:964, December 17, 1960.

Franco's executions, by W. F. Buckley, Jr. NATIONAL REVIEW 27:1193, October 24, 1975.

Gary Gilmore: death wish, by D. A. Williams, et al. NEWSWEEK 88:35-36, November 22, 1976.

Gilmore's future, by R. Rosenblatt. NEW REPUBLIC 176:32, January 1, 1977.

Goodbye, Uncle Tom, by E. Parr. NEW STATESMAN 70:692, November 5, 1965.

Grand success: first legal electrocution was fraught with controversy which flared between Edison and Westinghouse, by T. Bernstein. IEEE SPECTRUM 10:54-58, February, 1973.

Hangman's turn. NEWSWEEK 46:40-42, July 25, 1955.

Hypocrisy in high places; Senator Hughes public-execution amendment. CHRISTIAN CENTURY 91:357, April 3, 1974.

Killing in Cuba and a moral issue. LIFE 46:22-23, January 26, 1959.

Killing of Grimau, by J. M. Cohen. SPECTATOR 210:558, May 3, 1963.

Last firing squad; executioners of Utah, by G. Berriault. ESQUIRE 65:88-91+, June, 1966.

Maimed rites; Gilmore case. NATIONAL REVIEW 28:1335-1336, December 10, 1976.

Man of conviction: Aaron C. Mitchell's execution. NEWSWEEK 69: 29, April 24, 1967.

Marina's maidenhead, by A. Easson. SHAKESPEARE QUARTERLY 24:328-329, Summer, 1973.

Mass public executions in Iraq deplored by United States; text of letter to the president of the Security council, January 29, 1969, by C. W. Yost. DEPARTMENT OF STATE BULLETIN 60:145-146, February 17, 1969.

Much ado about Gary. TIME 108:85-87, December 13, 1976.

Nation is victorious; Tudeh plotters. TIME 64:36+, November 1, 1954.

Nigeria; time to stop [public executions]. ECONOMIST 244:37, July 29, 1972.

Night's work for Mr. Ellis. TIME 55:38, March 6, 1950.

No. 77; execution of Luis José Monge in Colorado. TIME 89:33, June 9, 1967.

Numeiry's justice; mass executions in Sudan, by J. Pringle. NEWS-WEEK 88:36-37+, August 16, 1976.

Open and concealed dramaturgic strategies: the case of the state execution, by J. Lofland. URBAN LIFE 4:272-295, October, 1975.

Pierrepoint papers, by R. Reynolds. NEW STATESMAN 51:409-410, April 21, 1956.

Playboy interview: Gary Gilmore. PLAYBOY 24:69+, April, 1977.

Right to die; case of G. Gilmore, by T. Szasz. NEW REPUBLIC 175:8-9, December 11, 1976; Reply by H. Schwarzschild, 175:32, December 18, 1976.

Russia shoots its business crooks; executions for economic crimes, by G. Feifer. NEW YORK TIMES MAGAZINE pp. 32-33+, May 2, 1965.

Should there be live TV coverage of an execution?, by M. Weiss. TV GUIDE 25:A5+, January 1, 1977.

Slaughterhouse in Santiago, by J. Barnes. NEWSWEEK 82:53-54, October 8, 1973.

Stay of execution; Supreme court ordering indefinite stay of execution in the G. Gilmore case, by D. A. Williams, et al. NEWSWEEK 88:37, December 13, 1976.

Sudden rush for blood; murderer G. M. Gilmore's desire to be executed. TIME 108:56, November 22, 1976.

Test for the doomed; executions in California. NEWSWEEK 59:22+, January 22, 1962.

Warning to renegades: Haiti's first public execution in thirty years. TIME 84:44+, November 27, 1964.

When and why did Hastings lose his head?, by B. P. Wolffe. ENGLISH HISTORICAL REVIEW 89:835-844, October, 1974; Reply by

A. Hanham, 90:821-826, October, 1975.

When a condemned man wants to die; case of G. M. Gilmore. U. S. NEWS AND WORLD REPORT 81:19, November 29, 1976.

Witnessed 189 executions [D. Reid], by C. Tomkinson. EDITOR AND PUBLISHER 105:30, September 16, 1972.

World looks at Gilmore's execution. ATLAS WORLD PRESS REVIEW 24:9, March, 1977.

Young man, be an executioner, by G. Walker. ESQUIRE 60:62-63, August, 1963.

NEWSPAPER ARTICLES

ACLU and NAACP sue Federal court, to bar execution of 51 on grounds Florida death penalty laws are unconstituional. NEW YORK TIMES 35:3, April 5, 1967.

Article noting there were no executions in US in 1968 links recent court rulings that enable prisoners to forestall execution almost indefinitely; some rulings discussed. NEW YORK TIMES IV,11:1, January 5, 1969.

Assemblyman Bartlett says NYS Comm. on Revision of Penal Law will propose abolition; Senator Chrenstein demands Governor Rockefeller stay all executions pending Legis. decision; Senator Zaretzki sees 'good chance' of Senate approval of abolition; Assemblyman Weinstein undecided. NEW YORK TIMES 1:3, February 25, 1965.

California Attorney General Brown asks 5-year moratorium after Governor Knight stay arrives 2 minutes after B. W. Abbott execution; doubts death penalty has deterrent effect. NEW YORK TIMES 21:8, March 16, 1957.

California resumes executions after 3-month moratorium declared by Governor Brown. NEW YORK TIMES 48:4, April 23, 1960.

Capital punishment should not be abolished but limited to a specific list of crimes and executed without public fanfare. THE NATIONAL OBSERVER p. 11, January 8, 1972.

Colorado Governor Love withdraws indefinite stays of execution for 5. NEW YORK TIMES 75:2, January 5, 1967.

Convicted kidnapper and bank robber are executed by firing squad on December 20 in Algiers. NEW YORK TIMES 15:3, December 21, 1972.

Court temporarily bars executions; sets hearing on technical procedures involved in capital punishment cases. NEW YORK TIMES 24:2, April 14, 1967.

Critical look at execution. CHRISTIAN SCIENCE MONITOR 13:1, September 18, 1970, (Eastern Edition); 2:1, September 22, 1970, (Western Edition); 10:5, September 21, 1970, (Midwestern Edition); 13:1, September 18, 1970, (London and Overseas Editions).

Editorial hails report of no executions in US in 1968; urges Mitchell keep record intact. NEW YORK TIMES 26:1, January 23, 1969.

El Salvador has 1st execution in 20 years. NEW YORK TIMES 6:6, July 17, 1963.

Excerpts from convicted murder Gary Gilmore's remarks to an Oregon judge after a 1973 attempted robbery are published. THE NATIONAL OBSERVER p. 4, November 20, 1976.

Execution by electric chair is a method introduced and perfected at Sing Sing. THE NATIONAL OBSERVER p. 6, April 6, 1970.

Federal court ends blanket stay of execution for California death row inmates. NEW YORK TIMES 31:2, August 25, 1967.

Federal District Court extends moratorium on Florida executions pending ruling in case brought by NAACP and ACLU. NEW YORK TIMES 38:4, August 11, 1967.

Federal District Court stays all California executions pending hearings on NAACP charge that California death penalty law is unconstitutional. NEW YORK TIMES 27:3, July 6, 1967.

Federal Prisons Bureau reports 42 executions in US, 1961, lowest since Bureau began keeping records in 1930. NEW YORK TIMES 21:3, April 26, 1962.

Federal Prisons Bureau reports 1968 marks 1st year without an execution since bureau began collecting statistics in 1938; 3,859 persons were executed 1930-68; 199 executed in record year of 1935; NAACP Legal Defense Fund director J. Greenberg says situation represents 'de facto national abolition of the death penalty' that could become permanent; ACLU aide M. L. Wulf says executions have been 'de facto abolished by court stays'; campaign by 2 organizations against capital punishment cited; comment on some court cases involving capital punishment. NEW YORK TIMES 17:1, December 31, 1968.

Federal Prisons Bureau reports 65 executions in US, 1956; breakdown by states. NEW YORK TIMES 7:2, February 25, 1957.

1st Brahmin executed, Nepal, under new law making all Nepalese equal before law. NEW YORK TIMES 4:1, February 2, 1964.

Florida Governor Askew on December 8 signs death penalty into law making Florida 1st state in nation to restore capital punishment; executions have been halted throughout US since June as result of US Supreme Court ruling that declared capital punishment unconstitutional as presently applied; Florida's new law could decide ultimate fate of death penalty in US, since 1st case is expected to be appealed to Supreme Court, asking Justices to clarify their original decision. NEW YORK TIMES 32:7, December 9, 1972.

14 convicted armed robbers are reportedly executed on July 22 by firing squad in Nigeria before cheering crowd of thousands. NEW YORK TIMES 46:8, July 23, 1972.

Georgia Governor Maddox weighs delaying all executions until after proposed referendum on capital punishment. NEW YORK TIMES

24:4, April 11, 1967.

Governor Mandel (Maryland) orders all stays of execution to remain in effect, granting of automatic stays in any new cases until US Supreme Court disposes of all its capital punishment cases. NEW YORK TIMES 26:5, November 4, 1969.

Governor Rockefeller says he has no authority to declare moratorium on executions; bars further comment pending special Legis. com. study. NEW YORK TIMES 25:2, March 2, 1965.

Justice Douglas stays 3 California executions, Governor Brown stays 4th. NEW YORK TIMES 19:5, May 4, 1963.

Kansas Governor Docking offers ex-Governor Landon job of executioner after Landon scores him for communting death sentence of B. J. Spencer; Landon links commutation to Docking opposition to death penalty. NEW YORK TIMES 4:6, April 16, 1960.

Kentucky State Court of Appeals on August 25 stays September 1 execution of convicted murderer R. K. Call, in accord with recent US Supreme Court decision abolishing capital punishment. NEW YORK TIMES 37:1, August 26, 1972.

L. Rubin lr. states that US is now 1 of 40 countries that have abolished capital punishment; says that contrary to world trend, South African executions have increased over past 20 years, accounting for nearly half the executions carried out in the whole world. NEW YORK TIMES IV,12:4, July 9, 1972.

NAACP Legal Defense and Education Fund. director J. Greenberg says 90% of persons executed for rape since 1930 were Negroes, s, conference of experts on capital punishment, NYC; charges current procedures make the downtrodden and deprived objects of capital convictions; cites fund success in campaign against capital punishment. NEW YORK TIMES 23:5, May 4, 1968.

NAACP Legal Defense and Education Fund. to appeal to US Supreme Court to void death sentence imposed on Arkansas prisoner, rev. November 1968 ruling by California Supreme Court upholding capital punishment; Professor A. Amsterdam says aim is total abolition of capital punishment in US, news conference, NYC; hails fact that no one was executed in 1968; arguments to be presented to court detailed. NEW YORK TIMES 63:1, March 2, 1969.

New Jersey bars moratorium on executions pending Legis. action on bills; penalty backed by S. Bates, opposed by Professor Bedau, public hearing on bills. NEW YORK TIMES 25:1, June 20, 1958.

New York State Assembly, 70-64, defeats Lentol bill requiring judges to accept grand jury recommendation of life term rather than execution in murder case. NEW YORK TIMES 16:3, March 10, 1968.

Official Saigon newspaper Giai Phong reports 2 alleged robbers were executed over past weekend; newspaper publishes photos of what is described as execution, attending by large crowd of people (M). NEW YORK TIMES 5:1, May 28, 1975.

P. A. Dunford, 1st prisoner scheduled for execution since British Parliament began acting on bill to abolish death penalty, gets reprieve. NEW YORK TIMES 54:1, January 3, 1965.

Peru has 1st execution in 63 years. NEW YORK TIMES 12:5, December 13, 1957.

Reasons for Gary Gilmore's request to be executed are examined. THE NATIONAL OBSERVER p. 4, November 20, 1976.

The Rev. Paul Tinlin of Schaumburg, Illinois, says that murderers should be executed on prime-time television as a deterrent to crime. THE NATIONAL OBSERVER p. 5, November 8, 1975.

7 Americans executed in US, 1965, 1st time number fell below 10; record high for executions was 199 in 1935; New York, Vermont; Iowa and West Virginia abolished death penalty, 1965, making total of 13 states without capital punishment; other data. NEW YORK TIMES 14:1, February 18, 1966.

Stays all executions pending January hearing. NEW YORK TIMES 27:2, November 15, 1967.

This method of execution was introduced and perfected at Sing Sing. THE NATIONAL OBSERVER p. 6, April 6, 1970.

20,000 reported executed since 1966. CHRISTIAN SCIENCE MONITOR 2:1, December 13, 1976, (All Editions).

US Supreme Court rules California, which prohibits execution of insane criminals, can give prison wardens unreviewable decretion to determine sanity. NEW YORK TIMES 19:1, July 2, 1958.

EXECUTIVE CLEMENCY
see: Clemency

THE FAMILY AND CAPITAL PUNISHMENT
see: Society and Capital Punishment

THE FIRING SQUAD
Death by firing squad in Guatemala City; photographs. TIME 59:26-27, March 31, 1952.

Execution of Private Slovik; condensation, by W. B. Huie. LOOK 18:30-38, May 4, 1954.

Expedient bullets? ECONOMIST 203:229, April 21, 1962.

Last firing squad: executions of Utah, by G. Berriault. ESQUIRE 65:88-91+, June, 1966.

Notches on a chair; Utah firing squad, by C. P. Larrowe. NATION 182:291-293, April 14, 1956; Discussion, 182:289, April 14, 1956; 182:inside cover, May 12, 1956.

Tales of the firing squad in Utah. TIME 66:21, July 11, 1955.

To be shot for bribetaking [Russia; former Dushanbe official]. CURRENT DIGEST OF THE SOVIET PRESS 13:34-35, April 3, 1963.

Waiting for the firing squad, by A. Ladas. HARPER 229:87-90, November, 1964.

NEWSPAPER ARTICLES

Convicted kidnapper and bank robber are executed by firing squad on December 20 in Algiers. NEW YORK TIMES 15:3, December 21, 1972.

6 narcotics peddlers are executed by firing squad, Teheran, Iran, April 8. NEW YORK TIMES 69:6, April 9, 1972.

2 Ghanaians sentenced to die before firing squard for stealing underground telephone cables valued at $800 after being found guilty by mil tribunal on February 1. NEW YORK TIMES 13:8, February 4, 1973.

FOWLER, JESSE T.
see: Cases Involving Capital Punishment
The Law and Capital Punishment

FRANCE
Expedient bullets? ECONOMIST 203:229, April 21, 1962.

France; the power to start and end a life. ECONOMIST 245:45, December 2, 1972.

Hunting vengeance votes. ECONOMIST 258:44, February 28, 1976.

Power to start and end a life. ECONOMIST 245:5, December 3, 1972.

President and Madame Guillotine, by D. Leitch. NEW STATESMAN 84:423, September 29, 1972.

Return of the guillotine, by D. Leitch. NEW STATESMAN 84:800-802, December 1, 1972.

NEWSPAPER ARTICLES

French Government files suit against periodicals Paris-Match, Special-

Derniere and L'Express for publishing details about 2 recent executions by guillotine involving C. Buffet and R. Bontems; suit is filed under paragraph in Penal Code that makes it unlawful to publish anything about execution other than official communique on front door of prison where execution takes place; publics face maximum penalty of $1,400 fine; Paris daily Combat is also being investigated. NEW YORK TIMES 8:4, January 5, 1973.

French President Pompidou, opponent of capital punishment, is now faced with growing pressure to forgo his policy of commutation of death penalities in case of R. Bomtems and C. Buffet, who were convicted of killing a guard and a nurse they were holding hostage during escape attempt at Claivaux Prison in eastern France last September; death sentences in case are very popular and consideration of abolition of penalty has been set aside until Clairvaux case has been settled. NEW YORK TIMES 10:2, July 1, 1972.

FURMAN v. GEORGIA
 see: Cases Involving Capital Punishment
 The Law and Capital Punishment

THE GAS CHAMBER
 At San Quentin, gas chamber is back in use. U. S. NEWS AND WORLD REPORT 62:19, April 24, 1967.

 Window on a gas camber: Maryland penitentiary, by S. M. Shane. NATION 194:170-171, February 24, 1962; Correction, 194: inside cover, March 17, 1962.

NEWSPAPER ARTICLES

 Puts away the gas chamber. CHRISTIAN SCIENCE MONITOR 2:2, August 4, 1969, (Eastern and London and Overseas Editions).

GEARHART, DANIEL
 see: Cases Involving Capital Punishment

GERMANY
NEWSPAPER ARTICLES

Capital punishment penalty retained. CHRISTIAN SCIENCE MONITOR 2:3, February 21, 1967, (Eastern, and London and Overseas Editions); 4:5, February 21, 1967, (Western and Midwestern Editions).

Germany: West Berlin abolishes death penalty. NEW YORK TIMES 8:6, August 1, 1950.

—. NEW YORK TIMES 9:2, October 20, 1950.

New West German President Heinemann opposes reintroduction of death penalty, interview, Bonn. NEW YORK TIMES 7:1, July 2, 1969.

GHANA
NEWSPAPER ARTICLES

2 Ghanaians sentenced to die before firing squad for stealing underground telephone cables valued at $800 after being found guilty by mil tribunal on Feburary 1. NEW YORK TIMES 13:8, February 4, 1973.

GREAT BRITAIN
Abolition and after, by C. H. Rolph. NEW STATESMAN 51:267-268, March 24, 1956.

At the end of the rope; Britain is now to stop hanging its last two or three capital murderers a year. ECONOMIST 213:1414-1415, December 26, 1964.

Back to the gallows, by C. Adam. NEW STATESMAN 68:563, October 16, 1964.

Balcombe Street siege came at just the wrong moment. ECONOMIST 257:27, December 13, 1975.

Beastly business again. ECONOMIST 230:47, March 1, 1969.

Breathing space in England. TIME 68:24-25, July 23, 1956.

Britain abolishes the hangman's job. U. S. NEWS AND WORLD RE-PORT 59:16, November 8, 1965.

Britain and Hongkong; the Queen's hand. ECONOMIST 247:39, May 19, 1973.

Britain faces end of death penalty. CHRISTIAN CENTURY 73:259, February 29, 1956.

Britain reviews and the penalty of death. CHRISTIAN CENTURY 70: 1157, October 14, 1953.

British and the IRA, by T. Beeson. CHRISTIAN CENTURY 93:60-62, January 28, 1976.

British constitution and the capital punishment abolition controversy, by H. S. Albinski. JOURNAL OF PUBLIC LAW 12:193, 1963.

British cry murder as a boy is hanged. LIFE 34:22-23, February 9, 1953.

Canterbury convocation: no hanging bishops. ECONOMIST 202:212, January 20, 1962.

Capital punishment agreement in sight [bill abolishing death penalty]. ECONOMIST 216:592, August 14, 1965.

Capital punishment and British party responsibility, by J. B. Cristoph. POLITICAL SCIENCE QUARTERLY 77:19-35, March, 1962.

Capital punishment and open-end questions, by L. R. England. PUB-LIC OPINION QUARTERLY 12(3):412-416, 1948.

Capital punishment; death watch. ECONOMIST 255:79, April 26, 1975.

Capital punishment; effects of abolition. ECONOMIST 213:950+, November 28, 1964.

Capital punishment: Royal Commission's Report. LAW TIMES 216: 505-506, October 2, 1953.

Capital punishment [summary of recommendations in the report issued by the Royal commission on capital punishment, Great Britain, September 23, 1953]. LABOUR RESEARCH 42:173-175, November, 1953.

Capital punishment; voting again. ECONOMIST 247:18+, April 7, 1973.

Case for total abolition. ECONOMIST 191:609, May 16, 1959.

Case of James Weaver, by W. Teeling. SPECTATOR 195:213-214, August 12, 1955.

Challenge to abolitionists, by G. Playfair, et al. NEW STATESMAN 52:63-64, July 21, 1956; Discussion, 52, 104, 136, 162, 187, 215, 244, July 28-September 1, 1956.

Commons says it again: no return to hanging. ECONOMIST 247:17, April 14, 1973.

Comparative aspects of the English homicide act of 1957 [capital punishment; murder and manslaughter concepts], by M. Koessler. MISSOURI LAW REVIEW 25:107-154, April, 1960.

Crime and punishment: third reading [Mr. Silverman's bill abolishing capital punishment]. ECONOMIST 216:247, July 17, 1965.

Criminal law: capital punishment in Britain [recent history of the death penalty], by G. Gardiner. AMERICAN BAR ASSOCIATION JOURNAL 45:259-261, March, 1959.

Day at the Lords. SPECTATOR 198:263, March 1, 1957.

Dead men don't talk. NEW STATESMAN 60:909, December 10, 1960.

Death ends its holiday. ECONOMIST 260:25, July 10, 1976.

Death on Parliament Hill [status of the death penalty in Canada; conference paper], by W. T. McGrath. CANADIAN WELFARE 48:8-10+, November-December, 1972.

Death penalty dying? ECONOMIST 202:694+, February 24, 1962.

Death penalty in Britain [excerpt]. SOCIAL SERVICE REVIEW 23:394, September, 1949.

The death penalty in other countries. ANNALS OF THE AMERICAN ACADEMY OF POLITICAL AND SOCIAL SCIENCE pp. 137-166, November, 1952.

Death sentence. SPECTATOR 205:675, November 4, 1960.

Death to hanging; government resolution outlawing hanging in Great Britain. NEWSWEEK 74:28+, December 29, 1969.

Debate in London, by B. Moyers. NEWSWEEK 84:64, December 30, 1974.

Demise of the gallows; House of commons in London votes to abolish the death penalty for murder. AMERICA 112:99, January 23, 1965.

Diminished responsibility. SPECTATOR 204:128, January 29, 1960.

Effects of abolition. ECONOMIST 213:950+, November 28, 1964.

Ellis case. ECONOMIST 176:209, July 16, 1955.

End of the rope for Englishmen. LIFE 40:48, February 27, 1956.

End of the rope in Britain. NEWSWEEK 47:44, February 27, 1956.

End to hanging; bill passed in the House of commons. TIME 85:36-37, January 1, 1965.

The English homicide act of 1957: the capital punishment issue, and various reforms in the law of murder and manslaughter, by G.

Hughes. JOURNAL OF CRIMINAL LAW, CRIMINOLOGY, AND POLICE SCIENCE 49:521-532, March-April, 1959.

English ideas of punishment [review article] . TIMES LITERARY SUPPLEMENT 3095:381-382, June 23, 1961.

English treason trials and confessions in the sixteenth century, by L. B. Smith. JOURNAL OF THE HISTORY OF IDEAS 15:471-498, October, 1954.

Evans or Christie?, by L. Gilmore. SPECTATOR 195:270-273, August 26, 1955; Discussion, 195:331, September 9, 1955.

Even good governments forget, by Templewood. SPECTATOR 197: 560+, October 26, 1956.

Execution of Ruth Ellis. SPECTATOR 195:81, July 15, 1955; Discussion, 195:110, 120-121, 165, July 22-29, 1955.

The executioner: his place in English society, by G. D. Robin. BRITISH JOURNAL OF SOCIOLOGY 15:234-253, September, 1964.

Famous victory. ECONOMIST 233:12-13, December 20, 1969.

Gallows must go in Great Britain. TIME 67:29-30, February 27, 1956.

Government from the backwoods. NEW STATESMAN 52:29, July 14, 1956; Discussion 52:70, 104, July 21-28, 1956.

Hanging and public opinion. NEW STATESMAN 50:142, August 6, 1955; Discussion, 50:187, 216, 272, 298, August 13-20, September 3-10, 1955.

Hanging and the timetable. ECONOMIST 179:672, May 19, 1956.

Hanging in the balance. ECONOMIST 178:543, March 3, 1956.

Hanging is dead in Britain. CHRISTIANITY TODAY 14:37, January 16, 1970.

Hanging on [moves to abolish death penalty] . ECONOMIST 177:639, November 19, 1955.

Hanging or rotting alive? NEW STATESMAN 77:345, March 14, 1969.

Hanging question, by J. Bentham. NEW STATESMAN 92:743, November 26, 1976.

Hanging reprieved again. ECONOMIST 174:611, February 19, 1955.

Hanging the sick. NEW STATESMAN 46:96+, July 25, 1953; Discussion, 46:130-131, 158, August 1-8, 1953.

Hanging's no answer, by C. H. Rolph. NEW STATESMAN 61:578, April 14, 1961.

Hangmen fight back, by C. H. Rolph. NEW STATESMAN 78:681, November 14, 1969.

Homicide in the Lords. ECONOMIST 182:710, March 2, 1957.

Hundred years on. SPECTATOR 205:763, November 18, 1960.

I am ashamed of my country. . ., by B. Woottoon. SPECTATOR 205:765, November 18, 1960.

In Britain, an end to hangings. U. S. NEWS AND WORLD REPORT 67:6, December 29, 1969.

Indecent haste. SPECTATOR 199:124, July 26, 1957.

Jenkins's passage. ECONOMIST 253:23-24, November 30, 1974.

Judicial barbarism. SPECTATOR 194:141, February 11, 1950.

Keeping a cool head. NEW STATESMAN 90:697, December 5, 1975.

Last twist of the rope, by C. H. Rolph. NEW STATESMAN 62:880, December 8, 1961.

Law of murder: the prospects of abolishing capital punishment are not necessarily being improved by the tactics of some abolitionists [Great Britain]. ECONOMIST 198:436-437, February 4, 1961.

Less than four hangings a year? ECONOMIST 181:671-672, November 24, 1956.

Letter from London, by M. Panter-Downes. NEW YORKER 36:85-86, February 11, 1961.

Letter from London; House of lords throws out Commons' bill to abolish penalty, by M. Panter-Downes. NEW YORKER 32:62, July 28, 1956.

Loop and lash. SPECTATOR 201:472, October 10, 1958.

Lord Chief on hanging, by C. H. Rolph. NEW STATESMAN 61:777, May 19, 1961.

Lords and the constitution; Fate of the Bill—and the varying tune. ECONOMIST 180:110, July 14, 1956.

The lords who said "no" [characteristics of the British peers who voted on the Death penalty (abolition) bill, House of lords, July 9-10, 1956]. LABOUR RESEARCH 45:113-114, August, 1956.

Mr. Callaghan's nettle. ECONOMIST 233:24, December 13, 1969.

Murder. SPECTATOR 207:564, October 27, 1961.

Murder and the constitution, by S. Silverman. NEW STATESMAN 52:618, November 17, 1956.

Murder and the principles of punishment: England and the United States, by H. L. A. Hart. NORTHWESTERN UNIVERSITY LAW REVIEW 52:433, September-October, 1957.

Murder; how long is life? [debate on bill to abolish capital punishment]. ECONOMIST 214:1277-1278, March 20, 1965.

Murderers' reminiscences [abolition of capital punishment will end demand for such articles], by C. Hollis. SPECTATOR 195:37-39, July 8, 1955.

Must night fall? [whether terrorist murders in Britain will lead to restoration of capital punishment]. ECONOMIST 257:9-10, December 6, 1975.

Night the hangman was turned away. ECONOMIST 253:17-18, December 14, 1974.

No answer. SPECTATOR 206:463, April 7, 1961.

No hanging by degrees. ECONOMIST 179:364+, April 28, 1956.

Not to worry, by A. Waugh. NEW STATESMAN 87:442, March 29, 1974.

Or such less penalty: if the British start hanging terrorists, they'll be out of Ulster in a year—which is just what the IRA [Irish republican army] wants. ECONOMIST 253:17-18, December 7, 1974.

Outside the walls, by C. Pannell. SPECTATOR 207:891, December 15, 1961.

Parliament and the gallows, by A. Howard. NEW STATESMAN 63:250, February 23, 1962.

Parliament and hanging: further episodes in an undying sage [parliamentary preoccupation with the issue of capital punishment; events since 1969], by G. Drewry. PARLIAMENTARY AFFAIRS 27:251-261, Summer, 1974.

Parliament: the beastly business again. ECONOMIST 230:47, March 1, 1969.

Parliament's agony over capital punishment: an inside view of an MP, his conscience and some rather disturbing mail [Canada], by P. Reilly. SATURDAY NIGHT 88:15-17, March, 1973.

Podola case. ECONOMIST 193:408, October 31, 1959.

Quare fellows, by C. Hitchens. NEW STATESMAN 87:917, June 28, 1974.

Reform of the law relating to capital punishment: a study in the operation of parliamentary institutions, by W. N. Ortved. FACULTY OF LAW REVIEW 29:73, August, 1971.

Report of the [British] royal commission on capital punishment (1949-1953): a review, by M. F. Wingersky. JOURNAL OF CRIMINAL LAW, CRIMINOLOGY AND POLICE SCIENCE 44:695-715, March, 1954.

—. JOURNAL OF CRIMINAL LAW AND CRIMINOLOGY 44:695-715, March-April, 1954.

Report of the Royal Commission on Capital Punishment, 1949-1953, Cmd. 8932, September 1953, by J. E. H. Williams. MODERN LAW REVIEW 17:57-65, January, 1954.

Restricted death in Great Britain. TIME 69:24, April 1, 1957.

Riley ruling. ECONOMIST 198:647, February 18, 1961.

Rope's end; Britain abolishes death penalty. NEWSWEEK 65:27, January 4, 1965.

Sacking the hangman: Great Britain. TIME 94:15-16, December 26, 1969.

Sentence for killing, by M. McNair-Wilson. CONTEMPORARY REVIEW 221:57-60, August, 1972.

Simcox case [doubly guilty of capital murder]. ECONOMIST 210:871, March 7, 1964.

Stride forward in Britain. COMMONWEAL 63:561, March 2, 1956; Discussion, 63:666, March 30, 1956; 64:123, May 4, 1956.

Thoughts on the Bentley case [brief history of the death penalty in England, and present weaknesses of the system, as shown in the recent execution of Derek Bentley], by H. Klare. SOCIALIST COMMENTARY 17:55-57, March, 1953.

Voting again. ECONOMIST 247:18+, April 7, 1973.

Weber's thesis as an historical explanation, by E. Sprinzak. HISTORY AND THEORY 11(3):294-320, 1972.

When will it end? ECONOMIST 203:24, April 7, 1962.

NEWSPAPER ARTICLES

A. Lewis discusses issue under study in Great Britain and US; holds death penalty has not proved to be an effective deterrent, serves mainly to satisfy obsessive public emotions. NEW YORK TIMES 32:6, December 22, 1969.

Abolished in Ulster. CHRISTIAN SCIENCE MONITOR 4:3, May 17, 1973, (Eastern and London and Overseas Editions); 4:4, May 17, 1973, (Western Edition); 10:5, May 18, 1973, (Midwestern Edition).

Bill rejected, 238-95; Commons can override Lords only after 1-year lapse; possible pol. implications of Lords action discussed; 1948 moves to suspend penalty reviewed. NEW YORK TIMES 1:1, July 11, 1956.

Bill to suspend death penalty passes 2d reading, British Commons; measure also specifies abolition unless both Houses request reinstatement within 10 years; Lords' action following 3d Commons hearing seen crucial test; continued controversy noted. NEW YORK TIMES 6:1, March 13, 1956.

British Commons approves abolition bill. NEW YORK TIMES 3:1, July 14, 1965.

British Commons approves amendment to retain death penalty for person who murders while serving life term for murder; 2d amendment to retain penalty for murder by armed robber defeated; complete abolition of penalty now out of question. NEW YORK TIMES 10:6, May 17, 1956.

British Commons approves Government plan to study abolition bill. NEW YORK TIMES 4:8, March 19, 1965.

British Commons gets bill to restore hanging for murders of police or prison officers. NEW YORK TIMES 23:8, October 20, 1966.

British Commons rejects MP D. Sandys effort to offer bill to restore capital punishment for murder of police and prison officers. NEW YORK TIMES 10:1, November 24, 1966.

British Commons, 343-185, votes to abolish death penalty in Great Britain; Home Secretary Callaghan discusses issue of public reference to restore hanging for some types of murders. NEW YORK TIMES 1:2, December 17, 1969.

British Commons votes 355-170 to abolish death penalty for murder; MP S. S. Silverman role in getting bill enacted noted. NEW YORK TIMES 1:2, December 22, 1964.

British Commons, 293-262, backs Laborite amendment to abolish or suspend capital punishment; pending executions canceled; Prime Minister Eden says Government will implement decision, make statement on resulting consequences; vote transcends party lines, defeating Government efforts to retain death penalty while revising law on murder; debate, past abolition efforts described. NEW YORK TIMES 1:4, February 17, 1956.

British Commons votes to retain death penalty for murder of police or jail officers; weighs abolition for most other murders. NEW YORK TIMES 2:6, January 25, 1957.

British Commons writes 5-year limit into bill to abolish penalty. NEW YORK TIMES 7:1, May 27, 1965.

British Conservative party conference delegates urge restoration of capital punishment for murder in Great Britain; party leader E.

Heath surprised by move; party's renewed interest in issue linked to fact that 5-year moratorium on hanging expires in 1970 and that general elections will be held in that year. NEW YORK TIMES 2:4, October 10, 1969.

British Conservative party rejects resolution to extend penalty, conference; New Zealand abolishes penalty. NEW YORK TIMES 3:2, October 13, 1961.

British debating reinstatement of capital punishment for terrorists in wake of bombing and murder campaign attributed to IRA; parliamentary vote on issue set; opponents of capital punishment say that middle-aged couple being held hostage in living room in central London would be in greater peril if gunmen knew they faced death; other MPs think siege will increase vote for death penalty (M). NEW YORK TIMES 15:1, December 11, 1975.

British Home Secretary Butler refuses to schedule Commons discussion on death penalty and his reprieve of slayer J. Rogers; Earl of Harewood named chairman of committee formed by National Campaign for Abolition of Capital Punishment. NEW YORK TIMES 9:3, December 9, 1960.

British Home Secretary R. Maudling reports number of murders in England and Wales in 1971 rose to 177, highest since 1965 abolition of punishment. NEW YORK TIMES 8:1, July 16, 1972.

British House of Commons refuses S. Silverman permission to offer bill banning death penalty for 5 years. NEW YORK TIMES 12:5, July 2, 1953.

British House of Commons, 253-94, on May 14 abolishes capital punishment in Northern Ireland; death penalty for murder will be replaced by sentence of life imprisonment; British Secretary for Northern Ireland W. Whitelaw, introducing no-hanging clause, rejects argument that its effect would be to encourage terrorism in Ulster. NEW YORK TIMES 4:6, May 15, 1973.

British House of Lords approves abolition bill sponsored by M. P. Silverman. NEW YORK TIMES 10:3, July 21, 1965.

British House of Lords debates bill to abolish death penalty; voting to be 'free,' not along party lines. NEW YORK TIMES 10:3, July 10, 1956.

British House of Lords passes bill restricting death penalty to certain types of murder. NEW YORK TIMES 21:4, March 20, 1957.

British Labor Government Legis. program includes proposal for free Commons vote on bill to abolish death penalty. NEW YORK TIMES 42:2, November 4, 1964.

British Labor Government suffers defeat, Commons, as Conservatives succeed in bringing abolition bill out of com.; long delay likely as Conservatives press for amendments. NEW YORK TIMES 8:3, March 6, 1965.

British official hangman A. Pierrepoint resigns; D. Middleton notes growing pol. dispute over legis.; reports abolitionists fear Government maneuvers to defeat bill in Commons by seeking to sway Conservatives who backed it; possible pol. repercussions discussed; case reviewed. NEW YORK TIMES 2:5, 6, February 27, 1956.

British Parliament rejects proposal to abolish death penalty in armed forces for crimes that are non-capital in civilian life. NEW YORK TIMES 2:4, May 3, 1961.

British Parliament to debate return of hanging; public indicates support of capital punishment for some types of murders, Labor party opposes it; pol. maneuvering by pol. parties discussed. NEW YORK TIMES 27:1, December 14, 1969.

British Royal Comm. ends study of methods. NEW YORK TIMES 15:1, May 27, 1951.

British Royal Comm. report recommends juries in murder trials be permitted to determine sentences; holds women should not be spared death penalty; compares methods; would raise age limit for imposition to 21 years. NEW YORK TIMES 35:2, September 24, 1953.

British reject attempt to restore death penalty. CHRISTIAN SCIENCE

MONITOR 4:4, December 13, 1974, (All Editions).

Commons resist series of amendments to qualify death penalty abolition. NEW YORK TIMES 3:6, April 26, 1956.

Commons spurs legis. action; Eden, citing Government opposition, says Government will not present bill as own measure; H. Gaitskell holds stand flaunts will of Commons; Eden holds Government not bound to introduce legis.; recalls pledge to give full weight to Commons decision; some fear abolition may be delayed 1 year by Lords veto. NEW YORK TIMES 3:1, February 24, 1956.

Commons votes its conscience. CHRISTIAN SCIENCE MONITOR E:1, December 24, 1964, (Eastern, Western, and Midwestern Editions).

Conservative candidates for Commons from Glasgow and P. Downey, bidding for Lancashire seat, seek return to capital punishment to remedy rise in capital crime rate, Great Britain. NEW YORK TIMES 11:4, March 26, 1966.

Editorial backs British move, notes only US and France among Western nations retain capital punishment. NEW YORK TIMES 30:1, December 20, 1969.

4 slayers reprieved, Great Britain, since Commons voted to end penalty. NEW YORK TIMES 27:1, March 25, 1956.

Government rejects royal comm. proposal to bar execution of murderers under 21 years old. NEW YORK TIMES 5:2, November 11, 1955.

Great Britain abolishes death penalty for 5 years; time limit seen device to assure passage of Silverman bill, under debate for 11 mo. NEW YORK TIMES 18:4, October 29, 1965.

Great Britain: British Royal Comm. ends study of US methods to help revise own procedures; Sir E. Gowers comment. NEW YORK TIMES 15:1, May 27, 1951.

Great Britain House of Commons on April 11 votes down proposal to restore capital punishment for murder by guns or explosives and for murder of policeman or prison officer; officials acknowledge that public in general undoubtedly favors return of penalty in face of rising crimes of violence and increase of armed crimes. NEW YORK TIMES 3:1, April 12, 1973; Comment on vote, IV,8:1, April 15, 1973.

Great Britain moves to abolish death penalty reviewed; cartoon. NEW YORK TIMES IV,4:1, July 15, 1956.

Great Britain Prime Minister Heath is under pressure from Parliament to restore death penalty, which was abolished in 1969 after 5-year experimental suspension; more than 100 MPs have signed motion urging restoration of penalty of hanging for murder involving firearms or explosives and for murder of policeman or prison officer; 1 member has proposed reviving beheading; Heath makes it clear that he will not yield to demands; emphasizes that best crime deterrent is likelihood of being caught. NEW YORK TIMES 2:4, April 3, 1973.

Hang down your head and die. CHRISTIAN SCIENCE MONITOR 6:4, March 26, 1964, (Eastern and Western Editions); 4:4, March 26, 1964, (Midwestern Edition).

House of Commons beats back 320 to 178. CHRISTIAN SCIENCE MONITOR 14:2, April 12, 1973, (Eastern Edition); 10:2, April 12, 1973, (Midwestern, and London and Overseas Editions); 10:3, April 12, 1973, (Western Edition).

House of Commons, 361-232, defeats motion to bring back death penalty for acts of terrorism causing loss of life; motion is introduced by Conservative MP Ivan Lawrence; Home Secretary Roy Jenkins argues that there is no evidence that prospect of hanging has deterrent effect, that it might cause even more violent reprisals while terrorists await trial and sentencing, and that terrorists have scant regard for their own self-preservation (M). NEW YORK TIMES 3:4, December 12, 1975.

House of Lords approves Government measure ending death penalty for murder; prior voting detailed. NEW YORK TIMES 9:1, December 19, 1969.

Killing in London of Ross McWhirter, co-editor of Guinness Book of Records and head of campaign to raise $100,000 for aid in capturing Irish bombers, provokes strongest demands for capital punishment since its abolishment in England 10 years ago (S). NEW YORK TIMES 3:1, November 29, 1975.

Lordly debate. CHRISTIAN SCIENCE MONITOR E:1, July 26, 1965, (Eastern, Western and Midwestern Editions).

Major Legge-Bourke says vote shows Lords in closer touch with people; recent public opinion poll cited. NEW YORK TIMES 4:3, July 14, 1956.

Malawi Parliament passes law giving local courts authority to try more serious types of criminal cases and to impose death penalty; under present system capital cases are tried only by British-trained judges of High Court. NEW YORK TIMES 2:3, November 19, 1969.

100 British clergymen, scientists, lawyers, others sign Howard League for Penal Reform plea to suspend death penalty; plea submitted to Secretary Lloyd-George. NEW YORK TIMES 7:3, August 4, 1955.

Ronnie Engle lr. comments on Tom Wicker's November 30 article on capital punishment (S). NEW YORK TIMES 30:5, December 15, 1975.

Tom Wicker article on US Supreme Court about to take up death penalty again, since it failed to settle matter with its 1972 ruling that capital punishment was too arbitrarily and capriciously imposed to be constitutional; holds that if Supreme Court intends to prohibit death penalty, which is not altogether clear, it will have to go beyond 1972 ruling and perhaps find death penalty 'cruel and unusual punishment,' which is barred by 8th Amendment; says it could also rule that unassailable record shows capital punishment to be racially discriminatory (M). NEW YORK TIMES 39:5, March 14, 1975.

Tom Wicker says that new demands in Great Britain for restoration of capital punishment because of outbreak of terrorism, presumed to be mostly work of IRA, are reminder that issue is 1 of most difficult before US Supreme Court that Judge John Paul Stevens will be joining; terrorism might be 1 crime most susceptible to supposed deterrent effect of death penalty, but men and women who devote lives to a cause are not necessarily 'deterred' by anything; US faces nothing like terrorist problem in Great Britain, but pressure for capital punishment has arisen for crimes clearly less 'deterrable' than terrorism; case that could settle issue is now before Court. NEW YORK TIMES IV,13:5, November 30, 1975.

Weighs capital punishment. CHRISTIAN SCIENCE MONITOR 2:5, December 16, 1964, (Eastern Edition); 6:4, December 17, 1964, (Western Edition); 4:5, December 16, 1964, (Midwestern Edition).

GRIMAU, JULIAN
see: Cases Involving Capital Punishment

GUATEMALA
Death by firing squad in Guatemala City: photographs. TIME 59:26-27, March 31, 1952.

NEWSPAPER ARTICLES

20,000 reported executed since 1966. CHRISTIAN SCIENCE MONITOR 2:1, December 13, 1976, (All Editions).

GUILLOTINE
President and Madame Guillotine, by D. Leitch. NEW STATESMAN 84:423, September 29, 1972.

Return of the guillotine, by D. Leitch. NEW STATESMAN 34:800-801, December 1, 1972.

NEWSPAPER ARTICLES

Article discusses French guillotine history and use; only 1 person executed in France in 1969. NEW YORK TIMES 20:1, December 28, 1969.

C. Buffet and R. Bontems are guillotined November 28 in Paris for murder of 2 hostages, N. Compte and G. Giradot, during prison riot; they are 1st men executed in France in more than 3½ years and deaths have stirred new debate over capital punishment; President Pompidou could have pardoned men but polls that showed well over half of the people favored capital punishment probably weighted in his decision to allow execution. NEW YORK TIMES 20:4, November 29, 1972.

Professor M. Foucault article on French prison system and continued use of guillotine for capital punishment; illus. NEW YORK TIMES IV,15:2, April 8, 1973.

HAITI

Warning to renegades: Haiti's first public execution in thirty years. TIME 84:44+, November 27, 1964.

HANGING

At the end of the rope; Britain is now to stop hanging its last two or three capital murderers a year. Economist 213:1414-1415, December 26, 1964.

Back to the gallows?, by C. Adam. NEW STATESMAN 68:563, October 16, 1964.

Britain abolishes the hangman's job. U. S. NEWS AND WORLD REPORT 59:16, November 8, 1965.

British cry murder as a boy is hanged. LIFE 34:22-23, February 9, 1953.

Canterbury convocation: no hanging bishops. ECONOMIST 202: 212, January 20, 1962.

Carnival in Baghdad; public hangings of Iraqi Jews in Baghdad. NEWSWEEK 73:31-32, February 10, 1969.

Come to a hanging, by R. Baker. NEW YORK TIMES MAGAZINE p. 6, May 11, 1975.

Day Judge Lynch cried hang!, by L. Elliott. CORONET 40:113-117, June, 1956.

Death to hanging; government resolution outlawing hanging in Great Britain. NEWSWEEK 74:28+, December 29, 1969.

Demise of the gallows; House of commons in London votes to abolish the death penalty for murder. AMERICA 112:99, January 23, 1965.

End of the rope for Englishmen. LIFE 40:48, February 27, 1956.

End of the rope in Britain. NEWSWEEK 47:44, February 27, 1956.

End to hanging; bill passed in the House of commons. TIME 85:36-37, January 1, 1965.

Execution, by P. Lewis. NEW STATESMAN 61:620+, April 21, 1961.

Gallows must go in Great Britain. TIME 67:29-30, February 27, 1956.

Hanged by the neck until. . ., by J. V. Barry. SYDNEY LAW REVIEW 2:401, March, 1958.

Hanging, by J. Bharier. NEW STATESMAN 65:828, May 31, 1963.

Hanging; abolition's progress. ECONOMIST 215:283, April 17, 1965.

Hanging and public opinion. NEW STATESMAN 50:152, August 6, 1955; Discussion, 50:187, 216, 272, 298, August 13-20 and September 3-10, 1955.

Hanging and the timetable. ECONOMIST 179:672, May 19, 1956.

Hanging in the balance. ECONOMIST 178:543, March 3, 1956.

Hanging in the balance, by R. Partridge. NEW STATESMAN AND NATION 39:480, April 29, 1950.

Hanging in New Zealand. ECONOMIST 179:804, May 26, 1956.

Hanging is dead in Britain. CHRISTIANITY TODAY 14:37, January 16, 1970.

Hanging on [moves to abolish death penalty]. ECONOMIST 177: 639, November 19, 1955.

Hanging or rotting alive? NEW STATESMAN 77:345, March 14, 1969.

Hanging question, by J. Bentham. NEW STATESMAN 92:743, November 26, 1976.

Hanging reprieval again. ECONOMIST 174:611, February 19, 1955.

Hanging the sick. NEW STATESMAN 46:96+, July 25, 1953; Discussion, 46:130-131, 153, August 1-8, 1953.

Hangings in Iraq. NATIONAL REVIEW 21:108, February 11, 1969.

The hangings in Iraq [possible motives for the public executions, January 27, 1969, of fifteen Iraqi citizens, nine of them Jews, condemned by a revolutionary tribunal for spying for Israel], by N. Rejwan. MIDSTREAM 15:16-23, March, 1969.

Hanging's no answer, by C. H. Rolph. NEW STATESMAN 61:578, April 14, 1961.

Hangman can relax. REPORTER 16:2, April 4, 1957.

Hangman stays: vote in Canada. TIME 87:40, April 15, 1966.

Hangman's turn. NEWSWEEK 46:40-42, July 25, 1955.

Hangmen fight back, by C. H. Rolph. NEW STATESMAN 78:681, November 14, 1969.

In Britain an end to hangings. U. S. NEWS AND WORLD REPORT 67:6, December 29, 1969.

Isle of Man; too much rope. ECONOMIST 226:22, February 17, 1968.

Last twist of the rope, by C. H. Rolph. NEW STATESMAN 62:880, December 8, 1961.

Law reform: to hang or not to hang? IRISH TIMES LAW 90:291, December 15, 1956.

Legacy of violence: the opera house lynching; Livermore, Kentucky, 1911, by J. M. Elliott. NEGRO HISTORY BULLETIN 37:303, October, 1974.

Less than four hangings a year? ECONOMIST 181:671-672, November 24, 1956.

Life without the hangman, by T. Beeson. CHRISTIAN CENTURY 90:468-469, April 25, 1973.

Lord Chief on hanging, by C. H. Rolph. NEW STATESMAN 61:777, May 19, 1961.

Mob still rides; with discussion, by M. Cartwright. NEGRO HISTORY BULLETIN 19:105-106, February, 1956.

Must the hangman go? AMERICA 105:3, April 1, 1961.

New deal for the hangman. NEW STATESMAN 46:364-365, October 3, 1953.

New handbook on hanging, a review by C. Duff. TIME 65:86, February 7, 1955; Discussion, 65:4, February 28, 1955.

Night the hangman was turned away. ECONOMIST 253:17-18, December 14, 1974.

No hanging by degrees. ECONOMIST 179:364+, April 28, 1956.

No remedy in law; case of E. Till. NEW REPUBLIC 133:5, November 21, 1955.

No work for the hangman, by E. Gertz. NATION 208:101-102, January 27, 1969.

Notes from the Temple—to hang or not to hang? IRISH LAW TIMES 90:49+, February 25, 1956.

One vote for the hangman, by P. Steinfels. COMMONWEAL 98:127+, April 13, 1973.

Or such less penalty: if the British start hanging terrorists, they'll be out of Ulster in a year—which is just what the IRA [Irish republican army] wants. ECONOMIST 253:17-18, December 7, 1974.

Parliament and the gallows, by A. Howard. NEW STATESMAN 63: 250, February 23, 1962.

Parliament and hanging: further episodes in an undying saga [parliamentary preoccupation with the issue of capital punishment; events since 1969], by G. Drewry. PARLIAMENTARY AFFAIRS 27:251-261, Summer, 1974.

Politics of the rope, by C. Bollinger. SPECTATOR 207:372, September 22, 1961.

Progress to the rope. SPECTATOR 206:668, May 12, 1961.

Reflections on hanging by A. Koestler, a review by D. R. Campion. AMERICA 97:446+, July 27, 1957.

—, by H. Weihofen. SATURDAY REVIEW 40:32, July 20, 1957.

—, by R. Hatch. NATION 185:54, August 3, 1957.

—, by R. Niebuhr. NEW REPUBLIC 137:18, August 26, 1957.

Rope and revenge in Nicosia, Cyprus. NEWSWEEK 47:50, May 21, 1956.

Rope's end: Britian abolishes death penalty. NEWSWEEK 65:27, January 4, 1965.

Sacking the hangman, Great Britain. TIME 94:15-16, December 26, 1969.

Should men hang?, by D. R. Campion. AMERICA 102:319-321, December 5, 1959; Discussion, 102:462-464, January 16, 1966.

Terrible myth of internal affairs; public hanging of fourteen men convicted of spying for Israel. CHRISTIAN CENTURY 86:205, February 12, 1969.

Thirteenpence-halfpenny for the hangman, by F. A. King. JUSTICE OF THE PEACE 122:216, April 5, 1958.

Throat trouble; photographs. AMERICAN WEST 7:22-23, January, 1970.

Trend against hanging. AMERICA 108:213, February 16, 1963.

Wrong end of the rope. ECONOMIST 178:449-450, February 18, 1956.

NEWSPAPER ARTICLES

Allen appointed official British hangman; illus. NEW YORK TIMES VI,20:3, April 15, 1956.

Article on history of hanging and other forms of capital punishment; illus. NEW YORK TIMES 4:2, February 17, 1956.

Article on re-erection of gallows used to hang triple slayer A. LeBlanc in Morristown, New Jersey, in 1933; restoration is accomplished at request of local historian who wishes to take photographs for book on LeBlanc case; gallows illus. NEW YORK TIMES 63:5, January 29, 1973.

British Commons gets bill to restore hanging for murderers of police or prison officers. NEW YORK TIMES 23:8, October 20, 1966.

British official hangman A. Pierrepoint resigns; D. Middleton notes growing pol. dispute over legis.; reports abolitionists fear Government maneuvers to defeat bill in Commons by seeking to sway Conservatives who backed it; possible pol. repercussions discussed; case reviewed. NEW YORK TIMES 5:6, February 27, 1956.

Canadian Parliamentary Committee urges retaining death penalty but abolishing hanging. NEW YORK TIMES 3:4, June 28, 1956.

Conservative Party conference approves motion condemning bill to abolish hanging, Great Britain. NEW YORK TIMES 3:1, October 13, 1956.

Keep curb on hanging. CHRISTIAN SCIENCE MONITOR 2:3, June 2, 1973, (Eastern, and London and Overseas Editions); 7:1, June 4, 1973, (Western Edition); 9:4, June 6, 1973, (Midwestern Edition).

Malawi Prime Minister Banda offers bill to permit public hangings. NEW YORK TIMES 55:7, November 11, 1965.

Plans for mock public hanging as part of Morristown, New Jersey, 250th anniversary celebration canceled as result of protests by church and civic groups. NEW YORK TIMES 41:1, May 18, 1965.

Rethink hangman's noose. CHRISTIAN SCIENCE MONITOR 2:1, December 13, 1972, (Western and Midwestern Editions).

Two hanged. CHRISTIAN SCIENCE MONITOR 2:1, November 14, 1970, (All Editions).

HARSH, G.

NEWSPAPER ARTICLES

C. Ebstein on G. Harsh's January 5 article on controversy over capital punishment; illus. NEW YORK TIMES 28:5, February 5, 1972.

HISTORY OF CAPITAL PUNISHMENT

Capital punishment after Furman (Furman v. Georgia, 92 Sup. Ct. 2726). JOURNAL OF CRIMINAL LAW AND CRIMINOLOGY 64:281-289, September, 1973.

Capital punishment and life imprisonment in North Carolina, 1946 to 1968: implications for abolition of the death penalty, by C. H. Patrick. WAKE FOREST INTERNATIONAL LAW REVIEW 6:417, May, 1970.

Capital punishment in Oregon, 1903-64, by H. A. Bedau. OREGON LAW REVIEW 45:1, December, 1965.

Capital punishment in the second half of the twentieth century: special study, by M. Ancel. BULLETIN OF THE INTERNATIONAL COMMISSION OF JURISTS: FOR THE RULE OF LAW pp. 33-48, June, 1969.

Capital punishment in South Carolina: the end of an era, by L. Mc-Donald. SOUTH CAROLINA LAW REVIEW 24:762, 1972.

Capital punishment in Texas, 1924-1968, by R. C. Koeninger. CRIME AND DELINQUENCY 15:132, January, 1969.

Capital punishment is on the way out, by D. M. Berman. PROGRES-SIVE 24:33-34, April, 1960.

Capital punishment: it's being revived in many states. U. S. NEWS AND WORLD REPORT 76:46, March 4, 1974.

Capital punishment: a sharp medicine reconsidered; historical background and the arguments pro and con, by E. J. Younger. AMERI-CAN BAR ASSOCIATION JOURNAL 42:113-116+, February, 1956.

Comparison of the executed and the commuted among admissions to death row: is a rational, fair scheme discernible in the commutation of death sentences? or does a selective system appear to operate, differentiating between the executed and commuted upon improper bases? [based on a study of] the case records of 439 persons sentenced to death for first degree murder and detained on death row in Pennsylvania between 1914 and 1958, by M. E. Wolfgang, et al. JOURNAL OF CRIMINAL LAW, CRIMINOLO-GY AND POLICE SCIENCE 53:301-311, September, 1962.

Criminal law: capital punishment in Britain [recent history of the death penalty], by G. Gardiner. AMERICAN BAR ASSOCIA-TION JOURNAL 45:259-261, March, 1959.

Death penalty after Furman (Furman v. Georgia, 92 Sup. Ct. 2726), by

C. S. Vance. NOTRE DAME LAWYER 48:850, April, 1973.

—, by L. A. Wollan, Jr. LOYOLA UNIVERSITY LAW JOURNAL 4:339-357, Summer, 1973.

The death penalty and the USSR: history of the death penalty in the USSR: the question of capital punishment and international organizations; countries having abolished capital punishment. BULLETIN OF THE INTERNATIONAL COMMISSION OF JURISTS; FOR THE RULE OF LAW pp. 55-64, November, 1961.

The death penalty in Virginia: its history and propsects, by N. D. Joyner. UNIVERSITY OF VIRGINIA NEWS LETTER 50:37-40, June 15, 1974.

Death penalty on the way out? U. S. NEWS AND WORLD REPORT 70:55, January 18, 1971.

Electricide: first use of the electric chair. SCIENTIFIC AMERICAN 228:45, April, 1973.

English treason trials and confessions in the sixteenth century, by L. B. Smith. JOURNAL OF THE HISTORY OF IDEAS 15:471-498, October, 1954.

L'exécution de Louis XVI] par Charles-Henri Sanson] (d'après des documents inédits) [excerpt], by R. Goulard. MERCURE DE FRANCE 313:470-481, November, 1951.

First electrocution, by A. Beichman. COMMENTARY 35:410-419, May, 1963.

Hundred years on. SPECTATOR 205:763, November 18, 1960.

Last firing squad; executioners of Utah, by G. Berriault. ESQUIRE 65:88-91+, June, 1966.

Mandatory capital punishment? The inutility of mandatory capital punishment: an historical note, by P. E. Mackey. BOSTON UNIVERSITY LAW REVIEW 54:30-35, January, 1974.

Spreading impact of a historic court decision: death penalty ruling. U. S. NEWS AND WORLD REPORT 81:49-51, July 12, 1976.

Thoughts on the Bentley case [brief history of the death penalty in England, and present weaknesses of the system, as shown in the recent execution of Derek Bentley], by H. Klare. SOCIALIST COMMENTARY 17:55-57, March, 1953.

Two myths in the history of capital punishment, by T. Sellin. JOURNAL OF CRIMINAL LAW AND CRIMINOLOGY 50:114, July-August, 1959.

Warning to renegades: Haiti's first public execution in thirty years. TIME 84:44+, November 27, 1964.

Weber's thesis as an historical explanation, by E. Sprinzak. HISTORY AND THEORY 11(3):294-320, 1972.

Witnessed 189 executions [D. Reid], by C. Tomkinson. EDITOR AND PUBLISHER 105:30, September 16, 1972.

NEWSPAPER ARTICLES

Article on history of hanging and other forms of capital punishment; illus. NEW YORK TIMES 4:2, February 17, 1956.

Capital punishment diminishing. CHRISTIAN SCIENCE MONITOR 4:5, November 4, 1968, (Eastern, and London and Overseas Editions); 8:1, November 7, 1968, (Midwestern Edition); 4:4, November 7, 1968, (Western Edition).

Losing support through world. CHRISTIAN SCIENCE MONITOR 2:1, May 12, 1973, (All Editions).

US TV program reviewing history of capital punishment reviewed. NEW YORK TIMES 55:4, October 27, 1958.

HOMICIDE
see: The Law and Capital Punishment

HONG KONG
Britain and Hongkong; the Queen's hand. ECONOMIST 247:39, May
19, 1973.

NEWSPAPER ARTICLES

Article discusses current conflict in Hong Kong concerning capital
punishment between progressive Western thinking that criminals
should receive humane treatment and traditional Chinese philosophy that they should be sternly punished; law and order is a major
issue in Hong Kong, following sharp rise in major crimes; 1st conflict arose when appeal of convicted murderer for communtation
of death sentence was denied by Hong Kong Government; reprieve
is granted by Queen Elizabeth on ground that death sentence is
outlawed in Britain, and so should be in colonies; decision sparked
adverse reaction in colony; 2d issue at stake is introduction of
new legis. to broaden sentencing powers of judges and magistrates,
introduce preventive detention for habitual criminals and provide
for corporal punishment for young offenders; legis. was welcomed
by Chinese community but sharply criticized by Hong Kong Bar
Association. NEW YORK TIMES 15:1, June 3, 1973.

Comment on growth of crime rate in Hong Kong resulting in strong
popular demand for renewed use of death penalty, still on statute
books but not enforced since 1966 (M). NEW YORK TIMES
7:1, August 5, 1975.

HONG KONG: authorities decree death penalty for using arms in
robberies or assaults, or for possession of grenade or mine. NEW
YORK TIMES 20:4, October 12, 1950.

INDIA
Government of India on December 11 introduces bill that would sharply curtail death penalty; capital punishment, now mandatory for
murder except in extenuating circumstances, will be limited to
slayings of police, armed forces members and public servants
charged with keeping order. NEW YORK TIMES 3:1, December
12, 1972.

IRAQ
Carnival in Baghdad; public hangings of Iraqi Jews in Baghdad. NEWS-
WEEK 73:31-32, February 10, 1969.

Comments on the executions in Iraq [January 27, 1969, on fourteen
Iraqi nationals. of the Muslim, Christian and Jewis faiths, all of
whom had been convicted of espionage], by F. Sayegh. ARAB
WORLD 15:18-20, January-February, 1969.

Hangings in Iraq. NATIONAL REVIEW 21:108, February 11, 1969.

The hangings in Iraq [possible motives for the public executions, January 27, 1969, of fifteen Iraqi citizens, nine of them Jews, condemned by a revolutionary tribunal for spying for Israel], by N.
Rejwan. MIDSTREAM 15:16-23, March, 1969.

Interfaith scaffold in Iraq. CHRISTIANITY TODAY 13:47, February
28, 1969.

ISRAEL
A case for capital punishment [for Arab terrorism in Israel], by G.
Weiler; A case against capital punishment, by L. Sheleif (Shaskol-
sky); A new high in ethnocentrism [commenting on the article by
Gershon Weiler], by D. Amit. NEW OUTLOOK 17:46-58, Octo-
ber, 1974.

Knesset [Israeli parliament] debates capital punishment [excerpts
from debate, July 24, 1950]. JEWISH FRONTIER pp. 6-9,
November, 1950.

NEWSPAPER ARTICLES

ISRAEL: Cabinet to submit low proposing abolition. NEW YORK
TIMES 8:7, October 30, 1951.

ISRAEL: Knesset (Parliament) debates issue; some members back
death for traitors but not murderers. NEW YORK TIMES 20:1,
August 6, 1950.

Many urge terrorists be executed. CHRISTIAN SCIENCE MONITOR

ISRAEL

2:1, May 21, 1974, (All Editions).

IRISH REPUBLICAN ARMY
British and the IRA, by T. Beeson. CHRISTIAN CENTURY 93:60-62, January 28, 1976.

ITALY

NEWSPAPER ARTICLES

L'Osservatore Romano sees move sign of 'disequilibrium'. NEW YORK TIMES 19:8, May 9, 1961.

JEWS AND CAPITAL PUNISHMENT
see also: Israel War Crimes

Carnival in Baghdad; public hangings of Iraqi Jews in Baghdad. NEWSWEEK 73:31-32, February 10, 1969.

JOSE, LUIS
see: Cases Involving Capital Punishment

THE JURY AND CAPITAL PUNISHMENT
American jury and the death penalty, by H. Kalven, Jr., et al. UNIVERSITY OF CHICAGO LAW REVIEW 33:769, Summer, 1966.

Competency of jurors who have conscientious scruples against capital punishment. WASHBURN LAW JOURNAL 8:352, Spring, 1969.

Constitutional invalidity of convictions imposed by death-qualified juries, by W. S. White. CORNELL LAW REVIEW 58:1176-1220, July, 1973.

Criminal law—exclusion for cause of prospective jurors with scruples against death penalty violates due process. VANDERBILT LAW REVIEW 21:864, October, 1968.

Death-oriented jury shall live. UNIVERSITY OF SAN FERNANDO VALLEY LAW REVIEW 1:253, January, 1968.

Due process standard of jury impartiality precludes death-qualification of jurors in capital cases. UTAH LAW REVIEW 1969:154, January, 1969.

Effects of a mandatory death penalty on the decision of simulated jurors as a function of heinousness of the crime, by R. K. Hester, et al. JOURNAL OF CRIMINAL JUSTICE 1(4):319-326, Winter, 1973.

Juries and the death penalty. NATION 206:814, June 24, 1968.

Jury challenges, capital punishment, and Labat v. Bennett (365 F 2d 298): a reconciliation. DUKE LAW JOURNAL 1968:283, April, 1968.

Jury discretion, provocation and insanity, by G. H. L. Fridman. SOLICITOR 22:107-110, April, 1955.

Jury said death, by G. Marine. NATION 182:424-426, May 19, 1956.

Jury selection and the death penalty: Witherspoon (Witherspoon v. Illinois, 88 Sup. Ct. 1770). UNIVERSITY OF CHICAGO LAW REVIEW 37:759, Summer, 1970.

New data on the effect of a "death qualified" jury on the guilt determination process, by G. L. Jurow. HARVARD LAW REVIEW 84:567, January, 1971.

Problems of jury discretion in capital cases [suggests legislation for minimizing the arbitrary character of the jury's decision], by R. E. Knowlton. UNIVERSITY OF PENNSYLVANIA LAW REVIEW 101:1099-1136, June, 1953.

Reprieve for juries. ECONOMIST 169:949, December 26, 1953.

Toward expansion of Witherspoon (Witherspoon v. Illinois, 88 Sup. Ct. 1770): capital scruples jury bias, and use of psychological data to raise presumptions in the law, by F. Goldberg. HARVARD CIVIL RIGHTS. CIVIL LIBERTIES LAW REVIEW 5:53, January, 1970.

Unanimity requirement of a jury's determination and the Witherspoon (Witherspoon v. Illinois, 88 Sup. Ct. 1770) exclusionary rule. TEMPLE LAW QUARTERLY 43:48, Fall, 1969.

NEWSPAPER ARTICLES

ACLU of Northern California and NAACP challenge capital punishment in California Supreme Court, Anderson and Saterfield cases; claim Death Row inmates are denied right to counsel after State Supreme Court review of their sentences, that so-called 'scrupled' jurors, those opposed to death penalty, are excluded from hearing capital cases, and that juries in such cases are without standards or guidelines in reaching decision. NEW YORK TIMES 67:1, June 9, 1968.

By a 6-to-3 vote, the Supreme Court concludes that the Constitution does not require that states provide standards to guide juries in sentencing. THE NATIONAL OBSERVER p. 3, May 10, 1971.

KETCH, JACK
see: Cases Involving Capital Punishment

KIDNAPPING
No death for kidnappers. TIME 91:86, April 19, 1968.

NEWSPAPER ARTICLES

Convicted kidnapper and bank robber are executed by firing squad on December 20 in Algiers. NEW YORK TIMES 15:3, December 21, 1972.

Kidnapping refocus spotlight on death penalty. CHRISTIAN SCIENCE MONITOR 2:1, February 25, 1974, (All Editions).

NAACP Legal Defense and Education Fund. and New Jersey Public Defender ask New Jersey Supreme Court to abolish state's death penalty; hold US Supreme Court ruling outlawing death penalty in Federal kidnapping cases applies to capital cases in New Jersey. NEW YORK TIMES 34:8, June 4 1968.

Nebraska reinstates death penalty for crimes of premediated murder, killing in course of rape, arson, robbery, kidnapping, hijacking and burglary. NEW YORK TIMES 23:8, April 20, 1973.

KOREA

NEWSPAPER ARTICLES

Seoul, South Korea, court imposes death sentences on 2 American soldiers convicted of murdering South Korean couple in March; sentence is 1st involving capital punishment since 1967 US-South Korea status of forces agreement. NEW YORK TIMES 8:3, December 5, 1970.

South Korean Assembly passes bill to extend death penalty to various crimes. NEW YORK TIMES 3:5, February 15, 1966.

THE LAW AND CAPITAL PUNISHMENT
see also: Police

Abolition of capital punishment—a symposium (Feinberg, Haines, Kelly, McGeachy, Mackay, MacLean, Maloney, Martin, Parsons, Sedgwick, Snell). CANADIAN BAR REVIEW 32:485-519, May, 1954.

American jury and the death penalty, by H. Kalven, Jr., et al. UNIVERSITY OF CHICAGO LAW REVIEW 33:769, Summer, 1966.

American Law Institute proceedings, May 20, 1954. Crime and punishment, by A. J. Harno; A thoughtful code of substantive law, by H. Wechsler; Sentencing function of the judge, by G. F. Flood; After sentence—what?, by J. V. Bennett. JOURNAL OF CRIMINAL LAW AND CRIMINOLOGY 45:520-540, January-February, 1955.

Bastard or legitimate child of Furman (Furman v. Georgia, 92 Sup. Ct. 2726)? An analysis of Wyoming's new capital punishment law. LAND AND WATER REVIEW 9:209-236, 1974.

Bill to abolish capital punishment in Pennsylvania, by F. Worley. DICKINSON LAW REVIEW 60:167, January, 1956.

Bringing back death; Supreme court decisions, by R. A. Pugsley. COMMONWEAL 103:518-519, August 13, 1976.

British constitution and the capital punishment abolition controversy, by H. S. Albinski. JOURNAL OF PUBLIC LAW 12:193, 1963.

Capital crimes as defined in American statutory law, by L. D. Savitz. JOURNAL OF CRIMINAL LAW, CRIMINOLOGY AND POLICE SCIENCE 46:355-363, September-October, 1955.

Capital punishment. IRISH LAW TIMES 92:17, April 13, 1957.

—. SCOTTISH LAW REVIEW 69:241-246, November, 1953.

—. SOUTH AFRICAN LAW JOURNAL 73:344, August, 1956.

—. TENNESSEE LAW REVIEW 29:534, Summer, 1962.

—, by A. O'Halloran. FEDERAL PROBATION 29:33, June, 1965.

—, by D. F. McMahon. FBI LAW ENFORCEMENT BULLETIN 42(2):20-21, February, 1973.

—, by J. F. Coakley. AMERICAN CRIMINAL LAW QUARTERLY 1:27, May, 1963.

—, by K. Soelling. CHITTY'S LAW JOURNAL 8:146, February, 1959.

—, by L. T. Pennell. ALBERTA LAW REVIEW 5:167, 1967.

—, by S. W. Karge. JOURNAL OF CRIMINAL LAW AND CRIMINOLOGY 67:437-449, December, 1976.

—, by T. B. Smith. SCOTTISH LAW REVIEW 1953:197-204, November 7, 1953.

—, by T. Sellin. CRIMINAL LAW QUARTERLY 8:36, June, 1965.

—. FEDERAL PROBATION 25:3, September, 1961.

Capital punishment agreement in sight [bill abolishing death penalty] . ECONOMIST 216:592, August 14, 1965.

Capital punishment and its alternatives in ancient Near Eastern law, by E. M. Good. STANFORD LAW REVIEW 19:947, May, 1967.

Capital punishment and life imprisonment in North Carolina, 1946 to 1968: implications for abolition of the death penalty, by C. H. Patrick. WAKE FOREST INTERNATIONAL LAW REVIEW 6:417, May, 1970.

Capital punishment controversy, by W. O. Hochkammer, Jr. JOURNAL OF CRIMINAL LAW AND CRIMINOLOGY 60:360, September, 1969.

Capital punishment: does it deter or degrade? [with a list entitled] , "Where the states stand on capital punishment—two years after U.S. Supreme court decision." CONGRESSIONAL QUARTERLY WEEKLY REPORT 32:1419-1422, June 1, 1974.

Capital punishment in the building of communism, by B. A. Ramundo. AMERICAN BAR ASSOCIATION. SECTION OF INTERNATIONAL AND COMPARATIVE LAW BULLETIN 1963:215, 1963.

Capital punishment in imperial and Soviet criminal law, by W. Adams. AMERICAN JOURNAL OF COMPARATIVE LAW 18(3):474-594, 1970.

Capital punishment in its legal and social aspects, by J. S. Roucek. THE INTERNATIONAL JOURNAL OF LEGAL RESEARCH 6:np, December, 1971.

Capital punishment in the light of constitutional evolution: an analysis of distinctions between Furman and Gregg [Gregg v. Georgia, 96 Sup. Ct. 2909), by J. C. England. NOTRE DAME LAWYER 52: 596-610, April, 1977.

Capital punishment in Northern Ireland, by J. K. J. Edwards. CRIMINAL LAW REVIEW 1956:750, November, 1956.

Capital punishment in South Carolina: the end of an era, by L. Mc-Donald. SOUTH CAROLINA LAW REVIEW 24:762, 1972.

Capital punishment in Virginia. VIRGINIA LAW REVIEW 58:97-142, January, 1972.

Capital punishment is constitutional: California state Supreme court decision. TIME 92:93, November 29, 1968.

Capital punishment: a model for reform. KENTUCKY LAW JOURNAL 57:508, 1968-1969.

Capital punishment—a practical viewpoint, by D. E. W. Tisdale. CANADIAN BAR JOURNAL 2:255, August, 1959.

Capital punishment: a reaction from a member of the clergy, by L. Kinsolving. AMERICAN BAR ASSOCIATION JOURNAL 42: 850-852, September, 1956.

Capital punishment reconsidered [social and political aspects], by W. O. Reichert. KENTUCKY LAW JOURNAL 47:397-417, Spring, 1959.

Capital punishment under the UCMJ after Furman, by R. E. Tragolo. AIR FORCE LAW REVIEW 16(4):86-95, Winter, 1974.

Capital punishment; voting again. ECONOMIST 247:18+, April 7, 1973.

The Capitall Lawes of New-England, by G. L. Haskins. HARVARD LAW SCHOOL BULLETIN 7:10, February, 1956.

Case for the abolition of capital punishment. LOUISIANA LAW REVIEW 29:396, February, 1969.

Children of Cain? Senate vote and H. Hughes' amendment. Sisyphus. COMMONWEAL 100:107-108, April 5, 1974.

Commons says it again: no return to hanging. ECONOMIST 247:17, April 14, 1973.

Comparative aspects of the English homicide act of 1957 [capital punishment; murder and manslaughter concepts], by M. Koessler. MISSOURI LAW REVIEW 25:107-154, April, 1960.

Comparison of punishments in Soviet criminal law and American military law, by A. Avins. SOUTH TEXAS LAW JOURNAL 2:303, Summer-Fall, 1956.

Constitutional invalidity of convictions imposed by death-qualified juries, by W. S. White. CORNELL LAW REVIEW 58:1176-1220, July, 1973.

Constitutional law—Arkansas state penitentiary transgresses constitutional proscription against cruel and unusual punishment. SETON HALL LAW REVIEW 3:159, Fall, 1971.

Constitutional law: capital punishment—the current status of the death penalty in North Carolina. WAKE FOREST LAW REVIEW 9:135, December, 1972.

Constitutional law—capital punishment—death penalty as presently administered held unconstitutional. FORDHAM LAW REVIEW 41:671, March, 1973.

Constitutional law: capital punishment for rape constitutes cruel and unusual punishment when no life is taken or endangered. MINNESOTA LAW REVIEW 56:95, November, 1971.

Constitutional law—capital punishment—Furman v. Georgia (92 Sup. Ct. 2726) and Georgia's statutory response. MERCER LAW REVIEW 24:891, Summer, 1973.

Constitutional law—challenge for cause on the ground of conscientious scruples against capital punishment. ARKANSAS LAW REVIEW 23:108, Spring, 1969.

Constitutional law—cruel and unusual—capital punishment. NORTH CAROLINA LAW REVIEW 42:909, June, 1964.

Constitutional law—cruel or unusual punishment: the death penalty.

SUFFOLK UNIVERSITY LAW REVIEW 6:1045, Summer, 1972.

Constitutional law—cruel and unusual punishments—the imposition and carrying out of the death penalty under current discretionary sentencing statutes constitutes cruel and unusual punishment in violation of the eighth and fourteenth amendments. UNIVERSITY OF CINCINNATI LAW REVIEW 42:172-178, 1973.

Constitutional law—death penalty—Texas death penalty statutes comply with the discretion requirements of the United States Supreme Court. ST. MARY'S LAW JOURNAL 7:454-462, 1975.

Constitutional law—eighth amendment: cruel and unusual punishment; a vehicle for reappraising the application of the criminal law to the individual. CONNECTICUT BAR JOURNAL 40:521, September, 1966.

Constitutional law—eighth amendment—death penalty as currently administered constitutes cruel and unusual punishment. TULANE LAW REVIEW 47:1167-1184, June, 1973.

Constitutional law—eighth amendment—the death penalty as presently administered under discretionary sentencing statutes is cruel and unusual. SETON HALL LAW REVIEW 4:244, Fall-Winter, 1972.

Constitutional law—the eighth amendment's proscription of cruel and unusual punishment precludes imposition of the death sentence for rape when the victim's life is neither taken nor endangered. GEORGE WASHINGTON LAW REVIEW 40:161, October, 1971.

Constitutional law—the remains of the death peanalty: Furman v. Georgia (92 Sup. Ct. 2726). DE PAUL LAW REVIEW 22:481, Winter, 1972.

The constitutional status of the death penalty in New Jersey, by H. A. Cohen. CRIMINAL JUSTICE QUARTERLY 2:5-24, Winter, 1974.

Constitutionality of the Connecticut penal code (title 53a) guilt plea/ capital punishment provisions. CONNECTICUT BAR JOURNAL

45:414, December, 1971.

Constitutionality of the death penalty for non-aggravated rape. WASHINGTON UNIVERSITY LAW QUARTERLY 1972:170, Winter, 1972.

Corporal punishment and courts, by A. J. W. Taylor. NEW ZEALAND LAW JOURNAL 1963:407, July 23, 1963.

Corporal punishment in Northern Ireland, by J. L. J. Edwards. CRIMINAL LAW REVIEW 1956:814, December 1956.

Corporal punishment in South Australia. ADELAIDE LAW REVIEW 2:83, June, 1963.

Counsel for the doomed. NEWSWEEK 61:36-37, March 25, 1963.

Courts, the Constitution, and capital punishment, by H. A. Bedau. UTAH LAW REVIEW 1968:201, May, 1968.

Crime and punishment [Russia] : Execution: hallmark of "socialist legality," by L. Lipson; The wages of economic sin, by H. Willets. PROBLEMS OF COMMUNISM 11:21-32, September-October, 1962.

Crime and punishment. Sentencing: a reply, by H. Mannheim. JUSTICE OF THE PEACE 122:102, February 15, 1958.

Crime and punishment: third reading [Mr. Silverman's bill abolishing capital punishment] . ECONOMIST 216:247, July 17, 1965.

Crimes on violence and the sentencing policy of the courts, by T. E. James. CRIMINAL LAW REVIEW 1960:678, October, 1960.

Criminal law—capital punishment. UNIVERSITY OF KANSAS CITY LAW REVIEW 28:170, Summer, 1960.

Criminal law—capital punishment—corporal punishment—lotteries— joint committee reports, by P. J. O'Hearn. CANADIAN BAR REVIEW 34:844, August-September, 1956.

Criminal law: capital punishment in Britain [recent history of the death penalty], by G. Gardiner. AMERICAN BAR ASSOCIATION JOURNAL 45:259-261, March, 1959.

Criminal law—capital punishment—the Texas statutes authorizing the death penalty do not violate the eighth amendment's prohibition of cruel and unusual punishment. TEXAS LAW REVIEW 7:170-181, Fall, 1975.

Criminal law—the limited application of the eighth amendment's cruel and unusual punishment clause to the death penalty. WAKE FOREST LAW REVIEW 7:494, June, 1971.

Criminal law—rape—death penalty—eighth amendment prohibition against cruel and unusual punishments forbids execution when the victim's life was neither taken nor endangered. UNIVERSITY OF CINCINNATI LAW REVIEW 40:396, Summer, 1971.

The crisis in capital punishment [based on address], by C. L. Black, Jr. MARYLAND LAW REVIEW 31(4):289-311, 1971.

Cruel and unusual punishment—constitutionality of the death penalty for rape where victim's life neither taken nor endangered. UNIVERSITY OF RICHMOND LAW REVIEW 5:392, Spring, 1971.

Day at the Lords. SPECTATOR 108:268, March 1, 1957.

De facto abolition of the death penalty in Louisiana?, by W. H. Forman, Jr. LOUISIANA BAR JOURNAL 18:199, December, 1970.

Death dealing, case before the Supreme court. TIME 105:58+, April 21, 1975.

Death delayed: Supreme court decision. PROGRESSIVE 40:8-9, September, 1976.

Death in court. ECONOMIST 224:1199, September 30, 1967.

Death killers: Cruel and unusual, story behind Supreme court's abolition of the death penalty. TIME 102:94, September 17, 1973.

Death of capital punishment? Furman v. Georgia (92 Sup. Ct. 2726), by D. D. Polsby. SUPREME COURT REVIEW 1972:1, 1972.

Death on Parliament Hill [status of the death penalty in Canada, conference paper], by W. T. McGrath. CANADIAN WELFARE 48:8-10+, November-December, 1972.

Death penalty—the alternatives left after Furman v. Georgia (92 Sup. Ct. 2726). ALBANY LAW REVIEW 37:344, 1973.

Death penalty and the Supreme Court, by A. J. Goldberg. ARIZONA LAW REVIEW 15:355-368, 1973.

Death penalty: bill to abolish execution. NEWSWEEK 72:28, July 15, 1968.

Death penalty: Chinese style, by C. Douglas. TRIAL 13:44-46, February, 1977.

Death penalty; haunting the court. ECONOMIST 259:45-46, April 10, 1976.

The death penalty in the United States. ANNALS OF THE AMERICAN ACADEMY OF POLITICAL AND SOCIAL SCIENCE pp. 45-100, November, 1952.

Death penalty provision of the new penal code, by J. M. Carroll. KENTUCKY BAR JOURNAL 38:15-21, October, 1974.

Death penalty revived: Supreme court decision. TIME 108:35-37, July 12, 1976.

Death to hanging; government resolution outlawing hanging in Great Britain. NEWSWEEK 74:28+, December 29, 1969.

Declaring the death penalty unconstitutional, by A. J. Goldberg, et al. HARVARD LAW REVIEW 83:1773, June, 1970.

Decree of presidium of U.S.S.R. Supreme Soviet: on intensifying the struggle against especially dangerous crimes [to permit application of capital punishment: for, pilfering of state or public property in large amounts; counterfeiting of money or securities; with respect to habitual offenders and persons convicted of serious crimes who in places of detention terrorize prisoners endeavoring to reform, commit attacks on the administration, organize criminal groups for this purpose or actively participate in such groupings]. CURRENT DIGEST OF THE SOVIET PRESS 13:8, May 24, 1961.

Demise of the gallows; House of commons in London votes to abolish the death penalty for murder. AMERICA 112:99, January 23, 1965.

Discretion and the constitutionality of the new death penalty statutes. HARVARD LAW REVIEW 87:1690-1719, June, 1974.

Effectiveness of the eighth amendment: an appraisal of cruel and unusual punishment. NEW YORK UNIVERSITY LAW REVIEW 36:846, April, 1961.

Eighth amendment and Kentucky's new capital punishment provisions —waiting for the other shoe to drop. KENTUCKY LAW JOURNAL 63:399-429, 1974-1975.

An end to "death row"? what Supreme court ruled. U. S. NEWS AND WORLD REPORT 73:25-27, July 10, 1972.

End to hanging; bill passed in the House of commons. TIME 85:36-37, January 1, 1965.

The English homicide act of 1957: the capital punishment issue, and various reforms in the law of murder and manslaughter, by G. Hughes. JOURNAL OF CRIMINAL LAW, CRIMINOLOGY AND POLICE SCIENCE 49:521-532, March-April, 1959.

Footnote to Furman (Furman v. Georgia, 92 Sup. Ct. 2726): failing justification for the capital case exception to the right to bail after abolition of the death penalty. SAN DIEGO LAW REVIEW 10:349, February, 1973.

Furman (Furman v. Georgia, 92 Sup. Ct. 2726) Case: what life is left in the death penalty? CATHOLIC UNIVERSITY LAW REVIEW 22:651, Spring, 1973.

Furman v. Georgia (92 Sup. Ct. 2726) and Kentucky statutory law, by L. M. T. Reed. KENTUCKY BAR JOURNAL 37:25, January, 1973.

Furman v. Georgia (92 Sup. Ct. 2726): the Burger court looks at judicial review, by D. Victor. LAW AND THE SOCIAL ORDER 1972:393, 1972.

Furman v. Georgia (92 Sup. Ct. 2726): will the death of capital punishment mean a new life for bail? HOFSTRA LAW REVIEW 2:432-443, Winter, 1974.

Government from the backwoods. NEW STATESMAN 52:29, July 14, 1956; Discussion, 52:70, 104, July 21-28, 1956.

Haunting the court. ECONOMIST 259:45-46, April 10, 1976.

Homicide in the Lords. ECONOMIST 182:710, March 2, 1957.

House bill 200: the legislative attempt to reinstate capital punishment in Texas. HOUSTON LAW REVIEW 11:410-423, January, 1974.

Hypocrisy in high paces; Senator Hughes public-execution amendment. CHRISTIAN CENTURY 91:357, April 3, 1974.

Judicial barbarism. SPECTATOR 194:141, February 11, 1950.

Jury challenges, capital punishment, and Labat v. Bennett (365 F 2d 698): a reconciliation. DUKE LAW JOURNAL 1968:283, April, 1968.

Jury selection and the death penalty: Witherspoon (Witherspoon v. Illinois, 88 Sup. Ct. 1770). UNIVERSITY OF CHICAGO LAW REVIEW 37:759, Summer, 1970.

Law of murder and the death sentence. JUSTICE OF THE PEACE

120:83, February 11, 1956.

Law of murder: the prospects of abolishing capital punishment are not necessarily being improved by the tactics of some abolitionists [Great Britain]. ECONOMIST 198:436-437, February 4, 1961.

Law reform: capital punishment. IRISH LAW TIMES 91:79, March 23, 1957+.

Law reform: to hang or not to hang? IRISH LAW TIMES 90:291, December 15, 1956.

Letter from London; House of lords throws out Commons' bill to abolish death penalty, by M. Panter-Downes. NEW YORKER 32:62, July 23, 1956.

Life or death, by L. R. Friedman; Another view by R. Kinglsey. JOURNAL OF THE STATE BAR OF CALIFORNIA 35:543, September-October, 1960.

Lindbergh law revised. NEWSWEEK 71:38A, April 22, 1968.

Litigating against the death penalty: the strategy behind Furman (Furman v. Georgia, 92 Sup. Ct. 2726), by M. Meltsner. YALE LAW JOURNAL 82:111, May, 1973.

Lords and the constitution; Fate of the Bill—and the varying tune. ECONOMIST 180:110, July 14, 1956.

The lords who said "no" [characteristics of the British peers who voted on the Death penalty (abolition) bill, House of lords, July 9-10, 1956]. LABOUR RESEARCH 45:113-114, August, 1956.

McGautha. v. California, May, 1971: on May 3, 1971, the Supreme court handed down a far-reaching decision that capital punishment procedures in general use throughout the United States today do not violate the constitution [excerpts from the text of the decision]. CURRENT HISTORY 61:40-42+, July, 1971.

Making the punishment fit the crime [critical comment on Justice

Arthur Goldberg's questioning of the propriety of imposing the death penalty on convicted rapists], by H. L. Packer. HARVARD LAW REVIEW 77:1071-1082, April, 1964.

A matter of conviction, by E. G. Brown. FELLOWSHIP 26:14-16, July 1, 1960.

Montana's death penalty after State v. McKenzie [33 St. Reptr. 1043 (1976)]. MONTANA LAW REVIEW 38:209-220, Winter, 1977.

Mr. Chief Justice. . .reason proves a sorry substitute for revelation, by J. R. Spon, Jr. OHIO NORTHERN UNIVERSITY LAW REVIEW 1:130-142, 1973.

Murder. SPECTATOR 207:564, October 27, 1961.

Murder and capital punishment: some further evidence, by W. C. Bailey. AMERICAN JOURNAL OF ORTHOPSYCHIATRY 45(4):669-688, July, 1975.

Murder and the constitution, by S. Silverman. NEW STATESMAN 52: 618, November 17, 1956.

Murder and the death penalty, by C. M. Craven. NEW STATESMAN AND NATION 37:154, February 12, 1949.

—, by W. C. Bailey. JOURNAL OF CRIMINAL LAW AND CRIM-INOLOGY 65:416-423, September, 1974.

Murder and the death penalty: a case report, by B. L. Diamond. AMERICAN JOURNAL OF ORTHOPSYCHIATRY 45(4):712-722, July, 1975.

Murder and the penalty of death, by T. Sellin. ANNALS OF THE AMERICAN ACADEMY OF POLITICAL AND SOCIAL SCIENCE 284:1-166, November, 1952.

Murder and the principles of punishment: England and the United States, by H. L. A. Hart. NORTHWESTERN UNIVERSITY LAW

REVIEW 52:433, September-October, 1957.

Murder: how long is life? [debates on bill to abolish capital punishment]. ECONOMIST 214:1277-1278, March 20, 1965.

Murder in New Hampshire [1843], by D. B. Davis. NEW ENGLAND QUARTERLY 28:147-163, June, 1955.

Murder more and less foul; committee stage of government's homicide bill. ECONOMIST 181:863, December 8, 1956.

Murder: Mr. Callaghan's nettle. ECONOMIST 233:24, December 13, 1969.

Murder [the public inquiry of the Royal commission on capital punishment in its attempt to define degrees of murder is seeking alternatives to death by hanging]. ECONOMIST 157:333-334, August 13, 1949.

Murderers' reminiscences [abolition of capital punishment will end demand for such articles], by C. Hollis. SPECTATOR 195:37-39, July 8, 1955.

The new Soviet legislation concerning the death penalty, by Y. Mironenko. SOVIET AFFAIRS ANALYSIS SERVICE 37:1-4, 1960-1961.

Nixon administration and the deterrent effect of the death penalty, by H. A. Bedau. UNIVERSITY OF PITTSBURGH LAW REVIEW 34:557-566, Summer, 1973.

Parliament and the gallows, by A. Howard. NEW STATESMAN 63: 250, February 23, 1962.

Parliament and hanging: further episodes in an undying saga [parliamentary preoccupation with the issue of capital punishment; events since 1969], by G. Drewry. PARLIAMENTARY AFFAIRS 27:251-261, Summer, 1974.

Parliament: the beastly business again. ECONOMIST 230:47, March

1, 1969.

Parliament's agony over capital punishment: an inside view of an MP, his conscience and some rather disturbing mail [Canada], by P. Reilly. SATURDAY NIGHT 88:15-17, March, 1973.

Pittman v. State [(Texas) 434 S W 2d 352] : the death penalty and Texas jurors. SOUTHWESTERN LAW JOURNAL 23:405, May, 1969.

The proposed federal criminal codes: a prosecutor's point of view [focuses on federal law relating to tax offenses, the death penalty and entrapment], by D. A. Connelly. NORTHWESTERN UNIVERSITY LAW REVIEW 68:826-849, November-December, 1973.

Prosecutor looks at capital punishment, by R. M. Gerstein. JOURNAL OF CRIMINAL LAW AND CRIMINOLOGY 51:252, July-August, 1960.

Prosecutors may no longer tell juries capital punishment is a known deterrent: historic California Supreme court decision. CALIFORNIAN 3:5, February, 1962.

Punishment: current survey of philosophy and law, by R. J. Gerber, et al. ST. LOUIS UNIVERSITY LAW JOURNAL 11:491, Summer, 1967.

Recent changes in California law regarding jury's discretion in selecting first degree murder penalty [People v. Green (California) 302 P 2d 307]. SOUTHERN CALIFORNIA LAW REVIEW 31:200, February, 1958.

Recent judicial concepts of "cruel and unusual punishment", by A. Sultan. VILLANOVA LAW REVIEW 10:271, Winter, 1965.

Reflections on crime and punishment in China, with appended sentencing documents, by R. Edwards. COLUMBIA JOURNAL OF TRANSNATIONAL LAW 16:45-103, 1977.

Reform of the law relating to capital punishment: a study in the operation of parliamentary institutions, by W. N. Ortved. FACULTY OF LAW REVIEW 29:73, August, 1971.

Response to Furman (Furman v. Georgia, 92 Sup. Ct. 2726): can legislators breathe life back into death? CLEVELAND STATE LAW REVIEW 23:172-189, Winter, 1974.

Resurrection of capital punishment—the 1976 death penalty cases. DICKINSON LAW REVIEW 81:543-573, Spring, 1977.

Resurrection of the death penalty: the validity of Arizona's response to [the U.S. supreme court's decision, June 29, 1972, in the case of] Furman v. Georgia, by G. Forster. ARIZONA STATE LAW JOURNAL 1974(2):257-296, 1974.

Reviving the death penalty: Supreme court decision, by S. Fraker, et al. NEWSWEEK 88:14-15, July 12, 1976.

Right of the state to inflict capital punishment, by T. J. Riley. CATHOLIC LAWYER 6:279, Autumn, 1960.

The role of the social science in determining the constitutionality and capital punishment, by W. S. White. AMERICAN JOURNAL OF ORTHOPSYCHIATRY 45(4):581-595, July, 1975.

Someone had a good idea: New York Law. NATION 196:298, April 13, 1963; Reply by N. Redlich, 196:inside cover, April 27, 1963.

Spreading impact of a historic court decision: death penalty ruling. U. S. NEWS AND WORLD REPORT 81:49-51, July 12, 1976.

State supreme court rules death penalty unconstitutional in California. CALIFORNIA JOURNAL 3:51, February, 1972.

State v. Laws [(New Jersey) 242 A 2d 333] : appellate power to reduce jury determined death sentences. RUTGERS LAW REVIEW 23: 490, Spring, 1969.

Statistical evidence on the deterrent effect of capital punishment—A comparison of the work of Thorsten Sellin and Isaac Ehrlich on the deterrent effect of capital punishment, by D. C. Baldus, et al.; The illusion of deterrence in Isaac Ehrlich's research on capital punishment, by W. J. Bowers, et al.; Deterrence: evidence and inference, by I. Ehrlich. YALE LAW JOURNAL 85:164-227, December, 1975.

Still cruel and unusual; arguments on capital punishment before the Court, by H. A. Bedau. NATION 220:612-613, May 24, 1975.

The strength of sin is the law [opposes capital punishments], by A. Burdett. LIBERATION: AN INDEPENDENT MONTHLY 5:17-18, November, 1960.

Supreme Court and capital punishment—from Wilkerson to Witherspoon (Witherspoon v. Illinois, 88 Sup. Ct. 1770). ST. LOUIS UNIVERSITY LAW JOURNAL 14:463, Spring, 1970.

Supreme Court rulings on capital punishment, 1976. CURRENT HISTORY 71:30-31, July, 1976.

Supreme judicial court and the death penalty: the effects of judicial choice on legislative options. BOSTON UNIVERSITY LAW REVIEW 54:158-185, January, 1974.

Survival of the death penalty. BAYLOR LAW REVIEW 23:499, Summer, 1971.

Tennessee v. Walsh Jones: the closing argument for the defense, by J. W. Henry, Jr. AMERICAN BAR ASSOCIATION JOURNAL 46:52, January, 1960.

Testing the death penalty, by G. H. Gottlieb. SOUTHERN CALIFORNIA LAW REVIEW 34:268, Spring, 1961.

13 states restore death penalty. STATE GOVERNMENT NEWS 16:2-5, May, 1973.

Unconstitutional punishment, by R. A. Tingler. CRIMINAL LAW BULLETIN 6:311, July-August, 1970.

United States v. Jackson (88 Sup. Ct. 1209): guilty pleas and replacement capital punishment provisions. CORNELL LAW REVIEW 54:448, February, 1969.

Use of the death penalty v. outrage at murder, by D. Glaser, et al. CRIME AND DELINQUENCY 20:333-338, October, 1974; Reply with rejoinder by W. C. Bailey, 22:31-43, January, 1976.

Why was capital punishment restored in Delaware?, by G. W. Samuelson. JOURNAL OF CRIMINAL LAW, CRIMINOLOGY AND POLICE SCIENCE 60(2):148-151, June, 1960.

Witherspoon revisited: exploring the tension between Witherspoon and Furman, by W. S. White. UNIVERSITY OF CINCINNATI LAW REVIEW 45:19-36, 1976.

NEWSPAPER ARTICLES

A. Lewis article discusses U.S. Supreme Court decision to abolish capital punishment; states court has a history of overturning and reinterpreting "traditional" practices and laws. . . NEW YORK TIMES 21:1, July 1, 1972.

ACLU, New Jersey State Association on Correction and Coalition on Penal Reform attack plan for public hearing on death penalty proposal, saying it is pol. motivated because it comes in midst of gubernatorial and legis. election campaign; hearing is set for September 13. NEW YORK TIMES 74:2, September 10, 1973.

Abolition bill assured of floor action in New York State legislature. NEW YORK TIMES 23:1, April 21, 1965.

Alabama conviction reversed. CHRISTIAN SCIENCE MONITOR 16:1, June 4, 1969, (Western Edition).

Alabama Governor Wallace supporters file minority report with Democratic Platform Com. defending capital punishment. NEW YORK TIMES 1:4, June 28, 1972.

American Bar Association, meeting on February 12 in Cleveland, votes to postpone for 1 year any action on proposed state legis. to reinstate capital punishment on ground that law remains unsettled in wake of 1972 Supreme Court decision. NEW YORK TIMES 11:1, February 13, 1973.

Approves bill limiting death penalty to 5 types of homicide; would impose death sentence for multiple murders. NEW YORK TIMES 29:3, February 7, 1957.

The Arkansas legislature was asked to substitute drawing and quartering for the electric chair as it debated how to retain capital punishment despite recent Federal court decisions. THE NATIONAL OBSERVER p. 3, March 24, 1973.

Article reviews status of capital punishment in NYS in light of last weeks court ruling outlawing last discretionary instances of death penalty in state—law giving juries option to decree death in murder of on-duty police or prison officers and in murders committed by convicts serving life sentences; proponents of capital punishment now contend that making sentence mandatory instead of optional will satisfy Supreme Court, and are preparing to launch campaign in December at legis. hearing; Assemblyman D. L. DiCarlo and Senator H. D. Barclay comment; drawing. NEW YORK TIMES IV,8:1, November 18, 1973.

Assembly, 78-67, approves bill. NEW YORK TIMES 1:5, May 20, 1965.

Baltimore grand jury, in report issued on May 12, urges restoration of death penalty for 1st degree murder, to apply for taking life of all citizens and not just prison officials. NEW YORK TIMES 44:4, May 13, 1973.

Bill for 6-year moratorium on death penalty with some exceptions backed by California Assembly. NEW YORK TIMES 53:4, May 10, 1957.

Bill is introduced in Massachusetts Legis. on December 31 that would establish death penalty for murder of law enforcement and correctional officers and for rape. NEW YORK TIMES 32:2, December 14, 1973.

Bill modifiying Massachusetts mandatory death-peanlty law in certain cases signed. NEW YORK TIMES 20:6, April 4, 1951.

Bill to abolish death penalty passes 3d and final reading. NEW YORK TIMES 12:7, June 29, 1956.

Bill to end penalty in Indiana approved by State Senate, 27-19. NEW YORK TIMES 55:3, February 19, 1967.

Bill voted. CHRISTIAN SCIENCE MONITOR 7:5, March 14, 1963, (Eastern Edition); 2:6, March 14, 1963, (Western Edition).

British Commons gets bill to abolish death penalty. NEW YORK TIMES 10:3, December 5, 1964.

By a 6-to-3 vote, the Supreme Court concludes that the Constitution does not require that states provide standards to guide juries in sentencing. THE NATIONAL OBSERVER p. 3, May 10, 1971.

California Assembly defeats bills for repeal and 4-year moratorium on penalty. NEW YORK TIMES 28:3, April 26, 1961.

California Governor Brown says he will call special Legis. session to study death peanlty, statement following Chessman reprieve. NEW YORK TIMES 16:5, February 19, 1960.

California Governor Reagan on September 24 signs bill restoring death penalty in state on limited basis; bill makes execution mandatory in 11 categories of murder committed after January 1, 1974; Reagan says he regrets step, but believes measure will save lives. NEW YORK TIMES 6:4, September 25, 1973.

California Legis. rejects abolition bill and amendment to end bill's effective date July 1963; adjourns special session; Brown regrets decision. NEW YORK TIMES 1:8, March 11, 1960.

California Legis. to begin special session; Senator Kuchel opposes abolition, radio program; stresses deterrent value; abolition urged by New York Correction Comr. Kross and New York Com. to Abolish Capital Punishment chairman Nathanson. NEW YORK TIMES 28:1, February 29, 1960.

California Senator com. kills bill to abolish penalty; demonstrators outside San Quentin prison, State Capitol and Governor Reagan's home protest execution of A. C. Mitchell, convicted in February 1963 murder. NEW YORK TIMES 50:2, April 13, 1967.

The California Supreme Court has ruled that capital punishment is cruel and unusual punishment and therefore is in violation of the state's constitution. THE NATIONAL OBSERVER p. 5, February 26, 1972.

California Supreme Court to hear attacks on constitution of death penalty. NEW YORK TIMES 10:1, November 10, 1967.

Capital punishment appeal ruling. CHRISTIAN SCIENCE MONITOR 5:1, October 19, 1967, (Eastern, Western, Midwestern, and London and Overseas Editions).

Comment on bill's passage details Senator debate that preceded vote; illus. of J. Taborsky, last man to be executed in Connecticut. NEW YORK TIMES IV,7:1, April 22, 1973.

Comment on massive and controversial revision of Federal Criminal Code approaching its 1st test in Congress notes that 1 of provisions would reinstate capital punishment (S). NEW YORK TIMES 24:3, April 24, 1975.

Comment on recent US Supreme Court decision abolishing capital punishment; notes narrow margin of decision, individual opinions written by justices, Nixon's influence on his appointees, and possibility that states will reinstitute their own death penalties. NEW YORK TIMES IV,1:1, July 2, 1972.

Comr. Broderick urges closing loophole in law. NEW YORK TIMES 20:5, January 31, 1966.

Congress has begun an attempt to rewrite entire Federal Criminal

Code, including issue of capital punishment; bill, sponsored by Senator McClellan, would reinstate death penalty for crimes of murder and treason; is attempt to override Supreme Court's ban on such punishment by establishing 2-stage trial procedure in which death sentence could be imposed only in 2d stage. NEW YORK TIMES 17:3, January 15, 1973.

Connecticut Governor Meskill on May 4 signs bill restoring death penalty in state effective on October 1. NEW YORK TIMES 43:6, May 5, 1973.

Connecticut Governor Meskill says on December 1 that he expects Connecticut General Assembly in next 2 years to enact legis. that will widen death penalty to cover rapists and possibly to cover illegal drug traffickers; says that despite June 29 US Supreme Court ruling virtually eliminating death penalty, constitutional question of 'cruel and unusual' punishment remains open. NEW YORK TIMES 83:1, December 3, 1972.

Connecticut HR on April 11 votes to restore death penalty for sale of heroin, cocaine or methadone by unaddicted person where death of buyer results; bill provides for divided verdict, with jury or 3-judge panel first determining guilt or innocence, and court then considering specific mitigating circumstances before imposing death sentence. NEW YORK TIMES 9:1, April 12, 1973.

Connecticut House rejects death penalty abolition bill. NEW YORK TIMES 53:3, May 19, 1965.

Connecticut legis. com. backs bill to eliminate death penalty; House reportedly favors amendment to continue it for killing prison guards or attendants during escape attempts; Governor Ribicoff reports he will follow General Assembly action. NEW YORK TIMES 65:1, April 24, 1955.

Connecticut Senator rejects bill to abolish it. NEW YORK TIMES 18:3, June 4, 1955.

Conservative NYC mayoral candidate Representative Biaggi on September 15 calls on NYS Legis. to adopt law providing mandatory death penalty for murderers of police officers and prison guards, for hired assassins, for murderers of witnesses to serious crimes and for those committing murder during rape, robbery or kidnapping; says California has recently approved similar law and 20 other states have adopted measures to reinstitute penalty; Biaggi illus. NEW YORK TIMES 53:1, September 16, 1973.

Constitutionality of death penalty seen facing challenge in October 13 reargument before US Supreme Court of Maxwell v. Bishop. NEW YORK TIMES 1:2, July 28, 1969.

Court ruling. CHRISTIAN SCIENCE MONITOR 27:4, August 11, 1976, (Midwestern, and Eastern Editions); 25:4, August 11, 1976, (Western Edition).

Court ruling clears way. CHRISTIAN SCIENCE MONITOR 6:1, May 6, 1971, (Eastern Edition); 3:1, May 7, 1971, (Western Edition); 5:1, May 6, 1971, (Midwestern Edition); 6:1, May 6, 1971, (London and Overseas Editions).

The courts v. the people. CHRISTIAN SCIENCE MONITOR E:2, December 15, 1972, (Eastern, and London and Overseas Editions); E:2, December 16, 1972, (Western and Midwestern Editions).

Death penalty abolition proponents confident of NYS Senate approval this year but unsure of Assembly. NEW YORK TIMES 16:4, March 5, 1965.

Death penalty arguments this week. CHRISTIAN SCIENCE MONITOR 2:5, March 29, 1976, (All Editions).

Delaware Assembly overrides veto. NEW YORK TIMES 24:4, December 20, 1961.

Delaware Senate votes to restore penalty banned in 1958. NEW YORK TIMES 40:8, December 8, 1961.

Deputy Attorney General Clark says Justice Department favors abolition, lr. to Representative McMillan who sought department view on bill to end death penalty for 1st-degree murder in DC. NEW YORK TIMES 1:5, July 24, 1965.

Dr. D. T. Nash lr. on recent US Supreme Court decision to abolish capital punishment holds that further legis. is needed to protect rights of persons who have not committed crimes, instead of focusing attention on rights of criminals; illus. NEW YORK TIMES IV,12:3, July 9, 1972.

Editorial on case of G. Whitmore, wrongly indicted for murder, NYC, raising fresh doubts about death penalty. NEW YORK TIMES 26:2, January 30, 1965.

Excerpts from US Supreme Court opinion on capital punishment. NEW YORK TIMES 14:5, June 30, 1972.

F. P. Graham comments on upcoming US Supreme Court ruling on constitutionality of capital punishment. NEW YORK TIMES IV,2:1, January 23, 1972.

Fails. CHRISTIAN SCIENCE MONITOR 8:1, November 13, 1973, (Eastern Edition); 12:1, November 13, 1973, (Midwestern, and London and Overseas Editions); 14:1, November 13, 1973, (Western Edition).

Fate of Illinois proposition to new state Constitution that will abolish death penalty in doubt. NEW YORK TIMES 22:1, December 16, 1970.

Federal court rejects plea. CHRISTIAN SCIENCE MONITOR 13:4, August 31, 1967, (Eastern Edition); 6:4, August 30, 1967, (Western Edition); 3:1, August 30, 1967, (Midwestern Edition).

Fight looms on "New" penalty. CHRISTIAN SCIENCE MONITOR 6:2, January 6, 1973, (Eastern, and London and Overseas Editions); 2:2, January 8, 1973, (Western Edition).

Florida may soon pass the first law that would authorize the death penalty within the limits set by the Supreme Court. THE NATIONAL OBSERVER p. 6, December 9, 1972.

Florida State Supreme Court on July 26 upholds, 5 to 2, state's new capital punishment law; law sets up separate trial procedure after person has been convicted of a capital crime; jury, after hearing extenuating circumstances, recommends whether person should receive death penalty or life imprisonment; judge may then either accept or reverse decision and any death penalty decisions to automatically to State Supreme Court for review. NEW YORK TIMES 12:2, July 27, 1973.

Florida Supreme Court orders a new trial for two men on death row. THE NATIONAL OBSERVER p. 4, May 31, 1971.

Foes see none. CHRISTIAN SCIENCE MONITOR 1:4, September 5, 1973, (Eastern Edition); 1:4, September 6, 1973, (Western and Midwestern Editions); 1:4, September 5, 1973 (London and Overseas Editions).

Georgia Governor Carter on March 28 signs bill restoring death penalty. NEW YORK TIMES 51:3, March 29, 1973.

Georgia Legis. to review law. NEW YORK TIMES 33:1, October 10, 1961.

Georgia State Senate on February 22 votes, 47 to 7, to restore capital punishment in state; Governor Carter is expected to sign bill into law. NEW YORK TIMES 15:7, February 23, 1973.

Georgia Attorney General A. K. Bolton, Texas Attorney General C. C. Martin and Philadelphia District Attorney A. Spector file petition asking US Supreme Court to reconsider its historic 5 to 4 decision that sentences of death as now imposed under some state laws violate 8th and 14th Amendments to Constitution; petitions ask for rehearing of 16 capital cases in those 3 states; details. NEW YORK TIMES 20:1, July 25, 1972.

Governor Cargo signs bill banning death penalty in New Mexico except in 2 situations; bill commutes to life imprisonment sentences of 3 men now on Death Row. NEW YORK TIMES 38:2, April 1, 1969.

Governor Carvel vetoes bill. NEW YORK TIMES 42:4, December 15, 1961.

Governor McKeldin, testifying in favor of 2 bills to abolish capital punishment in Maryland, says he is ashamed he let 4 prisoners be executed during his term. NEW YORK TIMES 35:1, February 15, 1968.

High Court avoids decision on capital punishment, but will take up the issues with full court later. THE NATIONAL OBSERVER p. 7, June 8, 1970.

House sends it to com.; move seen ending hope of passage. NEW YORK TIMES 33:2, February 26, 1967.

If the Supreme Court upholds capital punishment, state courts immediately will set execution dates for some 550 prisoners sentenced to death. THE NATIONAL OBSERVER p. 1, November 16, 1970.

Illinois House votes, 102-36, to kill bill that would have restored death penalty in state (S). NEW YORK TIMES 37:8, May 18, 1975.

Illinois Senate com. rejects bill for 6-year moratorium. NEW YORK TIMES 36:6, June 16, 1965.

Illinois Supreme Court invalidates state's death penalty law that was passed in 1973 to cover certain types of murder; decision voids law on procedural ground, ruling that it violates state constitution; court, however, does not rule on constitutionality of capital punishment (M). NEW YORK TIMES 38:3, October 5, 1975.

Illinois Supreme Court rules that state's death penalty is unconstitutional (S). NEW YORK TIMES 34:3, September 30, 1975.

Indiana Governor Branigan vetoes bill, says abolition should be decided by referendum; Governor has been under pressure to veto bill since recent shooting of state trooper. NEW YORK TIMES 74:3, March 14, 1965.

Indiana Senator approves 2 bills abolishing penalty for 1st-degree murder and 4 other crimes. NEW YORK TIMES 14:3, February 10, 1965.

Indiana Supreme Court considers on July 17 whether to ban death penalty after lawyer asked that death sentence be overturned for client convicted of murder; court refers question to 5-judge panel; death sentence in Indiana now is given only to persons found guilty of murder or of abetting murder. NEW YORK TIMES 2:5, July 18, 1972.

Iowa Legis. abolishes penalty. NEW YORK TIMES 21:1, February 19, 1965.

The issue still confronts the Supreme Court in key cases. THE NATIONAL OBSERVER p. 12, October 2, 1971.

Ital. Penal Law Association President G. Persico urges elimination of death penalty, International Congress of Penal Law. NEW YORK TIMES 13:4, September 28, 1953.

Justice Department, in friend-of-court brief, notifies US Supreme Court that it does not support constitutional challenges to capital punishment that are now pending before Court; details. NEW YORK TIMES 23:2, October 16, 1970.

Justice Department neutral on Representative Multer bill to substitute life term for death sentence in Federal courts, reply to Representative Celler. NEW YORK TIMES 16:1, February 25, 1960.

Kentucky House approves bill to ban death penalty. NEW YORK TIMES 65:4, March 13, 1964.

Kentucky House considers legis. to abolish death penalty; defeats move to kill bill, 40-38; hears Tennessee convict who escaped electric chair. NEW YORK TIMES 17:4, February 16, 1966.

Kentucky House, 76-20, defeats bill to abolish death penalty. NEW YORK TIMES 14:2, February 18, 1966.

Legislatures in more than half the states are considering restitution of death penalty which was voided by US Supreme Court 5-4 decision. NEW YORK TIMES 1:7, March 11, 1973.

Louisiana Governor E. W. Edwards on June 20 signs bill restoring death penalty in state, saying that he has serious reservations as to whether Supreme Court would hold any bill constitutional which provides for capital punishment. NEW YORK TIMES 36:6, June 21, 1973.

Louisiana HR on June 11 re-enacts death penalty for 1st-degree murder and sends measure to Governor for signature. NEW YORK TIMES 61:1, June 13, 1973.

Louisiana House of Representatives, 68-26, defeats bill calling for a 6-year suspension of penalty. NEW YORK TIMES 35:4, June 28, 1968.

Maryland House of Delegates on March 22 approves, 90-41, bill mandating capital punishment for 7 kinds of murder (S). NEW YORK TIMES 49:1, March 23, 1975.

Maryland House of Delegates, 78-4, gives final legis. approval to bill backed by Governor Marvin Mandel to restore death penalty in Maryland for specified crimes (S). NEW YORK TIMES 30:8, March 30, 1975.

Massachusetts Governor Michael S. Dukakis on April 29 vetoes bill that would restore capital punishment in state; issuing veto minutes after state Senate had approved bill; bill, which would mandate capital punishment in 9 categories of murder, was previously approved by House; categories of murder requiring death penalty listed (M). NEW YORK TIMES 43:1, April 30, 1975.

Massachusetts House approves bill that would reinstate capital punishment for 9 categories of 1st-degree murder, Governor Dukakis expected to veto measure (S). NEW YORK TIMES 18:3, April 4, 1975.

Massachusetts House, with vote of 156-68, overrides Governor Michael

S. Dukakis' veto of bill to restore state's death penalty (S). NEW YORK TIMES 10:3, May 1, 1975.

Massachusetts Senate approves bill that would make death penalty mandatory in 7 categories of 1st-degree murder, including killing of policeman, fireman or correctional officer; bill as approved by House calls for mandatory death sentence in all 1st-degree murder cases; Senate bill now goes to House for vote. NEW YORK TIMES 26:1, October 11, 1973.

Massachusetts Senate rejects bill to require life terms in capital cases unless jury recommended death sentence. NEW YORK TIMES 18:7, April 4, 1961.

Massachusetts Senate, 26-14, sustains Governor Michael S. Dukakis' veto of bill providing death penalty for 9 types of murder; state House had earlier voted to override veto (S). NEW YORK TIMES 23:1, May 2, 1975.

Massachusetts Senate rejects House amendments to bill restoring death penalty; bill is sent to conf. com. NEW YORK TIMES 13:8, October 19, 1973.

Measure's opponents say bill will be challenged at 1st opportunity and carried back to US Supreme Court, which earlier had struck down state's death penalty law. NEW YORK TIMES 22:3, March 30, 1973.

The method of trying a murder defendant and of sentencing him to death is a key issue facing the Supreme Court beginning next week. THE NATIONAL OBSERVER p. 1, September 28, 1970.

Missouri House passes on June 3 bill making death penalty mandatory for anyone convicted of premeditated murder; Governor Christopher S. Bond says he will delay decision on whether to sign bill until he can consult his staff (S). NEW YORK TIMES 36:4, June 4, 1975.

NAACP Legal Defense and Education Fund. and New Jersey Public Defender ask New Jersey Supreme Court to abolish state's death penalty; hold US Supreme Court ruling outlawing death penalty in Federal kidnapping cases applies to capital cases in New Jersey. NEW YORK TIMES 34:8, June 4, 1968.

Nevada Supreme Court upholds secretary of state's capital punishment law that mandates death penalty for person convicted of killing more than 1 person in common plan or scheme (S). NEW YORK TIMES 72:7, November 16, 1975.

New Jersey Assembly com. hearing on bills to eliminate death penalty; most witnesses back bills, doubt penalty is crime deterrent. NEW YORK TIMES 25:1, June 6, 1958.

New Jersey Assembly Conference Com. shelves bill to restore capital punishment when bill receives only 36 of necessary 41 votes to send it to floor for vote; action seals fate of proposal in 1973, and it is not likely to be revived in 1974; Governor-elect B. T. Byrne has said he would be reluctant to sign bill reinstating death penalty. NEW YORK TIMES 154:1, December 2, 1973.

New Jersey Assembly delays vote on surprise proposal to reinstate death penalty (S). NEW YORK TIMES 83:6, December 2, 1975.

New Jersey Assembly Judiciary Com. chairman W. K. Dickey predicts that his panel will follow lead of Senate in approving measure to restore death penalty in state; public hearing on issue is scheduled for September 13; Dickey says he will lead drive for floor vote on measure when Legis. reconvenes in November; por. NEW YORK TIMES 97:1, September 9, 1973.

New Jersey Assembly Judiciary Com. on March 26 votes, 5-1, to proceed with consideration of death penalty bill. NEW YORK TIMES 100:1, March 27, 1973.

New Jersey Assembly Judiciary Com. schedules public hearing for September 13 on Senate-approved bill that would reinstate death penalty, despite recommendation by state Capital Punishment Study Comm. that Legis. put off any action toward restoration. NEW YORK TIMES 65:1, August 19, 1973.

New Jersey Assemblyman Haines confident of approval of his bills to drop death penalty; attorney for E. H. Smith, facing execution for murder, tries to get stay on basis of bills; death penalty in other states and nations noted. NEW YORK TIMES 64:1, August 17, 1958.

New Jersey Assembly's Conference Com. approves, 55-18, restoration of death penalty in state; action immediately precipitates legis. dispute over whether to vote on issue during summer session or to delay until after November Assembly elections; bill, sponsored by Assemblyman Richard J. Codey, would make death penalty mandatory for mass murderers and for anyone convicted of killing person in uniform (M). NEW YORK TIMES 83:1, June 10, 1975.

New Jersey Assembly's Judiciary Com. passes on April 17 legis. that would restore death penalty in New Jersey and abolish criminal penalties for use of marijuana; also approves proposed changes in state's Penal Code with regard to gambling, fornication and other nonviolent or victimless crimes. NEW YORK TIMES 71:1, April 18, 1975.

New Jersey Senate on May 3 rejects move to restore capital punishment in state; Senator J. Azzolina, principal sponsor of bill, says that he will seek to bring it to vote in future. NEW YORK TIMES 1:1, May 5, 1972.

New Jersey Supreme Court rules it has 'inherent' power to modify sentences, including reducing death penalty to life imprisonment. NEW YORK TIMES 1:7, May 7, 1968.

New Mexico HR passes bill to abolish capital punishment for almost all crimes. NEW YORK TIMES 91:4, March 18, 1969.

New Mexico Senate, 26-12, passes bill to abolish death penalty, except on convictions for killing policemen or jail guards. NEW YORK TIMES 19:1, March 1, 1969.

New York State Appeals Court on June 7 rules that law allowing execution of convicted murderers of policemen is unconstitutional because it gives too much discretion to juries. NEW YORK TIMES

1:3, June 8, 1973.

New York State Assembly, after 5 hours of debate, defeats, 65-69, on April 27 bill that would have restored death penalty for most persons convicted of murder; measure, sponsored by Assemblyman Kelly, would have nullified virtual abolition of capital punishment by Legis. in 1965. NEW YORK TIMES 1:1, April 28, 1972.

New York State Assemblymen R. F. Kelly and A. Hochberg on April 6 announce bipartisan drive for legis. to restore death penalty in NYS. NEW YORK TIMES 41:2, April 7, 1973.

New York State Assemblyman R. F. Kelly on February 14 introduces bill to restore death penalty for most persons convicted of first-degree murder; Kelly notes that violent crimes have increased since repeal of death penalty; bill is identical to one which failed in 1972 by 11 votes. NEW YORK TIMES 37:2, February 15, 1973.

New York State bill abolishing death penalty signed; provisions, exceptions outlined; Rockefeller to commute to life terms sentences of 17 men awaiting execution; will review cases of 3 others whose crimes were covered by exceptions. NEW YORK TIMES 1:1, June 2, 1965.

New York State Governor Dem. aspirant Goldberg, in article written with Harvard Professor A. Dershowitz for current Harvard Law Review, says that he believes that capital punishment is unconstitutional. NEW YORK TIMES 68:4, June 21, 1970.

New York State Governor Rockefeller declares that if Legis. passes bill reinstating death penalty he will sign it, but he will not propose bill, speech, September 11, Los Angeles; says he personally would prefer to deal with crime problem without penalty; he originally approved abolition of capital punishment in NYS except for those convicted of premeditated murder of policemen and prison guards. NEW YORK TIMES 31:1, September 12, 1973.

New York State Senate Codes Com. rejects all pending bills to expand capital punishment law to more crimes. NEW YORK TIMES 21:4, February 5, 1969.

New York State Senate codes com. reported out bill. NEW YORK
TIMES 40:5, April 30, 1965.

New York State Senate, 47-9, approves bill to abolish death penalty for
murder, kidnapping and treason and to substitute life imprisonment; would retain death sentence for murder of peace officer
acting in line of duty and murder by life-term convict in course of
escape; Senator Zaretzki and Assemblyman Bartlett hail vote;
Governor Rockefeller stand uncertain; he terms measure a curtailment rather than abolition bill. NEW YORK TIMES 1:5,
May 13, 1965; roll-call, 28:3, May 13, 1965.

New York State Senate votes to reinstate death penalty when a murder
victim is killed while aiding a policeman; move reflects growing
sentiment against 1965 legis. abolishing capital punishment in all
cases except killing of a policeman or prison guard. NEW YORK
TIMES 44:1, February 28, 1968.

19 states have revived death penalty since it was struck down in June
19, 1972 by US Supreme Court; Florida was 1st state to re-estab-
lish it; its new law may be 1st one to be reviewed by Court; other
states that have re-established capital punishment noted. NEW
YORK TIMES 21:3, August 25, 1973.

Ohio HR com. defeats Governor DiSalle bill to abolish death penalty.
NEW YORK TIMES 14:5, April 20, 1961.

1 of most significant actions of California Legis. in 1972-73 session was
passage or bill restoring death penalty, which Governor Reagan
says he will sign within week; bill provides death in gas chamber
for hired assassins, police killers, life-term convicts who slay
guards, mass and repeat murders, train wreckers, persons who
commit murder during rape, robbery, kidnapping, burglary and
lewd acts involving children, and those who kill witnesses to
crimes. NEW YORK TIMES 62:1, September 16, 1973.

Outlook for 1975-76 US Supreme Court session notes that capital
punishment is 1 of major issues facing Supreme Court this term(S).
NEW YORK TIMES 39:3, October 5, 1975.

Penalty falls before court. CHRISTIAN SCIENCE MONITOR 1:4, June 30, 1972, (Eastern Edition); 1:3, June 30, 1973, (Western and Midwestern Editions); 1:4, June 30, 1972, (London and Overseas Edition).

Pennsylvania Senate on November 28 passes bill to restore capital punishment; House has passed different version; bill would make Pennsylvania 22d state to restore death penalty since US Supreme Court decision outlawing it last year. NEW YORK TIMES 46:2, November 29, 1973.

R. H. Wels lr. on Professor L. Pfeffer's March 12 lr. on legality of death penalty. NEW YORK TIMES IV,12:5, April 2, 1972.

Readers Write. Prudent. CHRISTIAN SCIENCE MONITOR E:4, February 24, 1972, (Eastern, and London and Overseas Editions); E:4, February 25, 1972, (Western and Midwestern Editions).

Refuses review. CHRISTIAN SCIENCE MONITOR 2:1, October 12, 1972, (Midwestern Edition).

Representative Drinan introduces bill on March 14 that would abolish death penalty under Federal law; says that President Nixon is exploiting people's fear of crime; contends that capital punishment is ineffective as deterrent to crime. NEW YORK TIMES 25:7, March 15, 1973.

Representative Kastenmeler offers bill to abolish penalty for Federal crimes. NEW YORK TIMES 36:5, June 10, 1966.

A review of cruel and unusual: the Supreme court and capital punishment by M. Meltsner, by J. W. Bishop, Jr. COMMENTARY 57:32+, February, 1974; Reply with rejoinder by M. Meltsner, 57:17-18, May, 1974.

Revival. CHRISTIAN SCIENCE MONITOR 3:1, August 3, 1972, (Eastern and London and Overseas Editions); 3:4, August 4, 1972, (Western and Midwestern Editions).

Rules appeals must be treated separately. NEW YORK TIMES 23:5,

August 26, 1967.

Ruling on capital punishment. CHRISTIAN SCIENCE MONITOR E:1, May 5, 1971, (Eastern, and London and Overseas Editions); E:1, May 6, 1971, (Western and Midwestern Editions).

Russell Baker article on US Supreme Court hearing capital punishment case; cartoon (M). NEW YORK TIMES VI:6, May 11, 1975.

Seems unjust to reader. CHRISTIAN SCIENCE MONITOR E:4, May 7, 1976, (All Editions).

Senate Judiciary Com. hearings on nomination of Deputy Attorney General Kleindienst to succeed Mitchell as Attorney General continue; Kleindienst testifies concerning his attitude on law and order, saying that he has reservations on elimination of capital punishment and that he is in favor of use of wiretapping 'sparingly' with 'most fundamental regard for rights of individuals'; testimoney detailed. NEW YORK TIMES 26:3, February 23, 1972.

Senate passes bill. NEW YORK TIMES 1:3, October 9, 1970.

Solicitor General Griswold urges US Supreme Court to leave it to state legislatures and Congress to decide how capital punishment should be handled by trial juries; says that 2 death penalty appeals currently before Court are diversionary tactic by anticapital punishment reformers who hope eventually to end executions through court action; argues that Justices are now being asked to make changes that are not required by Constitution and would encroach on authority of states and legis. branches of government; appeals reviewed. NEW YORK TIMES 40:1, November 10, 1970.

Stanford University Professor A. G. Amsterdam article backing decisions in which California Supreme Court and US Supreme Court invalidated death penalty. NEW YORK TIMES 33:2, November 4, 1972.

State legislators review laws involving capital punishment in light of recent US Supreme Court decision barring death penalty as it is now imposed; Chief Justice Burger, in dissenting opinion, noted possibility of retaining capital punishment if laws make sentence mandatory or set down firm guidelines for its imposition; legislators in 5 states say they will press for death penalty, at least 2 other states tend to favor mandatory life sentences with no possibility of parole; comments by various state officials. NEW YORK TIMES 10:1, July 1, 1972.

State of California, in petition signed by Deputy Attorney General R. M. George, asks US Supreme Court to stay, pending appeal, enforcement of California Supreme Court ruling that death sentence violates California Constitution. NEW YORK TIMES 28:5, March 18, 1972.

Support grows in US for capital punishment. CHRISTIAN SCIENCE MONITOR 2:5, April 25, 1974, (All Editions).

The Supreme Court has abolished the death penalty in the United States except under laws that absolutely require death for all persons convicted of a specific crime. THE NATIONAL OBSERVER p. 3, July 8, 1972.

The Supreme Court has upheld the death penalty in murder convictions and specified clear guidelines for state legislatures to draw up capital-punishment laws. THE NATIONAL OBSERVER p. 2, July 10, 1976.

Supreme Court to weigh constitution of 'plea bargaining' when a defendant is faced with possible death sentence if he pleads not guilty but cannot be sentenced to death if he pleads guilty, C. Parker case. NEW YORK TIMES 25:8, June 24, 1969.

Tennessee Governor Clement in effect abolishes capital punishment for remaining 2 years of term by commuting 5 death sentences, news conference after House rejects his abolition plea. NEW YORK TIMES 1:7, March 20, 1965.

Tests capital penalty. CHRISTIAN SCIENCE MONITOR 2:2, December 29, 1971, (Eastern Edition); 2:2, December 23, 1971, (Western Edition); 6:1, December 23, 1971, (Midwestern Edition); 6:1, December 23, 1971, (London and Overseas Edition).

Texas Court of Criminal Appeals upholds state's death penalty law, passed in 1973, as constitutional and valid under latest US Supreme Court ruling (S). NEW YORK TIMES 26:5, April 17, 1975.

US Appeals Court rules North Carolina legal provisions for imposing death penalty are unconstitutional. NEW YORK TIMES 26:8, November 27, 1968.

US: bill offered, NYS, to substitute life imprisonment for death in treason and 1st-degree murder cases. NEW YORK TIMES 19:1, January 17, 1951.

US Supreme Court announces it will consider constitution of traditional procedure in which prosecutors may remove from juries in capital cases all persons opposed to death penalty, D. Bumper and W. C. Witherspoon cases. NEW YORK TIMES 20:3, January 16, 1968.

US Supreme Court, 5 to 4, abolishes on June 29 death peanlty as it is imposed under present statutes, ruling it is 'cruel and unusual'; decision will save 600 persons now on death rows in US. NEW YORK TIMES 1:8, June 30, 1972.

US Supreme Court on April 2 refuses to allow Pennsylvania prosecutor to attempt to reinstate death penalty by arguing at sentencing hearing for convicted murderer that penalty had not been imposed arbitrarily or capriciously in past; prosecutor was attempting to prove practice in Pennsylvania fell outside Supreme Court's area of objection to penalty. NEW YORK TIMES 22:1, April 3, 1973.

US Supreme Court on June 23 postpones any re-examination of its 1972 ruling that capital punishment is unconstitutional; ruling is now unlikely before early 1976. NEW YORK TIMES 1:2, June 24, 1975.

US Supreme Court on November 12 declines to review ruling by NYS Appeals Court that NYS death penalty statute is unconstitutional. NEW YORK TIMES 1:8, November 13, 1973.

US Supreme Court sets review of death sentence imposed on Jesse T. Fowler in North Carolina for shooting companion in dice-game brawl for April 21, virtually committing self to new ruling on capital punishment before mid-June summer recess. NEW YORK TIMES 13:1, March 31, 1975.

US Supreme Court, 6-3, rules persons who oppose death penalty or have general conscientious scruples against it cannot automatically be kept off of juries in capital cases. NEW YORK TIMES IV,7:1, June 9, 1968.

US Supreme Court to begin hearing arguments on April 21 on capital punishment case from North Carolina which may ultimately resolve question of whether new death penalty laws are constitutional. NEW YORK TIMES 1:6, April 21, 1975.

Under the Federal Constitution, the death penalty is a legitimate punishment, says M. Stanton Evans, editor of the Indianapolis News. THE NATIONAL OBSERVER p. 17, June 10, 1972.

Ups age. CHRISTIAN SCIENCE MONITOR 7:6, March 16, 1963, (Eastern Edition); 14:1, March 16, 1963, (Western Edition).

Vermont House approves abolition bill. NEW YORK TIMES 32:2, April 14, 1965.

Vermont House approves bill to abolish death penalty except in murder convictions for 2d offense unrelated to 1st slaying. NEW YORK TIMES 11:2, March 6, 1965.

Washington State Supreme Court on September 28 strikes down state laws allowing capital punishment, following recent US Supreme Court ruling that death penalty is unconstitutional. NEW YORK TIMES 29:1, September 29, 1972.

West Virginia Legis. approves abolition bill. NEW YORK TIMES 8:8, March 13, 1965.

Wicker article says that death sentences have been imposed on 20 people in North Carolina since 1972 Supreme Court ruling outlawing it; says as many as 40 persons are on new Death Row in US; 21 states have passead mandatory death penalty laws in last 18 months and 14 more are expected to do so in 1974; history of penalty in North Carolina noted; article says that characteristics of new Death Row are much like those of old Death Row, with most of sentences imposed on blacks and poor; case of Vernon L. Brown, Bobby Hines and J. L. Walston, sentenced for rape of white woman in Tarboro, North Carolina, on August 22, noted. NEW YORK TIMES 21:1, December 25, 1973.

Will hear arguments on constitutionality. CHRISTIAN SCIENCE MONITOR 6:6, March 31, 1975, (All Editions).

LAWS AND LEGISLATION
see: The Law and Capital Punishment

LEGALIZED MURDER
see: Capital Punishment—Against

LEGISLATION
see: The Law and Capital Punishment

LEIF, NETTIE
see: Women and Capital Punishment

LINDBERG LAW
see: The Law and Capital Punishment

LIVINGSTON, EDWARD
Edward Livingston on the punishment of death, by P. E. Mackey. TULANE LAW REVIEW 48:25-42, December, 1973.

LYNCHING
see: Hanging

McGAUTHA v. CALIFORNIA
see: Cases Involving Capital Punishment
The Law and Capital Punishment

MALIK, MICHAEL ABDUL
see: Clemency

MEDICINE AND CAPITAL PUNISHMENT
Paradigm of religion, medicine, and capital punishment, by I. I. Lasky.
MEDICINE, SCIENCE, AND THE LAW 14:26-31, January, 1974.

MEXICO

NEWSPAPER ARTICLES

State of Mexico ends penalty. NEW YORK TIMES 6:8, March 19, 1961.

MIDEAST
Nixon's first foreign crisis: the boiling Mideast: public hangings in Baghdad. U. S. NEWS AND WORLD REPORT 66:35-36, February 10, 1969.

MITCHELE, AARON C.
see: Cases Involving Capital Punishment

THE MORALITY OF CAPITAL PUNISHMENT
see also: Cruel and Unusual Punishment

Answers for J. W. CHRISTIAN CENTURY 84:131-132, February 1, 1967.

Assessment of capital punishment, by W. H. Dempsey, Jr. COMMONWEAL 75:496-497, February 2, 1962.

Bishops v. the death penalty. SENIOR SCHOLASTIC 78:10-11, May 17, 1961.

Britain reviews the penalty of death. CHRISTIAN CENTURY 70: 1157, October 14, 1953.

British and the IRA, by T. Beeson. CHRISTIAN CENTURY 93:60-62, January 28, 1976.

Camus on capital punishment, by P. Henry. MIDWEST QUARTERLY

16:362-370, July, 1975.

Canterbury convocation: no hanging bishops. ECONOMIST 202:212, January 20, 1962.

Capital punishment, by R. Mathias. CHRISTIAN CENTURY 79:1542-1543, December 12, 1962.

Capital punishment as a human rights issue before the United Nations, by L. E. Landerer. HUMAN RIGHTS JOURNAL 4:511-534, July, 1971.

Capital punishment as seen by a correctional administrator, by R. A. McGee. FEDERAL PROBATION 28:11, June, 1964.

Capital punishment confronted, by J. A. Joyce. CHRISTIAN CENTURY 78:900-901, July 26, 1961.

Capital punishment—cruel and unusual?, by M. S. Enslin. RELIGION IN LIFE 41:251-258, Summer, 1972.

—, by T. A. Long. ETHICS 83:214-223, April, 1973; Reply by R. S. Gerstein, 85:75-79, October, 1974.

Capital punishment is legalized murder, by A. Kohn. SEVENTEEN 32:248, August, 1973.

Capital punishment is murder!, by D. Dressler. CORONET 47:135-140, January, 1960.

Capital punishment is necessary, by J. Rawitsch. SEVENTEEN 32:248, August, 1973.

Capital punishment: a moral consensus?, by J. M. Wall. CHRISTIAN CENTURY 92:483-484, May 14, 1975.

Capital punishment: the moral issue, by O. C. Snyder. WEST VIRGINIA LAW REVIEW 63:99, February, 1961.

Capital punishment: a reaction from a member of the clergy, by L.

Kinsolving. AMERICAN BAR ASSOCIATION JOURNAL 42: 850-852, September, 1956.

Capital punishment revisited, by H. Moody. CHRISTIANITY AND CRISIS 34:66, April 15, 1974.

Christianity and capital punishment, by L. Kinsolving. PASTORAL PSYCHOLOGY 11:33-42, June, 1960.

Churches and capital punishment, by J. A. Lazell. NATIONAL COUNCIL OUTLOOK 9:21-22, March, 1959.

Comments on the executions in Iraq [January 27, 1969, on fourteen Iraqi nationals. of the Muslim, Christian and Jewish faiths, all of whom had been convicted of espionage], by F. Sayegh. ARAB WORLD 15:18-20, January-February, 1969.

Constitutional law—Arkansas state penitentiary transgresses constitutional proscription against cruel and unusual punishment. SETON HALL LAW REVIEW 3:159, Fall, 1971.

Constitutional law: capital punishment for rape constitutes cruel and unusual punishment when no life is taken or endangered. MINNESOTA LAW REVIEW 56:95, November, 1971.

Cruel and unusual punishments. CATHOLIC UNIVERSITY LAW REVIEW 3:117-121, May, 1953.

Death penalty abolished: action in Iowa, by P. B. Mather. CHRISTIAN CENTURY 82:382, March 24, 1965.

Death penalty must go. CHRISTIAN CENTURY 74:412-413, April 3, 1957.

Death penalty today, by H. A. Bedau. CHRISTIAN CENTURY 76: 320-322, March 18, 1959.

The development of moral judgments concerning capital punishment, by L. Kohlberg, et al. AMERICAN JOURNAL OF ORTHOPSYCHIATRY 45(4):614-640, July, 1975.

Does society have the moral right to take human life?, by L. Kinsolving, et al. TOGETHER 6:34-36, May, 1962.

Does *tlb* in the Temple scroll refer to crucifixion?, by J. M. Baumgarten. JOURNAL OF BIBLICAL LITERATURE 91:472-481, December, 1972.

Espiscopalians oppose the death penalty. CHRISTIAN CENTURY 78:382, March 29, 1961.

Executive clemency and the death penalty, by W. Rockefeller. CATHOLIC UNIVERSITY LAW REVIEW 21:94, Fall, 1971.

Forbidding fruits of capital punishment, by J. E. Starrs. CATHOLIC WORLD 205:286-292, August, 1967.

Genesis and capital punishment; theme of Msgr. Kuhn's sermon at White House service. CHRISTIAN CENTURY 90:355-356, March 28, 1973.

Hanging is dead in Britain. CHRISTIANITY TODAY 14:37, January 16, 1970.

Immorality and the death penalty, by D. R. Burrill. CHRISTIAN CENTURY 90:99-101, January 24, 1973; Discussion, 90:325, March 14, 1973.

Injustice of the death penalty; discussion. AMERICA 136:41, January 22, 1977.

Interfaith scaffold in Iraq. CHRISTIANITY TODAY 13:47, February 28, 1969.

Judicial barbarism. SPECTATOR 194:141, February 11, 1950.

Justice and the death penalty, by D. R. Gordon. CHRISTIAN CENTURY 80:955, July 31, 1963.

Justice, Georgia style. COMMONWEAL 75:84, October 20, 1961.

Justice or revenge? DICKINSON LAW REVIEW 60:342, June, 1956.

Life without the hangman, by T. Beeson. CHRISTIAN CENTURY 90:468-469, April 25, 1978.

May ban death penalty, California, by D. L. Gardner. CHRISTIAN CENTURY 74:575, May 1, 1957.

Morality and retribution (in favor of CP), by T. Quist. NEW GUARD 17:20, April, 1977.

New York Senate would curtail capital punishment. CHRISTIAN CENTURY 82:669, May 26, 1965.

Une obsession d'Albert Camus: la peine de mort, by R. Legeais. REVUE DU NOTARIAT 67:450, April, 1965.

On capital punishment, by S. Goldberg. ETHICS 85:67-74, October, 1974.

On deterrence and the death penalty, by E. van den Haag. ETHICS 78:280-288, July, 1968.

Paradigm of religion, medicine, and capital punishment, by I. I. Lasky. MEDICINE, SCIENCE, AND THE LAW 14:26-31, January, 1974.

Playing God, by E. G. Brown. NATION 207:166, September 2, 1968.

Pleasure, punishment and moral indignation, by G. Johnson, et al. SOCIOLOGY AND SOCIAL RESEARCH 59:82-95, January, 1975.

Public opinion and the death penalty in South Africa, by J. Midgley. BRITISH JOURNAL OF CRIMINOLOGY 14:345-358, October, 1974.

Punishment: a symposium. Crime and punishment. Pope Pius XII; Criminal punishment—legal and moral considerations, by S. O. Cutler; Punishment from the viewpoint of psychiatry, by R. P. Odenwald. CATHOLIC LAWYER 6:92, Spring, 1960.

Restoring the death penalty: proceed with caution, by D. Llewellyn. CHRISTIANITY TODAY 19:10-12+, May 23, 1975.

Right of the state to inflict capital punishment, by T. J. Riley. CATHOLIC LAWYER 6:279, Autumn, 1960.

Taming the beast in man. CHRISTIAN CENTURY 83:1593-1594, December 28, 1966.

Terrible myth of internal affairs; public hanging of fourteen men convicted of spying for Israel. CHRISTIAN CENTURY 86:205, February 12, 1968.

Thou shalt not kill, by D. Lawrence. U. S. NEWS AND WORLD REPORT 48:152, March 14, 1960.

—, by L. Woolf. NEW STATESMAN 50:608+, November 12, 1955.

Twenty-five minutes to live; excerpt from Death row chaplain, by F. Riley, et al. READER'S DIGEST 81:265-266+, November, 1962.

What about capital punishment?, by P. A. Remick. GOSPEL MESSENGER pp. 6-8, July 12, 1958.

You may kill, but you must promise not to use discretion: Furman v. Georgia (92 Sup. Ct. 2726). LOYOLA UNIVERSITY LAW REVIEW 6:526-555, September, 1973.

NEWSPAPER ARTICLES

Abolition urged by NY Episc. Diocese. NEW YORK TIMES 18:5, March 27, 1965.

Anglican bishops back British campaign to abolish death penalty. NEW YORK TIMES 10:4, January 18, 1962.

Annual convention of Episcopal Diocese of NY on May 8 adopts resolution reaffirming opposition to death penalty for any crime. NEW YORK TIMES 34:4, May 9, 1973.

Baptist ministers in Tennessee disagree on punishment, survey. NEW YORK TIMES 24:1, December 16, 1956.

Biennial convention of American Lutheran Church adopts statement on capital punishment that criticizes 'mandatory punishments,' is skeptical of deterrent effect of death penalty; urges attention to root causes of crime and asks for overhaul of criminal justice system. NEW YORK TIMES 46:1, October 11, 1972.

Cain and Abel, 1972. CHRISTIAN SCIENCE MONITOR E:1, January 20, 1972, (Eastern, Western, and Midwestern Editions); E:1, January 20, 1972, (London and Overseas Edition).

Chaplains at Massachusetts State Prison sponsor bill to eliminate penalty in state. NEW YORK TIMES 24:8, December 7, 1955.

Governor Rockefeller says exceptions negate intent and moral principles of bill's proponents, news conference, but avoids saying whether he will veto it. NEW YORK TIMES 53:2, May 19, 1965.

A humane decision. CHRISTIAN SCIENCE MONITOR E:1, July 1, 1972, (Eastern, and London and Overseas Editions); E:1, July 3, 1972, (Western and Midwestern Editions).

J. Breuer lr. on murder of Rabbi S. R. Hirsch questions giving death penalty only for killing of policemen. NEW YORK TIMES 24:4, July 29, 1972.

Luthern Church in America urges abolition; discounts 5th Commandment as basis for move; denies it repudiates power of state to take life. NEW YORK TIMES 26:3, June 30, 1966.

National Federation of Priests' Councils adopts resolution calling for abolition of death penalty, convention, Denver. NEW YORK TIMES 20:4, March 17, 1972.

Newark, New Jersey, Human Rights Comm. head Rev. John Sharp issues report condemning concept of capital punishment and calling on State Legis. to defeat proposed bill that would reinstate death penalty for persons convicted for killing law enforcement officials (S). NEW YORK TIMES 80:7, September 30, 1975.

PE Bishops House opposes death penalty. NEW YORK TIMES 20:2, October 11, 1958.

PE Church opens drive for abolition; ends to all dioceses compilation of theological cand other arguments by public by National Council; scores Director Hoover stand; views of other Protestant churches, RC Church and Jewish authorities on death penalty noted. NEW YORK TIMES 1:2, March 20, 1961.

The Rev. Paul Tinlin of Schaumburg, Illinois, says that murderers should be executed on prime-time television as a deterrent to crime. THE NATIONAL OBSERVER p. 5, November 8, 1975.

Right or wrong? CHRISTIAN SCIENCE MONITOR 15:1, March 29, 1965, (Eastern Edition); 13:1, March 29, 1965, (Western Edition); 11:1, March 29, 1965, (Midwestern Edition).

Rockefeller says he will seek views of legal and religious leaders before deciding; holds present wording does not adhere to arguments that death penalty is immoral. NEW YORK TIMES 21:1, May 21, 1965.

Sing Sing chaplain Rev. L. K. Hannum opposes death penalty, interview. NEW YORK TIMES 18:4, August 29, 1960.

Southern Presb. Church General Assembly upholds death penalty, tabling Millard comm. report urging abolition on Scriptural grounds. NEW YORK TIMES 33:6, May 3, 1961.

20 leaders of Boston church and civic groups meet with Massachusetts Governor F. W. Sargent on December 6 to urge him not to sign death penalty bill that awaits decision by December 10. NEW YORK TIMES 55:6, December 7, 1973.

United Luthern Church Social Missions Board urges death penalty abolition. NEW YORK TIMES 63:5, April 29, 1960.

United Luthern Church, 248-238, rejects Social Missions Board proposal urging abolition. NEW YORK TIMES 26:8, October 21, 1960.

United Methodist Church, holding convict in Atlanta, Georgia, adopts doctrine of soc. principles that includes opposition to capital punishment. NEW YORK TIMES 16:2, April 27, 1972.

MURDER
see: The Law and Capital Punishment

NAACP

NEWSPAPER ARTICLES

NAACP begins survey on death penalty for rape convictions in South; study, headed by Pennsylvnaia University Professors Wolfgang and Amsterday, covers 2,600 cases in 225 counties of 11 states. NEW YORK TIMES 66:1, April 24, 1966.

NAACP fights to abolish. CHRISTIAN SCIENCE MONITOR 14:1, May 29, 1971, (Eastern, and London and Overseas Editions); 2:1, June 7, 1971, (Midwestern Edition).

NAACP holds attorneys often stop representing death row inmates when case has gone beyond state supreme court appeals and execution is pending; urges Federal District Court to order hearings on contention that legal rights of 59 San Quentin Prison inmates were violated. NEW YORK TIMES 38:4, August 11, 1967.

NAACP Legal Defense and Education Fund. and New Jersey Public Defender ask New Jersey Supreme Court to abolish state's death penalty; hold US Supreme Court ruling outlawing death penalty in Federal kidnapping cases applies to capital cases in New Jersey. NEW YORK TIMES 34:8, June 4, 1968.

NAACP Legal Defense Fund., charging there is disproportionate number of Negroes in San Quentin death row, sues in US court, San Francisco, to block executions of all inmates. NEW YORK TIMES 41:2, June 28, 1967.

US Appeals Court refuses Attorney General Lynch request that it set aside stays; NAACP Legal Defense Fund and ACLU aides hail move. NEW YORK TIMES 20:1, July 11, 1967.

NEW ZEALAND
Hanging in New Zealand. ECONOMIST 179:804, May 26, 1956.

Politics of the rope, by C. Bollinger. SPECTATOR 207:372, September 22, 1961.

NEWSPAPER ARTICLES

New Zealand abolishes death penalty for all crimes except treason. NEW YORK TIMES 10:5, November 2, 1961.

New Zealand National Party conference rejects proposal for reintroduction. NEW YORK TIMES 8:2, August 25, 1963.

New Zealand plans referendum on abolition. NEW YORK TIMES 6:7, May 2, 1956.

New Zealand—rejected. CHRISTIAN SCIENCE MONITOR 2:6, August 29, 1963, (Eastern Edition).

NIGERIA
Nigeria; time to stop [public executions]. ECONOMIST 244:37, July 29, 1972.

NEWSPAPER ARTICLES

Nigerian Government executes 14 men convicted of armed robbery on July 22; 170 have been executed for armed robbery since August 1970, when Government decreed death for the crime; prisoners illus. NEW YORK TIMES 3:1, July 27, 1972.

Nigerians debate issue of capital punishment for armed robbery and kidnapping; on July 22, 14 men were executed for armed robbery; 170 have been executed since decree was issued 2 years ago. NEW YORK TIMES 17:1, August 20, 1972.

NIXON ADMINISTRATION
Nixon administration and the deterrent effect of the death penalty, by

H. A. Bedau. UNIVERSITY OF PITTSBURGH LAW REVIEW 34:557-566, Summer, 1973.

Nixon and the death penalty, by W. Shawcross. NEW STATESMAN 86:366-367, March 16, 1973.

Nixon's first foreign crisis: the boiling Mideast: public hangings in Baghdad. U. S. NEWS AND WORLD REPORT 66:35-36, February 10, 1969.

NEWSPAPER ARTICLES

A. Lewis article discusses President Nixon's recent statements on crime, scoring his insistence that harsher penalties will discourage people from wrongdoing; decries his position on death penalty. NEW YORK TIMES 35:5, April 2, 1973.

American Hebrew Congregations Union Soc. Action Comm. executive director Vorspan scores Nixon stand; Reform Temple Fed. urges Governments of 41 states to abolish death penalty; asks major President candidates to take stand. NEW YORK TIMES 55:5, February 28, 1960.

Big stick approach dispute. CHRISTIAN SCIENCE MONITOR 1:2, March 12, 1973, (Eastern Edition); 1:2, March 13, 1973, (Western Edition); 1:2, March 13, 1973, (Midwestern Edition); 1:2, March 12, 1973, (London and Overseas Edition).

California Governor Reagan says on March 10 that many California residents agree with Nixon. NEW YORK TIMES 25:1, March 12, 1973.

Comment on President Nixon's tough new series of law enforcement proposals, including reinstitution of penalty; cartoon. NEW YORK TIMES IV,3:1, March 18, 1973.

Dame R. West article on Nixon's proposals notes current push to reinstate death penalty in Great Britain. NEW YORK TIMES IV,15:2, April 1, 1973.

Death penalty backed by Vice President Nixon, opposed by Senator Humphrey, replies to Union of American Hebrew Congregations questionnaire sent to major President contenders; both explain stands; Governor Rockefeller bars reply now; Union President Rabbi Eisendrath repeats Union view that penalty is morally unjustified. NEW YORK TIMES 57:1, April 10, 1960.

Death penalty favored by R. M. Nixon, opposed by Governor Brown, responses to queries by San Francisco Youth Association. NEW YORK TIMES 11:4, October 1, 1962.

Editorial opposes Nixon decision; believes criminal's actions do not absolve government from strictures of Sixth Commandment against killing. NEW YORK TIMES 38:1, March 13, 1973.

J. Hughes lr. lauds President Nixon for proposal to reinstate death penalty, holding that it acts as deterrent to crime. NEW YORK TIMES IV,14:4, April 1, 1973.

M. Maestro lr. notes that it has been announced that Attorney General Kleindienst, on behalf of President Nixon, will ask Congress to enact law reinstating death penalty for certain crimes; says Supreme Court ruled that death penalty is 'cruel and unusual punishment in violation of the 8th Amendment to the Constitution'; holds that only way to reinstate death penalty, besides reversal by Supreme Court would be to amend Constitution, so as to permit infliction of cruel and unusual punishment for certain crimes. NEW YORK TIMES IV,16:5, January 21, 1973.

New Jersey Policemen's Benevolent Association endorses President Nixon's plan for return of capital punishment in certain cases; is also backing proposal by New Jersey Senator J. Azzolina to reinstate death penalty in New Jersey for murder. NEW YORK TIMES 90:5, April 10, 1973.

Nixon Administration, apparently reversing position it took 1 week ago, says on January 10 that it does not believe that mandatory death sentence should be imposed for 'cold blooded, premeditated' crimes. NEW YORK TIMES 51:3, January 11, 1973.

Nixon Administration on April 16 asks Congress to restore death penalty in cases of treason, sabotage, espionage and murder in testimony by Assistant Attorney General R. G. Dixon before Senate Criminal Laws Subcommittee. NEW YORK TIMES 13:1, April 17, 1973.

Nixon Administration on March 21 presents Congress with President Nixon's legis. proposal to restore death penalty for such crimes as aggravated homicide and wartime treason or espionage. NEW YORK TIMES 62:5, March 22, 1973.

Nixon bolsters view. CHRISTIAN SCIENCE MONITOR 8:4, April 10, 1973, (Midwestern Edition).

President Nixon, in message to Congress on March 14, details his proposed rules to revive death penalty by circumventing Supreme Court's opposition and establishing novel system for sentencing Federal criminals. NEW YORK TIMES 24:3, March 15, 1973.

President Nixon, in national radio speech on March 10, calls on Congress to restore death penalty for certain Federal crimes. NEW YORK TIMES 1:8, March 11, 1973.

President Nixon, in news conference, urges retention of death penalty for kidnapping and hijacking. NEW YORK TIMES 1:6, June 30, 1972.

President Nixon, in September 9 radio address, urges speedy Congress action on bills to restore death penalty, increase punishment of heroin dealers and to rewrite Federal criminal code. NEW YORK TIMES 29:4, September 10, 1973.

President Nixon, in 6th State of Union message on March 14, says that he favors automatic imposition of death penalty for number of crimes, including killing of law enforcement officials and prison guards. NEW YORK TIMES 1:7, March 15, 1973.

President Nixon on March 22 asks Congress to restore death penalty as part of criminal code revision; prolonged debate is expected; penalty would be mandatory if there are aggravating factors in such 'class A' felonies as treason, sabotage, espionage and murder.

NEW YORK TIMES 19:2, March 23, 1973.

President Nixon urges capital punishment for illegal use of explosives to curb rise of bombings in cities, statement. NEW YORK TIMES 1:4, March 26, 1970; text, 24:1, March 26, 1970.

Readers write: crime and punishment. CHRISTIAN SCIENCE MONITOR E:5, April 23, 1973, (Eastern, Western and Midwestern Editions); E:5, April 21, 1973, (London and Overseas Editions).

Runs parallel to Nixon. CHRISTIAN SCIENCE MONITOR 10:6, April 3, 1973, (Midwestern Edition).

S. F. Baldwin lr. supports President Nixon in his statement that certain crimes demand death penalty, but does not support carrying out of such a sentence by traditional means; calls for practice of euthanasia. NEW YORK TIMES 42:4, March 22, 1973.

Senator G. S. McGovern, appearing on NCB's 'Meet the Press' on March 11, disagrees with Nixon. NEW YORK TIMES 25:1, March 12, 1973.

T. Wicker article holds Nixon stand is splendid way to reap pol. benefit from fear of crime that for good reason pervades nation; says that tough attitude will not do much about crime itself and that Nixon, in choosing pol. profit over President leadership, has sacrificed 1 more chance to talk sense to American people. NEW YORK TIMES 39:1, March 13, 1973.

Text of President Nixon's statement on US Supreme Court decision concerning capital punishment made during his June 29 news conference. NEW YORK TIMES 2:6, June 30, 1972.

US Attorney General Kleindienst says on January 4 that he expects Nixon Administration to ask Congress to reinstate death penalty, which was in effect struck down by US Supreme Court on June 29; says that death sentence will probably be asked for in restricted number and kinds of cases. NEW YORK TIMES 1:8, January 5, 1973.

What about political corruption. CHRISTIAN SCIENCE MONITOR E:5, April 14, 1973, (Eastern, and London and Overseas Editions); E:5, April 16, 1973, (Western and Midwestern Editions).

NORTHERN IRELAND

Capital punishment in Northern Ireland, by J. L. J. Edwards. CRIMINAL LAW REVIEW 1956:750, November, 1956.

Ulster on the tightrope, by A. Milner. SPECTATOR 208:263+, March 2, 1962.

NEWSPAPER ARTICLES

Northern Ireland to retain death penalty for murder. NEW YORK TIMES 4:6, March 22, 1956.

NORWAY

Punishment for murder in Norway, by A. Maddison. JUSTICE OF THE PEACE 120:147, March 10, 1956.

O'NEIL, R. I.

see: Cases Involving Capital Punishment

PERU

NEWSPAPER ARTICLES

Peru has 1st execution in 63 years. NEW YORK TIMES 12:5, December 13, 1957.

PHILOSOPHY

Une obsession d'Albert Camus: la peine de mort, by R. Legeais. REVUE DU NOTARIAT 67:450, April, 1965.

Philosopher's plea. TIME 79:28, March 23, 1962.

Punishment: current survey of philosophy and law, by R. J. Gerber, et al. ST. LOUIS UNIVERSITY LAW JOURNAL 11:491, Summer, 1967.

PIERREPOINT PAPERS
Pierrepoint papers, by R. Reynolds. NEW STATESMAN 51:409-410, April 21, 1956.

POLICE
Police: not a happy one [death penalty question]. STATIST 190: 442, August 19, 1966.

NEWSPAPER ARTICLES

Article reviews status of capital punishment in NYS in light of last weeks court ruling outlawing last discretionary instances of death penalty in state—law giving juries option to decree death in murder of on-duty police or prison officers and in murders committed by convicts serving life sentences; proponents of capital punishment now contend that making sentence mandatory instead of optional will satisfy Supreme Court, and are preparing to launch campaign in December at legis. hearing; Assemblyman D. L. Dicarlo and Senator H. D. Barclay comment; drawing. NEW YORK TIMES IV,8:1, November 18, 1973.

Bill introduced in NYS Legis. calls for mandatory death sentence for anyone convicted of killing policeman. NEW YORK TIMES 45:3, February 7, 1973.

California Senate approves mandatory death sentence for anyone who knowingly kills a police officer. NEW YORK TIMES 63:5, June 12, 1969.

Connecticut General Assembly debates use; Representative Parsells, State Police Comr. Kelly and police chiefs urge continuation; 2 attorneys and some mins. oppose it. NEW YORK TIMES 33:5, March 11, 1955.

Connecticut Senator on April 19 votes to restore death penalty for 6 types of crime. NEW YORK TIMES 1:7, April 20, 1973.

Conservatives call for return of death penalty, Great Britain, after slaying of 3 unarmed policemen. NEW YORK TIMES 10:1, August 14, 1966.

Continuing controversy over abolition in NYS discussed; law retains penalty only for murder of police officer or murder by convict under life term. NEW YORK TIMES 34:1, May 10, 1967.

Government of India on December 11 introduces bill that would sharply curtail death penalty; capital punishment, now mandatory for murder except in extenuating circumstances, will be limited to slayings of police, armed forces members and public servants charged with keeping order. NEW YORK TIMES 3:1, December 12, 1972.

J. Breuer lr. on murder of Rabbi S. R. Hirsch questions giving death penalty only for killing of policemen. NEW YORK TIMES 24:4, July 29, 1972.

Nevada Senate approves bill reinstating death peanlty for slaying of policemen and prison guards, contract killings and for killers already serving life terms. NEW YORK TIMES 27:4, April 7, 1973.

New Jersey Assembly Judiciary subcommittee removes from recommendations for changes in state criminal statutes portion of bill to reinstate death penalty for killing uniformed officer and mass murder; bill will be drafted separately and sponsored by Assemblyman Richard Codey (S). NEW YORK TIMES 84:3, March 12, 1975.

New Jersey Assembly expected to approve Assemblyman Richard J. Codey sponsored measure that would restore death penalty in state for anyone convicted of murdering policemen, firemen or prison officer; prospects for passage in Senate seen as less certain; por. of Codey (M). NEW YORK TIMES 73:1, April 13, 1975.

New York State Assembly Codes Com. holds hearing on October 16 on possibility of restoring death penalty; NYC Police Comr. Murphy sends statement to hearing urging legis. not to restore capital punishment; strong testimony is heard on both sides of issue. NEW YORK TIMES 26:2, October 17, 1972.

New York State bill providing death penalty for murder of policeman on duty signed; measure closes loophole in 1965 law abolishing capital punishment. NEW YORK TIMES 32:5, March 30, 1966.

New York State Legis. ends its 5th so-called 'work week' after Assembly engages in irate rhetoric over wording of resolution expressing 'deep feelings of sorrow and shock of members' over slayings of NYC Ptl. Laurie and Foster January 27 in East Village; resolution, which was supposed to be sent to families of slain ptl., finally withdrawn, but not until after it had engendered oratory about gun control, death penalty and mandatory sentences for criminals; details. NEW YORK TIMES 37:3, February 3, 1972.

New York State Senate, 59-40, votes to close loophole in 1965 law which makes police slayer subject to death penalty only if murder was premeditated; new bill prescribes death penalty for any murder of policeman acting in line of duty. NEW YORK TIMES 44:5, March 1, 1966.

New York State Sheriffs' Association unanimously passes resolution on August 9 calling for restoration of death penalty for premeditated murder, murder of law-enforcement officer and murder committed as part of a felony; also notes that England has experienced 'sharp increase' in homicides since it abolished capital punishment in 1965. NEW YORK TIMES 39:7, August 10, 1972.

New York State State Senator J. D. Calandra offers measure that would make death penalty mandatory for any person convicted of killing policeman if crime occurs while policeman is performing his duty. NEW YORK TIMES 40:7, February 9, 1972.

Newark Mayor Gibson delivers emotional denunciation of bill proposed by Assemblyman Richard Codey to reinstate capital punishment for murder of policemen and firemen slain in line of duty, May 12 hearing of Newark Human Rights Comm.; witnesses, 4-1, oppose bill, citing statistics to cast doubts on its value as deterrent to crime and show racist manner in which it is applied; Irv Joiner (United Church of Christ) and Councilman at Large Donald Tucker oppose death penalty; Newark Property Owners Protective Association pres. Michael Piccone supports it (M). NEW YORK TIMES 75:4, May 13, 1975.

Philadelphia District Attorney A. Spector asks Pennsylvania Legis. to reinstate death peanlty for 8 types of murder, including murder of policemen; action comes 2 weeks after US Supreme Court decision barring death penalty as it now is imposed; types of murders listed. NEW YORK TIMES 23:2, July 6, 1972.

Representative Cramer offers bill that will provide death penalty for killing policeman. NEW YORK TIMES 69:8, September 20, 1970.

Senator McGovern, speaking to NYC policemen June 15, says he does not favor capital punishment, although he would do 'anything up to that' to stop drug pushers. NEW YORK TIMES 22:1, June 16, 1972.

300 London policemen jeer Secretary Jenkins, Police Federal, over his opposition to bill, other moves. NEW YORK TIMES 6:1, October 21, 1966.

W. C. Henderson, convicted of killing San Diego, California, Police Sgt. F. Edwards, sentenced to death even though such a sentence has been held unconstitutional by California Supreme Court; Henderson granted stay of execution pending appeals of Supreme Court ruling. NEW YORK TIMES 29:1, March 16, 1972.

Washington State Senate votes 40-6 to require death penalty for killing unarmed policeman or fireman in performance of his duty; penalty would also be mandatory for killing prison guard. NEW YORK TIMES 17:2, February 10, 1973.

POLITICAL EXECUTIONS
see: Executions and Executioners

POLLS
see: Statistics and Surveys

THE PRISONER AND CAPITAL PUNISHMENT
Blunt talk of convict and accusers, by P. R. Brooke, et al. LIFE 48:29-32, February 22, 1960.

Capital punishment; death watch. ECONOMIST 255:79, April 26, 1975.

Death-cell inmates not devastatingly depressed. SCIENCE DIGEST 52:30, September, 1962.

The death penalty in the United States. ANNALS OF THE AMERICAN ACADEMY OF POLITICAL AND SOCIAL SCIENCE pp. 45-100, November, 1952.

Death row. ECONOMIST 223:355, April 22, 1967.

Death-row dramatics; case of G. M. Gilmore. TIME 108:46, November 29, 1976.

Death row for Robert Kennedy's killer, but. . . U. S. NEWS AND WORLD REPORT 66:16, June 2, 1969.

Death-row interviews: five under sentence to die speak out. U. S. NEWS AND WORLD REPORT 81:51-53, July 12, 1976.

Death row: a new kind of suspense. NEWSWEEK 77:23-24+, January 11, 1971.

Death row returns. NATION 217:356-357, October 15, 1973.

Death sentence. FORTNIGHTLY 180(174):289-290, November, 1953.

Eight years on death row: in the shadow of Chessman—Paul Crump, by W. Friedkin. CALIFORNIAN 2:6-15, October 1961.

An end to "death row"? what Supreme court ruled. U. S. NEWS AND WORLD REPORT 73:25-27, July 10, 1972.

Execution eve? NATIONAL REVIEW 28:1167, October 29, 1976.

Fifteen dates with the chair: P. Crump, by L. Robinson. EBONY 17:31-34+, July, 1962.

Green Haven prison and the death sentence, by C. M. Robinson. CHRISTIAN CENTURY 93:653-655, July 21, 1976.

Killing me solves nothing; interview, by J. Le Blanc, et al. EBONY 22:121-122+, June, 1967.

Last chance on death row, by H. Lavine. SATURDAY EVENING POST 236:76+, June 29, 1963.

Living on death row; inmates of Central prison, Raleigh, N.C., by J. White. TIME 104:75, December 16, 1974.

Michael X on death row, by G. Robertson. NEW STATESMAN 87:40-41, January 11, 1974.

Mike Bell is waiting; death row, Colorado state penitentiary, by D. Jackson. LIFE 64:92-98+, June 7, 1968.

Offender's attitude toward punishment, by M. Schmideberg. JOURNAL OF CRIMINAL LAW AND CRIMINOLOGY 51:328, September-October, 1960.

San Quentin is my home, by D. Jennings, et al. SATURDAY EVENING POST 222:42-43+, April 15, 1950.

Seven in death row: Connecticut state prison, by J. V. Hopkins, et al. NATION 183:476-478, December 1, 1956.

Signs of an end to "death row": U.S. joining trend? Death penalty: a word survey. U. S. NEWS AND WORLD REPORT 70:37-40, May 31, 1971.

Speaking out; I don't want to die; excerpts from Brief against death, by E. H. Smith. SATURDAY EVENING POST 241:10+, September 7, 1968.

Stirrings on death row: execution of Aaron Mitchell at San Quentin prison. TIME 89:25, April 21, 1967.

Sweating it out: on death row, a killer waits on high court and reads law books; one of 654, Fred Mefford, like others convicted, isn't likely to die soon, by L. Gapay. WALL STREET JOURNAL 178:1+, October 22, 1971.

Treatment of condemned prisoners, by T. Murton. CRIME AND DELINQUENCY 15:94, January, 1969.

Treatment of murderers, by H. J. Klare, et al. NEW STATESMAN 52:181-182, August 18, 1956.

Twenty-five minutes to live; excerpt from death row chaplain, by F. Riley, et al. READER'S DIGEST 81:265-266+, November, 1963.

Waiting for death. TIME 108:66, October 18, 1976.

Waiting on death row; case of G. Tyler, by B. Cory. PROGRESSIVE 40:30-31, August, 1976.

Waiting on death row: North Carolina, by L. Lopez. PROGRESSIVE 38:38, May, 1974.

NEWSPAPER ARTICLES

ACLU of Northern California and NAACP challenge capital punishment in California Supreme Court, Anderson and Saterfield cases; claim Death Row inmates are denied right to counsel after State Supreme Court review of their sentences, that so-called 'scrupled' jurors, those opposed to death penalty, are excluded from hearing capital cases, and that juries in such cases are without standards or guidelines in reaching decision. NEW YORK TIMES 67:1, June 9, 1968.

ACLU Southern California chapter voices doubt about constitution of voter-approved measure to restore death penalty in state for certain crimes, but does not plan to file suit against it at this time; death penalty issue was placed on ballot by California Prison Guards Association after US Supreme Court outlawed state's death penalty as unconstitutional; guards association measure establishes mandatory death penalty for killing prison guard, train wrecking with injuries, perjury resulting in death of innocent person and treason against California. NEW YORK TIMES 38:2, November 12, 1972.

Article reviews status of capital punishment in NYS in light of last week's court ruling outlawing last discretionary instances of death penalty in state—law giving juries option to decree death in murder of on-duty police or prison officers and in murders committed by convicts serving life sentences; proponents of capital punishment now contend that making sentence mandatory instead of optional will satisfy Supreme Court, and are preparing to launch campaign in December at legis. hearing; Assemblyman D. L. Di Carlo and Senator H. D. Barclay comment; drawing. NEW YORK TIMES IV,8:1, November 18, 1973.

Book by San Quentin ex-Warden C. Duffy opposing practice reviewed. NEW YORK TIMES VII:12, July 22, 1962.

Colorado Legis. will consider bill requiring mandatory death penalty in cases involving felony murders and for prison inmate killing a fellow prisoner, guard, hostage or bystander during escape attempt. NEW YORK TIMES 14:4, September 7, 1972.

Condemned men listed. NEW YORK TIMES 20:3, February 25, 1965.

Convict wins stay. CHRISTIAN SCIENCE MONITOR 6:4, October 26, 1967, (Eastern and London and Overseas Editions).

Edgar Smith, the longest inhabitant of death row in the United States says he admitted guilt only to win his freedom. THE NATIONAL OBSERVER p. 6, December 18, 1971.

Herkimer County (NY) District Attorney H. D. Blumberg lr. on T. Wicker's December 9 column says Wicker is wrong to suggest abandonment of death peanlty; holds it should be expanded to include persons who commit repeated acts of violence resulting in serious physical injury to others; cites death of A. DeSalvo and assault on J. V. Corona in prisons as examples of deficiencies in incarceration. NEW YORK TIMES IV,10:5, December 23, 1973.

Last 2 death row inmates at Ohio Penitentiary have been transferred to prison reception center; prison had 54 men on death row when US Supreme Court ruled death penalty unconstitutional. NEW YORK TIMES 34:5, October 22, 1972.

M. Waldron article examines reaction of prisoners on death row at Florida State Prison Farm at Raiford to US Supreme Court's decision declaring death penalty 'cruel and unusual'; illus. NEW YORK TIMES 14:2, June 30, 1972.

NAACP hold attorneys often stop representing death row inmates when case has gone beyond state supreme court appeals and execution is pending; urges Federal District Court to order hearings on contention that legal rights of 59 San Quentin Prison inmates were violated. NEW YORK TIMES 38:4, August 11, 1967.

NAACP Legal Defense Fund, charging there is disproportionate number of Negroes in San Quentin death row, sues in US court, San Francisco, to block executions of all inmates. NEW YORK TIMES 41:2, June 28, 1967.

NBC announces that W. Kelback and M. Lance, inmates on death row in Utah State Prison for murdering 6 persons in Salt Lake City in 1966, will be subject of TV documentary show entitled Thou Shall Not Kill; details. NEW YORK TIMES 82:7, March 17, 1972.

News Brief—convict faces. CHRISTIAN SCIENCE MONITOR 2:1, August 11, 1971, (Eastern, London and Overseas Editions).

118 prisoners, black Africans, remain on death row awaiting Government decision on their fate, Rhodesia; mandatory death sentence has been discarded, courts have been given discretion to impose death sentences as they see fit; Rhodesian press criticizes 'uncivilized' treatment of prisoners. NEW YORK TIMES 13:1, December 8, 1968.

Reaction, Sing Sing death house. NEW YORK TIMES 37:1, June 2, 1965.

San Quentin ex-warden Duffy among witnesses urging abolition, California Senate com. televised hearing; abolition cause seen doomed.

NEW YORK TIMES 17:1, March 10, 1960.

21 men now under death sentence in NYS; 17 in Sing Sing prison; 4 are out on court orders; 4 executions since 1961 is lowest 4-year total since 1891. NEW YORK TIMES 1:4, February 25, 1965.

US District Judge R. Peckham rules July 20 that death rows in California prisons must be abolished, following State Supreme Court decision last February that did away with capital punishment in California; says it is unconstitutional to treat capital offenders as a class differently from other prisoners. NEW YORK TIMES 31:4, July 22, 1972.

US Prisons Bureau reports 65 executions, 1957. NEW YORK TIMES 22:2, March 2, 1958.

US Supreme Court refuses again to delay temporarily effect of California Supreme Court decision invalidating death sentence under state's constitution; California Attorney General Younger has told court that denial of request would prejudice state's right to have Federal Court review decision before sentences of death row inmates are reduced to life imprisonment. NEW YORK TIMES 11:1, April 18, 1972.

PSYCHIATRY

Capital punishment; effects of the death penalty; data and deliberations from the social sciences; symposium, by H. Bedau. AMERICAN JOURNAL OF ORTHOPSYCHIATRY 45:580-726, July, 1975.

Hanging the sick. NEW STATESMAN 46:96+, July 25, 1953; Discussion, 46:130-131, 158, August 1-8, 1953.

A problem of simulation in modern legal history, by G. K. Stürup. ACTA PSYCHIATRICA ET NEUROLOGICA 30:343-350, 1955.

Psychiatric aspects of the report on capital punishment, by E. Glover. MODERN LAW REVIEW 17:329-335, July, 1954.

Psychiatric reflections on the death penalty, by L. J. West. AMERICAN JOURNAL OF ORTHOPSYCHIATRY 45(4):689-700, July,

1975.

Psychiatric review of capital punishment, by L. H. Gold. JOURNAL OF FORENSIC SCIENCE 6:465, October, 1961.

Psychiatrists condemn capital punishment. SCIENCE NEWS 89:386, May 21, 1966.

Punishment: a symposium. Crime and punishment. Pope Pius XII; Criminal and punishment—legal and moral considerations, by S. O. Cutler; Punishment from the viewpoint of psychiatry, by R. P. Odenwald. CATHOLIC LAWYER 6:92, Spring, 1960.

NEWSPAPER ARTICLES

American Psychiatric Association holds threat of death penalty may incite to crime rather than deter it among some persons, brief to Supreme Court in W. L. Maxwell case. NEW YORK TIMES 44:7, February 1, 1970.

Dr. K. Menninger and other psychiatrists score penalty, American Psychiatric Association panel. NEW YORK TIMES 27:1, May 13, 1960.

PSYCHOLOGY

Community psychology and correctional reform, by F. C. Thorne. JOURNAL OF COMMUNITY PSYCHOLOGY 3(2):163-165, April, 1975.

Effects of a mandatory death penalty on the discussions of simulated jurors as a function of heinousness of the crime, by R. K. Hester, et al. JOURNAL OF CRIMINAL JUSTICE 1(4):319-326, Winter, 1973.

Helping behavior and attitude congruence toward capital punishment, by S. A. Karabenick. JOURNAL OF SOCIAL PSYCHOLOGY 96(2):295-296, August, 1975.

Mental suffering under sentence of death: a cruel and unusual punishment. IOWA LAW REVIEW 57:814, February, 1972.

Retributive and utilitarian motives and other correlates of Canadian attitudes toward the death penalty, by N. Vidmar. CANADIAN PSYCHOLOGIST 15(4):337-356, October, 1974.

Strains and restraints. FORTUNE 70:27-28, October, 1964.

A symposium on the report of the Royal Commission on Capital Punishment, by E. Glover. BRITISH JOURNAL OF DELINQUENCY 4:163-168, 1954.

NEWSPAPER ARTICLES

Capital punishment (Readers write) rehabilitation. CHRISTIAN SCIENCE MONITOR E:3, August 19, 1968, (All Editions).

PUBLIC OPINION
   see: Society and Capital Punishment
   Statistics and Surveys

PUNISHMENT
   see: Cruel and Unusual Punishment

RAPE AND THE DEATH PENALTY
Arguing about death for rape. TIME 109:80, April 11, 1977.

Constitutional law—the eighth amendment's proscription of cruel and unusual punishment precludes imposition of the death sentence for rape when the victim's life is neither taken nor endangered. GEORGE WASHINGTON LAW REVIEW 40:161, October, 1971.

Constitutionality of the death penalty for non-aggravated rape. WASHINGTON UNIVERSITY LAW QUARTERLY 1972:170, Winter, 1972.

Criminal law—rape—death penalty—eighth amendment prohibition against cruel and unusual punishments forbids execution when the victim's life was neither taken nor endangered. UNIVERSITY OF CINCINNATI LAW REVIEW 40:396, Summer, 1971.

Cruel and unusual punishment—constitutionality of the death penalty for rape where victim's life neither taken nor endangered. UNI-VERSITY OF RICHMOND LAW REVIEW 5:392, Spring, 1971.

Death penalty for rape? case of Coker v. Georgia, by D. Leavy. MS 6:20, July, 1977.

Incidence of the death penalty for rape in Virginia, by D. H. Partington. WASHINGTON AND LEE LAW REVIEW 22:43, Spring, 1965.

Rape and death; Supreme Court decision on death penalty in rape cases. NEWSWEEK 90:48, July 11, 1977.

NEWSPAPER ARTICLES

Arkansas Supreme Court overturns death sentence imposed on Negro C. Jackson for rape of white woman because trial judge refused to allow Jackson's attorney to make opening statement to jury. NEW YORK TIMES 11:5, December 16, 1970.

Connecticut Governor Meskill says on December 1 that he expects Connecticut General Assembly in next 2 years to enact legis. that will widen death penalty to cover rapists and possibly to cover illegal drug traffickers; says that despite June 29 US Supreme Court ruling virtually eliminating death penalty, constitutional question of 'cruel and unusual' punishment remains open. NEW YORK TIMES 83:1, December 3, 1972.

Federal Appeals Court in Richmond, Virginia, holds that death penalty for rape when victim's life is neither taken nor endangered violates constitutional prohibition against cruel and unusual punishment; ruling upholds appeal of Negro W. Ralph who had been sentenced to death for raping white woman; case reviewed. NEW YORK TIMES 64:1, December 12, 1970.

Florida Legis. on December 1 votes to reinstate capital punishment for cases of premeditated murder and raping of child under 11 by person over 17; action seen as spurring another hearing in US Supreme Court on whether death penalty is 'cruel and unusual' punishment. NEW YORK TIMES 21:4, December 2, 1972.

Florida Supreme Court commutes death sentences of 40 convicted killers and rapists on September 8, changing sentences to life imprisonment with eligibility for parole; action comes after Florida Legis. enacted statute requiring all death row inmates to be given mandatory life sentences without eligibility for parole; court, fearing that law would prompt a rash of prison escapes and murder of guards, rendered law meaningless by its decision. NEW YORK TIMES 35:1, September 10, 1972.

Issues involved in W. L. Maxwell case, before US Supreme Court, discussed; question or procedure in imposing death penalty involved; Maxwell, a Negro, was condemned to death in 1961 for rape, Arkansas. NEW YORK TIMES IV,11:1, May 10, 1970.

Maryland Court of Special Appeals rules that state law imposing death sentence for rape convictions is unconstitutional. NEW YORK TIMES 66:4, October 29, 1972.

NAACP begins survey on death penalty for rape convictions in South; study, headed by Pennsylvania University Professors Wolfgang and Amsterday, covers 2,600 cases in 225 counties of 11 states. NEW YORK TIMES 66:1, April 24, 1966.

Nebraska reinstates death penalty for crimes of premeditated murder, killing in course of rape, arson, robbery, kidnapping, hijacking and burglary. NEW YORK TIMES 23:8, April 20, 1973.

RUSSIA

Arm of the red law, by R. J. Evans. NEW STATESMAN 65:486-487, April 5, 1963.

The campaign to extend the death penalty [Russia], by Y. P. Mironenko. INSTITUTE FOR THE STUDY OF THE USSR BULLETIN 6:25-30, January, 1959.

Capital punishment in imperial and Soviet criminal law, by W. Adams. AMERICAN JOURNAL OF COMPARATIVE LAW 18(3):575-594, 1970.

Capital punishment in the USSR, by J. S. Roucek. UKRANIAN

QUARTERLY 30:166-172, Summer, 1974.

Comparison of punishments in Soviet criminal law and American military law, by A. Avins. SOUTH TEXAS LAW JOURNAL 2:303, Summer-Fall, 1956.

Crime and punishment [Russia]: Execution: hallmark of "socialist legality", by L. Lipson; The wages of economic sin, by H. Willets. PROBLEMS OF COMMUNISM 11:21-23, September-October, 1962.

Crimes and punishments. NEW STATESMAN 61:738, May 12, 1961.

The death penalty and the USSR: history of the death penalty in the USSR; the question of capital punishment and international organizations; countries having abolished capital punishment. BULLETIN OF THE INTERNATIONAL COMMISSION OF JURISTS; FOR THE RULE OF LAW pp. 55-64, November, 1961.

Decree of presidium of U.S.S.R. Supreme Soviet: on intensifying the struggle against especially dangerous crimes [to permit application of capital punishment: for, pilfering of state or public property in large amounts; counterfeiting of money or securities; with respect of habitual offenders and persons convicted of serious crimes who in places of detention terrorize prisoners endeavoring to reform; commit attacks on the administration, organize criminal groups for this purpose or actively participate in such groupings]. CURRENT DIGEST OF THE SOVIET PRESS 13:8, May 24, 1961.

Moscow view. NEW STATESMAN 61:738, May 12, 1961.

The new Soviet legislation concerning the death penalty, by Y. Mironenko. SOVIET AFFAIRS ANALYSIS SERVICE 37:1-4, 1960-1961.

Progress to the rope. SPECTATOR 206:668, May 12, 1961.

The re-emergence of death penalty in the Soviet Union, by Y. P. Mironenko. SOVIET AFFAIRS ANALYSIS SERVICE 28:1-5,

1961-1962.

Russia shoots its business crooks; executions for economic crimes, by G. Feifer. NEW YORK TIMES MAGAZINE pp. 32-33+, May 2, 1965.

To be shot for bribetaking [Russia; former Dushanbe official]. CURRENT DIGEST OF THE SOVIET PRESS 15:34-35, April 3, 1963.

NEWSPAPER ARTICLES

Capital punishment—US—USSR spar. CHRISTIAN SCIENCE MONITOR 4:1, April 12, 1963, (Eastern Edition); 2:3, April 15, 1963, (Western Edition); 2:1, April 15, 1963, (Midwestern Edition).

Drunken driver, Kazakhstan, USSR, executed after car kills 1, injures several. NEW YORK TIMES 42:4, August 18, 1957.

Focus on Soviet punishment. CHRISTIAN SCIENCE MONITOR 1:1, February 23, 1972, (Eastern, London and Overseas Editions); 1:1, February 24, 1972, (Western and Midwestern Editions).

International League for Rights of Man protests USSR imposition for 'comparatively slight offenses' and without right of review by superior court, lr. to UN Acting Senator General Thant. NEW YORK TIMES 2:3, May 2, 1962.

Jewish Organizations Coordinating Board asks UN ECOSOC to review death penalty; request prompted by USSR execution of 141 persons for econ. crimes in last 2 years. NEW YORK TIMES 20:4, April 16, 1963.

USSR: Tass reports revival of death penalty for treason, espionage and sabotage. NEW YORK TIMES 3:6, January 13, 1950.

USSR weighs abolition of penalty for so-called econ. crimes and some rape and murder offenses. NEW YORK TIMES 26:8, October 27, 1967.

USSR widens capital punishment to include large-scale embezzlers of state property and counterfeiters. NEW YORK TIMES 28:1, May 7, 1961.

REID, DON, JR.
161 trips to the room to watch men die [Don Reid, Jr. battles capital punishment] , by R. Friedman. EDITOR AND PUBLISHER 93:72-73, May 7, 1960.

REID, JACK
see: Cases Involving Capital Punishment

RESTORATION OF DEATH PENALTY
see: The Law and Capital Punishment

RHODESIA
Death in Rhodesia. NATIONAL REVIEW 20:279, March 26, 1968.

Rhodesian fiasco, by W. F. Buckley, Jr. NATIONAL REVIEW 20: 310-311, March 26, 1963.

NEWSPAPER ARTICLES

Rhodesia to end curb on executions that has been in effect since declaration of independence. NEW YORK TIMES 9:1, September 1, 1967.

Rhodesian Parliament approves bill abolishing mandatory death sentence for acts of terrorism. NEW YORK TIMES 13:1, September 28, 1968.

RILEY
Riley ruling. ECONOMIST 198:647, February 18, 1961.

ROYAL COMMISSION ON CAPITAL PUNISHMENT
Death sentence report: report of the Royal commission on capital punishment, 1949-53, a review by Chorley. POLITICAL QUARTERLY 25:4-16, January, 1954.

Murder [the public inquiry of the Royal commission on capital punish-

ment in its attempt to define degrees of murder is seeking alternatives to death by hanging] . ECONOMIST 157:333-335, August
13, 1949.

Report of the [British] royal commission on capital punishment
(1919-1953): a review, by M. F. Wingersky. JOURNAL OF
CRIMINAL LAW, CRIMINOLOGY AND POLICE SCIENCE
44:695-715, March, 1954.

—. JOURNAL OF CRIMINAL LAW AND CRIMINOLOGY 44:695-
715, March-April, 1954.

Report of the Royal Commission on Capital Punishment, 1949-1953,
Cmd. 8932, September 1953, by J. E. H. Williams. MODERN
LAW REVIEW 17:57-65, January, 1954.

Royal Commission on capital punishment. LAW JOURNAL 103:713-
716, November 6, 1953.

Royal Commission on capital punishment—death and deterrence, by
G. H. L. Fridman. SOLICITOR 22:80-82, March, 1955.

A symposium on the report of the Royal Commission on capital
punishment, by E. Glover. BRITISH JOURNAL OF DELIN-
QUENCY 4:163-168, 1954.

SAN QUENTIN
see: United States

SANSON, CHARLES-HENRI
see: Cases Involving Capital Punishment

SANTIAGO
Slaughterhouse in Santiago, by J. Barnes. NEWSWEEK 82:53-54,
October 8, 1973.

SENTENCING
see: Cruel and Unusual Punishment
The Law and Capital Punishment

SKYJACKING

Deterrence: certainty, severity, and skyjacking [does the additional severity of capital punishment over life imprisonment serve to deter potential criminals, specifically skyjackers?], by R. Chauncey. CRIMINOLOGY 12:447-473, February, 1975.

NEWSPAPER ARTICLES

Nebraska reinstates death penalty for crimes of premeditated murder, killing in course of rape, arson, robbery, kidnapping, hijacking and burglary. NEW YORK TIMES 23:8, April 20, 1973.

Skyjacking—government penalty. CHRISTIAN SCIENCE MONITOR 2:1, January 12, 1973, (Easter, Western, London and Overseas Editions).

SLICING

Sung justice: death by slicing, by B. E. McKnight. AMERICAN ORIENTAL SOCIETY. JOURNAL 93:359-360, July, 1973.

SLOVIK, PRIVATE

see: Executions and Executioners

SOCIETY AND CAPITAL PUNISHMENT

Capital punishment in its legal and social aspects, by J. S. Roucek. THE INTERNATIONAL JOURNAL OF LEGAL RESEARCH 6:np, December, 1971.

Capital punishment reconsidered [social and political aspects], by W. O. Reichert. KENTUCKY LAW JOURNAL 47:397-417, Spring, 1959.

Death penalty and public knowledge, by G. Gregg. PSYCHOLOGY TODAY 10:16-17, September, 1976.

The executioner: his place in English society, by G. D. Robin. BRITISH JOURNAL OF SOCIOLOGY 15:234-253, September, 1964.

Family experience and public support of the death penalty, by R. J. Gelles. AMERICAN JOURNAL OF ORTHOPSYCHIATRY

45(4):596-613, July, 1975.

Hanging and public opinion. NEW STATESMAN 50:152, August 6, 1955; Discussion, 50:187, 216, 272, 298, August 13-20 and September 3-10, 1955.

Heirs of the widow. TIME 58:34+, October 15, 1951.

Helping behavior and attitude congruence toward capital punishment, by S. A. Karabenick. JOURNAL OF SOCIAL PSYCHOLOGY 96(2):295-296, August, 1975.

I am ashamed of my country. . ., by B. Wootton. SPECTATOR 205: 765, November 18, 1960.

People's bobbety, by Altrincham. SPECTATOR 197:88, July 20, 1956.

The poor and capital punishment: some notes on a social attitude, by M. Riedel. PRISON JOURNAL 45:24-28, Spring-Summer, 1965.

Public opinion and the death penalty [examination of public opinion polls and other social science studies on public attitudes toward capital punishment], by N. Vidmar, et al. STANFORD LAW RE- VIEW 26:1245-1270, June, 1974.

Race, judicial discretion, and the death penalty, by M. E. Wolfgang, et al. ANNALS OF THE AMERICAN ACADEMY OF POLITI- CAL AND SOCIAL SCIENCE 407:119-133, May, 1973.

The role of the social sciences in determining the constitutionality of capital punishment, by W. S. White. AMERICAN JOURNAL OF ORTHOPSYCHIATRY 45(4):581-595, July, 1975.

Scaling technique for measuring social attitudes toward capital punish- ment, by J. K. Balogh, et al. SOCIOLOGY AND SOCIAL RE- SEARCH 45:24-26, October, 1960.

A sociological perspective on public support for capital punishment, by C. W. Thomas. AMERICAN JOURNL OF ORTHOPSYCHI-

ATRY 45(4):641-657, July, 1975.

Welfare economic aspects of capital punishment, by D. L. McKee, et al. AMERICAN JOURNAL OF ECONOMICS AND SOCIOLOGY 35:41-47, January, 1976; Reply by M. O. Reynolds, 36:105-111, January, 1977.

Young man, be an executioner, by G. Walker. ESQUIRE 60:62-63, August, 1963.

NEWSPAPER ARTICLES

California voters have brought back the death penalty, and other states are likely to do likewise. THE NATIONAL OBSERVER p. 2, November 18, 1972.

Columnist Edwin A. Roberts, Jr., interviews himself on topics ranging from cancer research to violence on television. THE NATIONAL OBSERVER p. 11, June 26, 1976.

With an activated death penalty, society has some hope of making us all a little safer, says columnist Edwin A. Roberts, Jr. THE NATIONAL OBSERVER p. 13, May 1, 1976.

SOUTH VIETNAM
NEWSPAPER ARTICLES

South Vietnam widens number of crimes punishable by death. NEW YORK TIMES 2:3, July 24, 1965.

SPAIN

Executions and a rush of protest: Spain; with report by G. Scott. TIME 106:36-37, October 6, 1975.

Franco's apologists. NATION 221:356-357, October 18, 1975.

Franco's executions, by W. F. Buckley, Jr. NATIONAL REVIEW 27:1193, October 24, 1975.

Vengeance is whose? [political repression in Spain]. ECONOMIST

207:310, April 27, 1963.

STATISTICS AND SURVEYS
Attitude toward capital punishment: scale validation [Thurstone's scale], by M. Moore. PSYCHOLOGICAL REPORTS 37:21-22, August, 1975.

Attitudes to taking human life, by D. G. Beswick. AUSTRALIAN AND NEW ZEALAND JOURNAL OF SOCIOLOGY 6:120-130, October, 1970.

Capital punishment and open-end questions, by L. R. England. PUBLIC OPINION QUARTERLY 12(3):412-416, 1948.

Capital punishment; effects of the death penalty; data and deliberations from the social sciences; symposium, by H. Bedau. AMERICAN JOURNAL OF ORTHOPSYCHIATRY 45:580-726, July, 1975.

Capital punishment: amoral consensus?, by J. M. Wall. CHRISTIAN CENTURY 92:483-484, May 14, 1975.

Comparison of the executed and the commuted among admissions to death row: is a rational, fair scheme discernible in the commutation of death sentences? or does a selective system appear to operate, differentiating between the executed and commuted upon improper bases? [based on a study of] the case records of 439 persons sentenced to death for first degree murder and detained on death row in Pennsylvania between 1914 and 1958, by M. E. Wolfgang, et al. JOURNAL OF CRIMINAL LAW, CRIMINOLOGY, AND POLICE SCIENCE 53:301-311, September, 1962.

Crime up—punishment down [trend toward less severe punishment]. U. S. NEWS AND WORLD REPORT 62:72, April 10, 1967.

Deterrent effect of the death penalty: a statistical test, by P. Passell. STANFORD LAW REVIEW 28:61-80, November, 1975.

New attempts under way to abolish death penalty; What a poll shows. U. S. NEWS AND WORLD REPORT 58:13, April 5, 1965.

239

Petition. NATION 189:478, December 26, 1959.

Polls: capital punishment, by H. G. Erskine. PUBLIC OPINION QUARTERLY 34:290-307, Summer, 1970.

Public opinion and the death penalty [examination of public opinion polls and other social science studies on public attitudes toward capital punishment], by N. Vidmar, et al. STANFORD LAW REVIEW 26:1245-1270, June, 1974.

Public opinion and the death penalty in South Africa, by J. Midgley. BRITISH JOURNAL OF CRIMINOLOGY 14:345-358, October, 1974.

Punishment: current survey of philosophy and law, by R. J. Gerber, et al. ST. LOUIS UNIVERSITY LAW JOURNAL 11:491, Summer, 1967.

A rundown on the status of the death penalty in the 50 states and the District of Columbia. CONGRESSIONAL QUARTERLY. WEEKLY REPORT 31:602-603, March 17, 1973.

Scaling technique for measuring social attitudes toward capital punishment, by J. K. Balogh, et al. SOCIOLOGY AND SOCIAL RESEARCH 45:24-26, October, 1960.

Some official observations on murder and the death penalty [results of a questionnaire sent to prison officials], by P. A. Thomas. AMERICAN JOURNAL OF CORRECTION 19:16-17+, July-August, 1957.

Statistical evidence on the deterrent effect of capital punishment—A comparison of the work of Thorsten Sellin and Isaac Ehrlich on the deterrent effect of capital punishment, by D. C. Baldus, et al. YALE LAW JOURNAL 85:164-227, December, 1975.

A survey of recent literature on capital punishment, by D. E. J. MacNamara. AMERICAN JOURNAL OF CORRECTION 24:16-19, March-April, 1962.

Survey's only meeting, by R. Wilcove. NOAA QUARTERLY 3(4):61-63, October, 1973.

Time lapse between sentence and execution: the United States and Canada compared, by W. A. Lunden. AMERICAN BAR ASSOCIATION JOURNAL 48:1043-1045, November, 1962.

Trends in the use of capital punishment [United States], by F. E. Hartung. ANNALS OF THE AMERICAN ACADEMY OF POLITICAL AND SOCIAL SCIENCE pp. 8-19, November, 1952.

NEWSPAPER ARTICLES

American Institution of Public Opinion poll shows 42% of churchgoers favor penalty, 46% oppose it, as against 43% and 47% among nonchurchgoes. NEW YORK TIMES 10:8, January 19, 1967.

Article on results on ballot questions in elections throughout nation notes California voters favored reactivating death penalty for certain crimes; California Supreme Court outlawed death penalty last February as unconstitutional and US Supreme Court handed down qualified ruling supporting Supreme Court ruling. NEW YORK TIMES 40:4, November 9, 1972.

California law enforcement groups, State Attorney General Younger and thousands of volunteers begin campaign to gather more than ½ million signatures to restore death penalty in California. NEW YORK TIMES 63:1, March 19, 1972.

Comment on public opinion surveys finding throughout US that there is a resurgence in public support for retention of death penalty, despite US Supreme Court's ruling on June 29 that in effect ended capital punishment. NEW YORK TIMES IV,3:5, November 26, 1972.

Dr. B. van Niekerk reports survey of 430 South African lawyers reveals nonwhites convicted of capital crime in South Africa are more likely to be sentenced to death than whites; says majority back exhaustive government inquiry into death penalty. NEW YORK TIMES 26:1, December 14, 1969.

Editorial noting tide of conservatism sweeping US, cites recent increase in public opinion for reinstating capital punishment. NEW YORK TIMES 28:1, January 15, 1973.

Ex-Justice Leibowitz foresees capital punishment reinstated in NYS, TV interview; cites figure of 1,100 murders in NYC in 1969. NEW YORK TIMES 14:6, January 12, 1970.

Gallup Poll releases survey showing US public, by 5 to 4, favors death penalty for persons convicted of murder; survey detailed; chart. NEW YORK TIMES 29:2, March 16, 1972.

Gallup Poll survey finds growing support for death peanlty for murder among white citizens, opposition by majority of Negroes. NEW YORK TIMES 47:1, February 16, 1972.

Gallup Poll's latest survey finds that public support for capital punishment is currently at its highest point in nearly 2 decades, despite US Supreme Court's ruling striking down death penalty; figures show that 57% of adults 18 years old and older said that they favor death penalty for persons convicted of murder; previous high was recorded in 1953 when 68% were in favor of capital punishment; table. NEW YORK TIMES 18:4, November 23, 1972.

List of 31 states that have restored death penalty for some crimes since 1972 Supreme Court decision that held death penalty unconstitutional; Maryland soon to become 32 (S). NEW YORK TIMES 58:3, April 21, 1975.

Listing of 37 countries in which capital punishment has been abolished and dates of abolition. NEW YORK TIMES 14:3, June 30, 1972.

M. Belli charges that of 23 verdicts by Dallas juries entailing death sentences 7 were given after only 4-7 minutes of deliberation. NEW YORK TIMES 40:4, May 3, 1964.

Mervin D. Field poll finds that public support for capital punishment in California is stronger now than it has been in 20 years; finds that 74% of Californians surveyed wanted to retain death penalty compared with only 49% in 1956 (S). NEW YORK TIMES 47:8,

March 26, 1975.

NYC Mayor Lindsay decides to fight for liberal issues in next session of State Legis., despite indications that public opinion is shifting to conservatism; will push for liberal position on capital punishment. NEW YORK TIMES 1:3, October 22, 1972.

Newspaper score vote. NEW YORK TIMES 8:6, April 7, 1966.

Poll finds capital punishment favored. CHRISTIAN SCIENCE MONITOR 4:1, March 15, 1969, (Western Edition).

Poll indicates California legislators oppose abolition. NEW YORK TIMES 38:5, February 22, 1960.

Poll shows 66% of Californians favor retention of death penalty, 24% do not and 10% have no opinion; percentage in favor of capital punishment is largest in 16 years. NEW YORK TIMES 67:3, September 8, 1972.

Statistics, readers write specious logic. CHRISTIAN SCIENCE MONITOR E:5, July 20, 1972, (Eastern, and London and Overseas Editions); E:5, July 21, 1972 (Western and Midwestern Editions).

Tom Wicker article on injustice and repressiveness of North Carolina courts cites fact that there are more persons sentenced to die and awaiting executions in North Carolina than any other state (S). NEW YORK TIMES 31:1, December 26, 1975.

UN inquiry into death penalty shows that many governments are still reluctant to abolish capital punishment; replies from 69 countries show 75% still use death penalty, although fewer people are sentenced to death and even fewer executed; study's findings detailed. NEW YORK TIMES 8:1, April 3, 1972.

US: Federal Prisons Bureau reports 82 executed, 1950, 10-year low. NEW YORK TIMES 8:5, April 29, 1952.

STORY, JOHN
Joseph Story on capital punishment, by J. C. Hogan. CALIFORNIA

STORY, JOHN

LAW REVIEW 43:76-84, March, 1955.

SUDAN

Numeiry's justice; mass executions in Sudan, by J. Pringle. NEWS-
WEEK 88:36-37+, August 16, 1976.

SUICIDE

Capital punishment as suicide and as murder, by G. F. Salamon. AMER-
ICAN JOURNAL OF ORTHOPSYCHIATRY 45(4):701-711,
July, 1975.

Death wish; case of G. M. Gilmore, by P. Goldman, et al. NEWSWEEK
88:26-27+, November 29, 1976.

Gary Gilmore: death wish, by D. A. Williams, et al. NEWSWEEK
88:35-36, November 22, 1976.

Sudden rush for blood; murderer G. M. Gilmore's desire to be executed.
TIME 108:56, November 22, 1976.

When a condemned man wants to die; case of G. M. Gilmore. U. S.
NEWS AND WORLD REPORT 81:19, November 29, 1976.

TAIWAN

NEWSPAPER ARTICLES

Taiwan District Court sentences 3 smugglers to death and imprisons 22
others following seizure of more than 3 tons of contraband foods
and herbs in Keelung Harbor on May 20; case is 1st instance of
death penalty given to convicted smugglers. NEW YORK TIMES
9:1, July 16, 1972.

TANZANIA

NEWSPAPER ARTICLES

Zanzibar, Tanzania, introduces death penalty for persons convicted of
stealing cloves, island's main income source. NEW YORK TIMES
73:3, April 20, 1969.

TASMANIA

NEWSPAPER ARTICLES

Tasmania to abolish capital punishment. NEW YORK TIMES 28:4, December 15, 1968.

TAX EVASION

NEWSPAPER ARTICLES

Chad President Tombalbaye warns tax evaders now face death penalty. NEW YORK TIMES 40:1, February 8, 1970.

TERRORISM

A case for capital punishment [for Arab terrorism in Israel], by G. Weiler; A case against capital punishment, by L. Sheleff (Shaskolsky); A new high in ethnocentrism [commenting on the article by Gershon Weiler], by D. Amit. NEW OUTLOOK 17:46-58, October, 1974.

Death penalty for terrorists? CHRISTIAN CENTURY 90:333, March 21, 1973.

Must night fall? [whether terrorist murders in Britain will lead to restoration of capital punishment]. ECONOMIST 257:9-10, December 6, 1975.

Or such less penalty: if the British start hanging terrorists, they'll be out of Ulster in a year—which is just what the IRA [Irish republican army] wants. ECONOMIST 253:17-18, December 7, 1974.

NEWSPAPER ARTICLES

HR passes anticrime bill that includes provision calling for death penalty for those convicted of fatal bombings. NEW YORK TIMES 1:3, October 8, 1970.

Law that provides death penalty for bombings in effect, California. NEW YORK TIMES 58:6, August 23, 1970.

Many urge terrorists be executed. CHRISTIAN SCIENCE MONITOR

2:1, May 21, 1974, (All Editions).

Reinstatement of capital punishment for terrorists emerges as major pol issue in Great Britain in aftermath of bombing and murder campaign attributed to IRA; debate over death penalty, which was largely abolished in 1965, blurs party lines and involves government officials, police and politicians; parliamentary vote on capital punishment for terrorists is set for December 11; arguments for and against death penalty noted; bill to reinstate death penalty was defeated in 1974 (M). NEW YORK TIMES 15:1, December 11, 1975.

South Vietnamese President Thieu decrees death penalty for hijacking, armed robbery, rape, and for persons forcing women into prostitution; new laws are signed by Thieu under special powers granted him to deal with national emergency resulting from North Vietnamese offensive in South Vietnam. NEW YORK TIMES 2:7, September 4, 1972.

TREATMENT OF PRISONERS
    see: Cruel and Unusual Punishment
    The Prisoner and Capital Punishment

TRINIDAD
    Execution of Michael X, by J. Paine. NEW STATESMAN 89:681, May 23, 1975.

    Michael X on death row, by G. Robertson. NEW STATESMAN 87:40-41, January 11, 1974.

TURNER, HOSIE S.
    see: Cases Involving Capital Punishment

UN
    see: United Nations

U. S. SUPREME COURT
    see: The Law and Capital Punishment

UNITED NATIONS

Capital punishment: actions in UN third committee. UNITED NA-
TIONS MONTHLY CHRONICLE   5:39-41, November, 1968.

Capital punishment as a human rights issue before the United Nations,
by L. E. Landerer.   HUMAN RIGHTS JOURNAL   4:511-534,
July, 1971.

Capital punishment at UN, by J. A. Joyce.   CONTEMPORARY RE-
VIEW   201:120-123, March, 1962.

Capital punishment: report of the secretary-general [of the United
Nations, prepared as background for the discussion on capital
punishment which took place in the Economic and social council
during its fifty-fourth session in 1973].   INTERNATIONAL
REVIEW OF CRIMINAL POLICY   31:91-101, 1974.

United Nations and the issue of capital punishment.   UNITED NA-
TIONS MONTHLY CHRONICLE   3:53-58, February, 1966.

NEWSPAPER ARTICLES

Plans UN motion to ban.   CHRISTIAN SCIENCE MONITOR   11:1,
January 7, 1971, (Western Edition).

Studies penalties.   CHRISTIAN SCIENCE MONITOR   4:5, March 21,
1973, (Eastern Edition).

UN Assembly committee completes draft of covenant reconciling
statutes on imposing death sentence on pregnant women and those
under legal age.   NEW YORK TIMES   4:7, November 26, 1957.

UNITED STATES

Abolition of the death penalty in California, by C. Blease.   LAWYER
GUILD REVIEW   19:58, Summer, 1959.

Abolition or retention?   ANNALS OF THE AMERICAN ACADEMY
OF POLITICAL AND SOCIAL SCIENCE   pp. 101-136, November,
1952.

And the penalty is (sometimes) death [the death penalty and the incidence of actual executions; United States], by R. Slovenko.
ANTIOCH REVIEW 24:351-364, Fall, 1964.

At San Quentin, gas chamber is back in use. U. S. NEWS AND WORLD
REPORT 62:19, April 24, 1967.

Bastard or legitimate child of Furman (Furman v. Georgia, 92 Sup. Ct.
2726)? An analysis of Wyoming's new capital punishment law.
LAND AND WATER REVIEW 9:209-236, 1974.

Beating the rap, by R. H. Rovere. SPECTATOR 204:278, February
26, 1960.

Brown still astonishes. ECONOMIST 262:34, January 29, 1977.

California: death double-headers. NEWSWEEK 61:33, April 22,
1963.

California views the death penalty; discussion, by M. E. Leary. AMER-
ICA 127:53, 105, 189, 262-263; 128:95-97, August 5, September
23, October 7, 1972, February 3, 1973.

Capital punishment and life imprisonment in North Carolina, 1946
to 1968: implications for abolition of the death penalty, by C. H.
Patrick. WAKE FOREST INTERNATIONAL LAW REVIEW
6:417, May, 1970.

Capital punishment—cruel and unusual?, by T. A. Long. ETHICS
83:214-223, April, 1973.

Capital punishment: does it deter or degrade? [with a list entitled],
"Where the states stand on capital punishment—two years after
U. S. Supreme court decision." CONGRESSIONAL QUARTER-
LY WEEKLY REPORT 32:1419-1422, June 1, 1974.

Capital punishment in Connecticut, by R. C. Donnelly, et al. CON-
NECTICUT BAR JOURNAL 35:39, March, 1961.

Capital punishment in Oregon, 1903-64, by H. A. Bedau. OREGON

LAW REVIEW 45:1, December, 1965.

Capital punishment in South Carolina: the end of an era, by L. Mc-Donald. SOUTH CAROLINA LAW REVIEW 24:762, 1972.

Capital punishment in Texas, 1924-1968, by R. C. Koeninger. CRIME AND DELINQUENCY 15:132, January, 1969.

Capital punishment in Virginia. VIRGINIA LAW REVIEW 58:97-142, January, 1972.

Capital punishment in Virginia: a position paper, by V. C. Funk. CATHOLIC CHARITIES REVIEW 58:9-17, March 14-22, April, 1974.

Capital punishment is constitutional: California state Supreme court decision. TIME 92:92, November 29, 1963.

Capital punishment—the issues and the evidence [excerpt from the majority report to the Massachusetts legislature of the Special commission to investigate the abolition of the death penalty; recommends abolition] : The right of the state to inflict capital punishment, by T. J. Riley. CATHOLIC LAWYER 6:269-278+, Autumn, 1960.

Capital punishment: it's being revived in many states. U. S. NEWS AND WORLD REPORT 76:46, March 4, 1974.

Capital punishment statutes in the wake of United States v. Jackson: some unresolved questions [ruling concerning constitutionality of the death penalty provisions of the Federal kidnapping act], by D. A. Poe. GEORGE WASHINGTON LAW REVIEW 37:719-745, May, 1969.

Capital punishment [symposium]. AMERICAN JOURNAL OF OR-THOPSYCHIATRY 45:580-722, July, 1975.

Capital punishment under the UCMJ after Furman, by R. E. Tragolo. AIR FORCE LAW REVIEW 16(4):86-95, Winter, 1974.

Capital sentencing—effect of McGautha (McGautha v. California 91 Sup. Ct. 1454) and Furman (Furman v. Georgia 92 Sup. Ct. 2726). TEMPLE LAW QUARTERLY 45:619, Summer, 1972.

The Capitall Lawes of New-England, by G. L. Haskins. HARVARD LAW SCHOOL BULLETIN 7:10, February, 1956.

Chessman case. COMMONWEAL 71:616, March 4, 1960.

—. ECONOMIST 195:535, May 7, 1960.

Chessman case: when justice took 12 years. U. S. NEWS AND WORLD REPORT 48:73+, May 16, 1960.

Children of Cain? Senate vote and H. Hughes' amendment, by Sisyphus. COMMONWEAL 100:107-108, April 5, 1974.

Clemency in Arkansas. TIME 97:50, January 11, 1971.

Collector's choice: a first for law & order; execution of J. Forner in San Francisco, by R. Olmsted. AMERICAN WEST 7:11, January, 1970.

Comparison of punishments in Soviet criminal law and American military law, by A. Avins. SOUTH TEXAS LAW JOURNAL 2:303, Summer-Fall, 1956.

Consequences of Chessman, by R. Bendiner. NEW STATESMAN 59:351, March 12, 1960.

Constitutional law: capital punishment—the current status of the death penalty in North Carolina. WAKE FOREST LAW REVIEW 9:135, December, 1972.

Constitutional law—cruel and unusual—capital punishment. NORTH CAROLINA LAW REVIEW 42:909, June, 1964.

Constitutional law—death penalty—Texas death penalty statutes comply with the discretion requirements of the United States Supreme Court. ST. MARY'S LAW JOURNAL 7:454-462, 1975.

Constitutional law—the remains of the death penalty: Furman v. Georgia (92 Sup. Ct. 2726). DE PAUL LAW REVIEW 22:481, Winter, 1972.

The constitutional status of the death penalty in New Jersey, by H. A. Cohen. CRIMINAL JUSTICE QUARTERLY 2:5-24, Winter, 1974.

Constitutionality of the Connecticut penal code (title 53a) guilty plea/ capital punishment provisions. CONNECTICUT BAR JOURNAL 45:414, December, 1971.

Crime & punishment in Alabama. TIME 72:9, September 1, 1958.

Criminal law—capital punishment—the Texas statutes authorizing the death penalty do not violate the eighth amendment's prohibition of cruel and unusual punishment. TEXAS LAW REVIEW 7:170-181, Fall, 1975.

Crusading for death; J. F. Britt, district attorney of Lumberton, North Carolina, by J. K. Footlick, et al. NEWSWEEK 86:31, July 21, 1975.

De facto abolition of the death penalty in Louisiana?, by W. H. Forman, Jr. LOUISIANA BAR JOURNAL 18:199, December, 1970.

Death in court. ECONOMIST 224:1199, September 30, 1967.

Death in the dock. ECONOMIST 183:595-596, May 18, 1957.

Death on trial. ECONOMIST 230:41, January 11, 1969.

Death penalty, by H. B. Shaffer. EDITORIAL RESEARCH REPORTS pp. 573-588, August 14, 1953.

Death penalty abolished; action in Iowa, by P. B. Mather. CHRISTIAN CENTURY 82:283, March 24, 1965.

Death penalty after Furman (Furman v. Georgia, 92 Sup. Ct. 2726), by C. S. Vance. NOTRE DAME LAWYER 48:850, April, 1973.

—, by L. A. Wollan, Jr. LOYOLA UNIVERSITY LAW JOURNAL 4:339-357, Summer, 1973.

Death penalty—the alternatives left after Furman v. Georgia (92 Sup. Ct. 2726). ALBANY LAW REVIEW 37:344, 1973.

The death penalty [based on report prepared for the Iowa board of control of state institutions; address], by W. A. Lunden. POLICE 5:43-47, May-June, 1961.

Death penalty cases. CALIFORNIA LAW REVIEW 56:1270, October, 1968.

The death penalty cases [California]. CALIFORNIA LAW REVIEW 56:1268-1490, October, 1968.

Death penalty: continuing threat to America's poor, by L. S. Hinds. FREEDOMWAYS 16(1):39-43, 1976.

Death penalty: cruel, unusual, unethical, and futile, by L. H. Dewolf. RELIGION IN LIFE 42:37-41, Spring, 1973.

The death penalty gets a big push [United States]. U. S. NEWS AND WORLD REPORT 74:70, March 26, 1973.

Death penalty in America, by H. A. Bedau. FEDERAL PROBATION 35:32, June, 1971.

Death penalty in California, by M. Carter, et al. CRIME AND DE-LINQUENCY 15:62, January, 1969.

Death penalty in Massachusetts. SUFFOLK UNIVERSITY LAW RE-VIEW 8:632-681, Spring, 1974.

The death penalty in the United States. ANNALS OF THE AMERI-CAN ACADEMY OF POLITICAL AND SOCIAL SCIENCE pp. 45-100, November, 1952.

The death penalty in Virginia: its history and prospects, by N. D. Joyner. UNIVERSITY OF VIRGINIA NEWS LETTER 50:37-

40, June 15, 1974.

Death penalty provision of the new penal code, by J. M. Carroll. KEN-TUCKY BAR JOURNAL 38:15-21, October, 1974.

Death penalty reprieved? ECONOMIST 194:812, February 27, 1960.

Death penalty revived; Supreme court decision. TIME 108:35-37, July 12, 1976.

Death row. ECONOMIST 223:355, April 22, 1967.

The death sentence, by S. Hook. NEW LEADER 44:18-20, April 3, 1961.

Death sentences in New Jersey 1907-1960, by H. A. Bedau. RUTGERS LAW REVIEW 19:1, Fall, 1964.

Death watch. ECONOMIST 255:79, April 26, 1975.

Deterrent effect of the death penalty: facts v. faiths, by H. Zeisel. SUPREME COURT REVIEW 1976:317-343, 1976.

Eighth amendment and Kentucky's new capital punishment provisions —waiting for the other shoe to drop. KENTUCKY LAW JOUR-NAL 63:399-429, 1974-1975.

End of capital punishment in Delaware. SOCIAL SERVICE REVIEW 32:300, September, 1958.

An end to "death row"; what Supreme court ruled. U. S. NEWS AND WORLD REPORT 73:25-27, July 10, 1972.

Enquiry how far the punishment of death is necessary in Pennsylvania, by W. Bradford. AMERICAN JOURNAL OF LEGAL HISTORY 12:122, 245, April-July, 1968.

Entering wedge: death penalty in New York. NEWSWEEK 61:38, May 20, 1963.

Execution of Private Slovik, a review, by W. B. Huie. NEWSWEEK 43:107, April 26, 1954.

Execution of Private Slovik; condensation, by W. B. Huie. LOOK 18: 30-38, May 4, 1954.

Executions in America by W. J. Bowers, a review by E. Z. Friedenberg. SOCIETY 12:88-90, September, 1975.

Executive clemency in Wisconsin, by D. Adamany. WISCONSIN BAR BULLETIN 36:54, October, 1963.

Fight for life [Chessman case]. ECONOMIST 194:714+, February 20, 1960.

Footnote to Furman (Furman v. Georgia, 92 Sup. Ct. 2726): failing justification for the capital case exception to the right to bail after abolition of the death penalty. SAN DIEGO LAW REVIEW 10:349, February, 1973.

Furman v. Georgia (92 Sup. Ct. 2726) and Kentucky statutory law, by L. M. T. Reed. KENTUCKY BAR JOURNAL 37:25, January, 1973.

Furman v. Georgia (92 Sup. Ct. 2726): the Burger court looks at judicial review, by D. Victor. LAW AND THE SOCIAL ORDER 1972:393, 1972.

Furman (Furman v. Georgia, 92 Sup. Ct. 2726) Case: what life is left in the death penalty? CATHOLIC UNIVERSITY LAW REVIEW 22:651, Spring, 1973.

Furman v. Georgia (92 Sup. Ct. 2726)—death-knell for capital punishment? ST. JOHN'S LAW REVIEW 47:107, October, 1972.

Furman v. Georgia (92 Sup. Ct. 2726): a postmortem on the death penalty. VILLANOVA LAW REVIEW 18:678, March, 1973.

Furman v. Georgia (92 Sup. Ct. 2726): will the death of capital punishment mean a new life for bail? HOFSTRA LAW REVIEW 2:432-

443, Winter, 1974.

Haunting the court. ECONOMIST 259:45-46, April 10, 1976.

House bill 200: the legislative attempt to reinstate capital punishment in Texas. HOUSTON LAW REVIEW 11:410-423, January, 1974.

Hypocrisy in high places; Senator Hughes public-execution amendment. CHRISTIAN CENTURY 91:357, April 3, 1974.

Incidence of the death penalty for rape in Virginia, by D. H. Partington. WASHINGTON AND LEE LAW REVIEW 22:43, Spring, 1965.

The issue of capital punishment [United States], by H. A. Bedau. CURRENT HISTORY 53:82-87+, August, 1967.

Jury selection and the death penalty: Witherspoon (Witherspoon v. Illinois, 88 Sup. Ct. 1770). UNIVERSITY OF CHICAGO LAW REVIEW 37:759, Summer, 1970.

Last firing squad: executioners of Utah, by G. Berriault. ESQUIRE 65:88-91+, June, 1966.

Last mile? death sentence dying out in the U.S. NEWSWEEK 65:26+, March 8, 1965.

Legacy of violence: the opera house lynching; Livermore, Kentucky, 1911, by J. M. Elliott. NEGRO HISTORY BULLETIN 37:303, October, 1974.

Letter from Chessman, by C. H. Rolph. NEW STATESMAN 59:615-616, April 30, 1960.

Life and death of Caryl Chessman. NEW STATESMAN 59:653, May 7, 1960.

Life for Chessman, by C. H. Rolph. NEW STATESMAN 59:280+, February 27, 1960.

Litigating against the death penalty: the strategy behind Furman

(Furman v. Georgia, 92 Sup. Ct. 2726), by M. Meltsner. YALE LAW JOURNAL 82:1111, May, 1973.

McGautha v. California, May, 1971: on May 3, 1971, the Supreme court handed down a far-reaching decision that capital punishment procedures in general use throughout the United States today do not violate the constitution [excerpts from the text of the decision]. CURRENT HISTORY 61:40-42+, July, 1971.

Mandatory death: State v. Waddell [(North Carolina)–S E 2d–]. NORTH CAROLINA CENTRAL LAW JOURNAL 4:292, Spring, 1973.

Mass public executions in Iraq deplored by United States; text of letter to the president of the Security council, January 29, 1969, by C. W. Yost. DEPARTMENT OF STATE BULLETIN 60:145-146, February 17, 1969.

A matter of conviction, by E. G. Brown. FELLOWSHIP 26:14-16, July 1, 1960.

Montana's death penalty after State v. McKenzie [33 St. Reptr. 1043 (1976)]. MONTANA LAW REVIEW 38:209-220, Winter, 1977.

Movement to abolish capital punishment in America, 1787-1861, by D. B. Davis. AMERICAN HISTORICAL REVIEW 63:23-46, October, 1957.

Murder in New Hampshire [1843], by D. B. Davis. NEW ENGLAND QUARTERLY 28:147-163, June, 1955.

Must Chessman die? NATION 190:cover, 265, March 26, 1960; Discussion, 190:inside cover, April 9, 1960.

NEW REPUBLIC 142:3-4, March 28, 1960+; Reply by J. H. Sherman, 142:22-23, April 11, 1960; Discussion, 142:23, April 25, 1960.

New approach to M'Naghten v. Durham, by S. Rubin. JOURNAL OF THE AMERICAN JUDICATURE SOCIETY 45:133, December,

1961.

New debate on death penalty: major issue in California. U. S. NEWS AND WORLD REPORT 66:13, May 5, 1969.

New York abolishes death. TIME 85:61, June 11, 1965.

New York Senate would curtail capital punishment. CHRISTIAN CENTURY 82:669, May 26, 1965.

Nixon administration and the deterrent effect of the death penalty, by H. A. Bedau. UNIVERSITY OF PITTSBURGH LAW REVIEW 34:557-566, Summer, 1970.

Nixon and the death penalty, by W. Shawcross. NEW STATESMAN 85:366-367, March 16, 1973.

Not-so-new South: legal aid in the death belt; Team Defense Project, by M. Pinsky. NATION 224:367-368, March 26, 1977.

Notches on a chair; Utah firing squad, by C. P. Larrowe. NATION 182:291-293, April 14, 1956; Discussion, 182:inside cover, May 12, 1956; 182:289, April 14, 1956.

Now a new fight over the death penalty [campaign against capital punishment is now developing the United States]. U. S. NEWS AND WORLD REPORT 48:52, March 7, 1960.

On capital punishment. SOCIAL SERVICE REVIEW 47:426-427, September, 1973.

One, two, three, five! in Utah. NEWSWEEK 55:36-37, April 11, 1960.

Pleasure, punishment and moral indignation, by G. Johnson, et al. SOCIOLOGY AND SOCIAL RESEARCH 59:82-95, January, 1975.

Politics and Chessman, by R. Meister. NATION 190:275-277, March 26, 1960.

The proposed federal criminal codes: a prosecutor's point of view [focuses on federal law relating to tax offenses, the death penalty and entrapment], by D. A. Connelly. NORTHWESTERN UNIVERSITY LAW REVIEW 68:826-849, November-December, 1973.

Quality of mercy. SPECTATOR 204:648, May 6, 1960.

Quality of mercy [in California and Illinois]. ECONOMIST 204:525, August 11, 1962.

Recent changes in California law regarding jury's discretion in selecting first degree murder penalty [People v. Green (California) 302 P 2d 307]. SOUTHERN CALIFORNIA LAW REVIEW 31:200, February, 1958.

Response to Furman (Furman v. Georgia, 92 Sup. Ct. 2726): can legislators breathe life back into death? CLEVELAND STATE LAW REVIEW 23:172-189, Winter, 1974.

Resurrection of the death peanlty: the validity of Arizona's response to [the U.S. supreme court's decision, June 29, 1972, in the case of] Furman v. Georgia, by G. Forster. ARIZONA STATE LAW JOURNAL 1974(2):257-296, 1974.

Reviving the death penalty: Supreme court decision, by S. Fraker, et al. NEWSWEEK 88:14-15, July 12, 1976.

Road up from barbarism. SOCIAL SERVICE REVIEW 46:431-432, September, 1972.

A rundown on the status of the death penalty in the 50 states and the District of Columbia. CONGRESSIONAL QUARTERLY. WEEKLY REPORT 31:602-603, March 17, 1973.

Selective factors in capital punishment [study of convicted capital offenders, North Carolina, since 1909; adapted from address], by E. H. Johnson. SOCIAL FORCES 36:165-169, December, 1957.

Seven in death row: Connecticut state prison, by J. V. Hopkins, et al.

NATION 183:476-478, December 1, 1956.

Should Ohio abolish capital punishment? CLEVELAND-MARSHALL LAW REVIEW 10:365, May, 1961.

Should we abolish capital punishment in California? TRANSACTIONS OF THE COMMONWEALTH CLUB OF CALIFORNIA 58:17-37, November 11, 1963.

Signs of an end to "death row": U.S. joining trend? Death penalty: a world survey. U. S. NEWS AND WORLD REPORT 70:37-40, May 31, 1971.

Someone had a good idea: New York law. NATION 196:298, April 13, 1963; Reply by N. Redlich, 196:inside cover, April 27, 1963.

Staying the executioner; California. NEWSWEEK 49:43, May 20, 1957.

Tales of the firing squad in Utah. TIME 66:21, July 11, 1955.

Test for the doomed; executions in California. NEWSWEEK 59:22+, January 22, 1962.

Time lapse between sentence and execution: the United States and Canada compared, by W. A. Lunden. AMERICAN BAR ASSO-CIATION JOURNAL 48:1043-1045, November, 1962.

Toward abolition of capital punishment. SOCIAL SERVICE REVIEW 43:92, March, 1969.

Trends in the use of capital punishment [United States], by F. E. Hartung. ANNALS OF THE AMERICAN ACADEMY OF PO-LITICAL AND SOCIAL SCIENCE pp. 8-19, November, 1952.

United States v. Jackson (88 Sup. Ct. 1209): guilty pleas and replace-ment capital punishment provisions. CORNELL LAW REVIEW 54:448, February, 1969.

Use of the death penalty v. outrage at murder, by D. Glaser, et al.

CRIME AND DELINQUENCY 20:333-338, October, 1974; Reply with rejoinder by W. C. Bailey, 22:31-43, January, 1976.

Vanishing death sentence. ECONOMIST 214:671, February 13, 1965.

Waiting on death row: North Carolina, by L. Lopez. PROGRESSIVE 38:38, May, 1974.

Whatever happened to—capital punishment: it's being reviewed in many states. U. S. NEWS AND WORLD REPORT 76:46, March 4, 1974.

Who hates Chessman?, by R. Meister. NATION 190:167-169, February 20, 1960.

Why was capital punishment restored in Delaware?, by G. W. Samuelson. JOURNAL OF CRIMINAL LAW, CRIMINOLOGY AND POLICE SCIENCE 60(2):148-151, June, 1960.

Window on a gas chamber; Maryland penitentiary, by S. M. Shane. NATION 194:170-171, February 24, 1962; Correction, 194: inside cover, March 17, 1962.

Witherspoon revisited: exploring the tension between Witherspoon and Furman, by W. S. White. UNIVERSITY OF CINCINNATI LAW REVIEW 45:19-36, 1976.

NEWSPAPER ARTICLES

A. Lewis discusses issue under study in Great Britain and US; holds death penalty has not proved to be an effective deterrent, serves mainly to satisfy obsessive public emotions. NEW YORK TIMES 32:6, December 22, 1969.

ACLU of Northern California and NAACP challenge capital punishment in California Supreme Court, Anderson and Saterfield case; claim Death Row inmates are denied right to counsel after State Supreme Court review of their sentences, that so-called 'scrupled' jurors, those opposed to death penalty, are excluded from hearing capital cases, and that juries in such cases are without standards or guidelines in reaching decision. NEW YORK TIMES 67:1, June 9, 1968.

California Attorney General Younger asks State Supreme Court to reconsider its decision outlawing death penalty; accuses court of usurping legis. functions and eroding constitution separation of powers. NEW YORK TIMES 56:2, March 4, 1972.

California ban appeal denied. CHRISTIAN SCIENCE MONITOR 2:1, May 31, 1972, (All Editions).

California court kills. CHRISTIAN SCIENCE MONITOR 1:3, February 19, 1972, (Eastern Edition); 3:4, February 3, 1972, (Midwestern Edition); 1:5, February 19, 1972, (Western Edition); 1:3, February 19, 1972, (London and Overseas Edition).

California Governor Brown asks 4-year moratorium, message to legislature. NEW YORK TIMES 9:4, February 1, 1963.

California Supreme Court rules California death penalty is constitutional even in cases where murder has not been committed, ACLU suit; holds penalty does not constitute cruel and unusual punishment. NEW YORK TIMES 43:8, November 28, 1967.

California vote on reintroduction of death penalty in November noted. NEW YORK TIMES 27:6, June 27, 1972.

California will vote on whether to amend state constitution to reinstitute death penalty in November 7 election. NEW YORK TIMES 66:1, October 8, 1972.

Capital punishment drive spuds up in Michigan. CHRISTIAN SCIENCE MONITOR 9:5, September 12, 1973, (Eastern Edition); 2:1, September 11, 1973, (Western Edition); 2:4, September 11, 1973, (Midwestern Edition).

Capital punishment held legal. CHRISTIAN SCIENCE MONITOR 8:5, January 24, 1973.

Capital punishment limiting proposed in California. CHRISTIAN

SCIENCE MONITOR 3:6, February 12, 1963, (Eastern Edition); 1:1, February 8, 1963, (Western Edition); 4:1, February 12, 1963, (Midwestern Edition).

Capital punishment mandatory in eleven categories in California. CHRISTIAN SCIENCE MONITOR 8:5, September 26, 1973, (Eastern and London and Overseas Editions); 8:4, September 26, 1973, (Midwestern and Western Editions).

Capital punishment mandatory in New York. CHRISTIAN SCIENCE MONITOR 4:1, March 27, 1963, (Eastern Edition).

Capital punishment on trial in Cline case. CHRISTIAN SCIENCE MONITOR 3C:5, November 29, 1974, (Eastern Edition).

Capital punishment on trial in Rhode Island. CHRISTIAN SCIENCE MONITOR 3A:5, December 3, 1974, (Midwestern Edition); 5E:1, December 2, 1974, (Western Edition).

Capital punishment penalty law in Alabama. CHRISTIAN SCIENCE MONITOR 5C:4, August 2, 1974, (Midwestern Edition); 3A:3, August 1, 1974, (Western Edition).

Capital punishment repealers fail in California, Utah, and Oregon. CHRISTIAN SCIENCE MONITOR 1:4, July 22, 1963, (Western Edition); 3:5, July 22, 1963, (Midwestern Edition).

Capital punishment voted out in Oregon. CHRISTIAN SCIENCE MONITOR 7:1, November 13, 1964, (Eastern Edition); 5:7, November 13, 1964, (Western Edition); 3:3, November 13, 1964, (Midwestern Edition).

Comment on movement in US to abolish penalty; December 1964 lr. from late Justice Frankfurter to Mrs. S. Ehrmann, executive director of American League to Abolish Capital Punishment, hailing British Commons vote to abolish penalty quoted. NEW YORK TIMES IV,10:1, February 28, 1965.

Comment on number of controversial issues on calendar for 1973 New Jersey Legis., including State Senator Azzolina completion of number of amendments to bill that would restore death penalty in New Jersey. NEW YORK TIMES 49:8, December 24, 1972.

Comment on various states' minimum age limits. NEW YORK TIMES 81:1, January 7, 1962.

Connecticut Governor Meskill says on December 1 that he expects Connecticut General Assembly in next 2 years to enact legis. that will widen death penalty to cover rapists and possibly to cover illegal drug traffickers; says that despite June 29 US Supreme Court ruling virtually eliminating death penalty, constitutional question of 'cruel and unusual' punishment remains open. NEW YORK TIMES 83:1, December 3, 1972.

Death penalty law struck down. CHRISTIAN SCIENCE MONITOR 6:4, August 3, 1976, (All Editions).

Debates tough LW. CHRISTIAN SCIENCE MONITOR 5:1, July 14, 1973, (Eastern Edition).

Editorial comments, US and abroad; cartoon. NEW YORK TIMES IV,11:3, February 28, 1960.

Enlightened Oregon. CHRISTIAN SCIENCE MONITOR E:1, November 14, 1964, (All Editions).

Fails a 'cruel, unusual test'." CHRISTIAN SCIENCE MONITOR 3:2, October 28, 1976, (All Editions).

Florida comm. refuses to recommend abolition. NEW YORK TIMES 14:4, December 3, 1964.

Georgia may raise age. CHRISTIAN SCIENCE MONITOR 5:5, February 23, 1963, (Eastern Edition); 10:5, February 26, 1963, (Western and Midwestern Editions).

Georgia raises minimum age from 10 to 17. NEW YORK TIMES 5:4, March 15, 1963.

Georgia Senate defeats bill calling for death penalty for drug pushers.

263

NEW YORK TIMES 13:4, January 26, 1972.

Georgia Senate, 27-17, defeats bill providing death penalty for drug pushers. NEW YORK TIMES 17:1, January 27, 1972.

Governor Brown urges California Legis. approve 4-year moratorium on death penalty. NEW YORK TIMES 16:2, April 17, 1963.

Governor Bumpers on March 23 signs into law bill to reinstate death penalty in Arkansas; penalty will be reinstated for specific crimes, but capital punishment will not be mandatory; jury will have option of imposing sentence of death by electric chair or life imprisonment without chance of parole; among crimes subject to death penalty will be killing of policeman, fireman, court officials, publc officials and candidates and killing of persons while committing other major felonies. NEW YORK TIMES 22:4, March 24, 1973.

Governor Hughes urges New Jersey Legis. to set up new comm. to restudy capital punishment, legis. message. NEW YORK TIMES 32:4, January 14, 1970.

Governor Peabody hails Massachusetts Senate approval of to abolish penalty. NEW YORK TIMES 22:1, April 19, 1963.

Hawaii abolishes death penalty for capital crimes. NEW YORK TIMES 5:4, June 7, 1957.

Issue jars state. CHRISTIAN SCIENCE MONITOR 4:6, May 4, 1963.

Issue raised in robbery. CHRISTIAN SCIENCE MONITOR 5:2, March 8, 1969, (Western Edition).

J. M. Coale lr. expresses dismay at failure of US Supreme Court to achieve consensus of opinion in recent decision abolishing capital punishment. NEW YORK TIMES IV,12:5, July 9, 1972.

lr. scores death penalty in US. NEW YORK TIMES 46:6, April 30, 1969.

Maryland becomes 32nd state to reinstate capital punishment. CHRIS-TIAN SCIENCE MONITOR 6:3, August 24, 1975, (All Editions).

Massachusetts leans to penalty. CHRISTIAN SCIENCE MONITOR 5A:1, March 4, 1975, (Midwestern Edition); 3A:4, March 13, 1975, (Western Edition); 3D:1, March 12, 1975, (Eastern Edition).

Massachusetts legislators weigh mandatory capital punishment. CHRIS-TIAN SCIENCE MONITOR 8:4, March 29, 1973, (Eastern Edition).

Massachusetts repeal action. CHRISTIAN SCIENCE MONITOR 6:5, April 30, 1963, (Eastern Edition).

Montana voters, in June 6 primary election side issue, vote in favor of retaining state's death penalty. NEW YORK TIMES 28:8, June 7, 1972.

Move to return penalty. CHRISTIAN SCIENCE MONITOR 11:2, March 27, 1972, (Eastern Edition); 3:1, March 27, 1972, (Western and Midwestern Editions); 7:2, March 27, 1972, (London and Overseas Edition).

Nevada Senate approves bill reinstating death penalty for slaying of policemen and prison guards, contract killings and for killers already serving life terms. NEW YORK TIMES 27:4, April 7, 1973.

New Jersey Senator J. Azzolina introduces death-penalty bill that would force anyone charged with 1st-degree murder to stand trial and risk death in electric chair; bill also specifies that anyone sentenced for life must serve at least 30 years; convicts are now eligible for parole after 14 years and 10 months. NEW YORK TIMES 85:1, March 19, 1972.

New Jersey study comm. disagrees about death penalty but unanimously calls for minimum of 30 years imprisonment for 1st-degree murder; 7 of 9 members voted for retention of penalty. NEW YORK TIMES 39:5, November 12, 1964.

New Jersey Supreme Court rules 2 recent US Supreme Court decisions on death penalty do not outlaw capital punishment for state's 20 condemned men; upholds death sentences for 3 men, rules death penalty may not be excluded in 2 other cases. NEW YORK TIMES 17:6, July 4, 1968.

New York State Democratic Governor candidate O'Connor holds he favored abolition while Queens District Attorney, radio interview. NEW YORK TIMES 35:4, September 12, 1966.

News Brief: Capital punishment issue on ballot in California. CHRISTIAN SCIENCE MONITOR 2:1, August 5, 1972, (All Editions).

News Brief: Court upholds penalty. CHRISTIAN SCIENCE MONITOR 2:1, March 16, 1972, (All Editions).

News Brief: Judge delays. CHRISTIAN SCIENCE MONITOR 2:2, October 8, 1970, (All Editions).

Oregon watches California. CHRISTIAN SCIENCE MONITOR 10:7, February 26, 1963, (Western and Midwestern Editions).

Penalty cut back. CHRISTIAN SCIENCE MONITOR 3:1, May 7, 1968, (Eastern Edition).

Pennsylvania, Georgia, Texas defend capital punishment. CHRISTIAN SCIENCE MONITOR 2:1, July 25, 1972, (Eastern, Midwestern, and London and Overseas Editions).

Position in various states. CHRISTIAN SCIENCE MONITOR 11:2, September 23, 1963, (Western Edition).

Public pressure reviews. CHRISTIAN SCIENCE MONITOR 1:3, September 5, 1973, (All Editions).

Push on to abolish. CHRISTIAN SCIENCE MONITOR 1:1, November 18, 1965, (Eastern, Western, and Midwestern Editions).

Readers write—commuting. CHRISTIAN SCIENCE MONITOR 12:1, November 18, 1976, (Midwestern Edition); 17:1, November 15, 1976, (Western Edition); 23:1, November 19, 1976, (Eastern

Edition).

Reform hornets nest in west. CHRISTIAN SCIENCE MONITOR 3:3, January 12, 1973, (Eastern Edition); 3:1, January 13, 1973, (Western Edition); 3:1, January 13, 1973, (Midwestern Edition); 3:3, January 12, 1973, (London and Overseas Edition).

Revise penalty. CHRISTIAN SCIENCE MONITOR 2:2, November 10, 1972, (Eastern Edition); 2:2, November 11, 1972, (All Other Editions).

Ruling churns waves. CHRISTIAN SCIENCE MONITOR 5:3, February 25, 1972, (Eastern Edition); 2:2, February 25, 1972, (Western Edition); 5:3, February 25, 1972, (London and Overseas Edition).

San Quentin ex-warden Duffy among witnesses urging abolition, California Senate committee televised hearing; abolition cause seen doomed. NEW YORK TIMES 17:1, March 10, 1960.

Senate approves end to capital punishment. CHRISTIAN SCIENCE MONITOR 2:1, May 14, 1965, (Eastern Edition); 2:4, May 14, 1965, (Western and Midwestern Editions).

Tallahassee, Florida, blacked out for ½ hour on July 7 while Florida Attorney General R. L. Shevin outlines plan to restore capital punishment in electric chair at news conference. NEW YORK TIMES 26:6, July 8, 1972.

Tennessee keeps. CHRISTIAN SCIENCE MONITOR 15:3, March 26, 1963, (Western Edition).

Texas legislature on May 28 votes to reinstate death penalty for murder under 5 specific conditions. NEW YORK TIMES 5:1, May 30, 1973.

13 states have enacted laws to bring back death penalty; measures reinstating capital punishment are awaiting action by Governors of 2 other states, and issue is pending in 16 states; measures to restore penalty have been ·defeated in 8 states; issue has not been considered in 8 states; bill was passed and vetoed in Mississippi because

of unclear language; states that have restored death penalty are Arkansas, Colorado, Connecticut, Florida, Georgia, Indiana, Montana, Nebrasko, Nevada, New Mexico, Ohio, Utah and Wyoming; measures are waiting gubernatorial action in Arizona and Tennessee. NEW YORK TIMES 18:1, May 10, 1973.

Tom Wicker on indifference in US to recent execution in Spain says indifference partly reflects what appears to be rising American sentiment for return of capital punishment (S). NEW YORK TIMES 35:5, October 3, 1975.

Tough law urged. CHRISTIAN SCIENCE MONITOR 9:3, August 14, 1973, (London and Overseas Edition); 12:4, August 18, 1973, (Midwestern Edition).

US squashes move to abolish death penalty. NEW YORK TIMES 6:5, November 18, 1955.

US Supreme court agrees to review North Carolina case. CHRISTIAN SCIENCE MONITOR 6:1, October 30, 1974, (All Editions).

Urge revival of law. CHRISTIAN SCIENCE MONITOR 3:1, April 23, 1973, (Western Edition); 8:4, April 7, 1973, (London and Overseas Edition).

W. F. Tompkins heads comm. studying death penalty in New Jersey. NEW YORK TIMES 33:6, June 2, 1964.

West Virginia, New York, Kentucky, Illinois, Vermont and Indiana legislatures weigh ending death peanlty; Kentucky General Assembly stays 9 executions pending decision; NYS Trial Lawyers Association backs abolition. NEW YORK TIMES 23:4, March 8, 1965.

Will California vote to restore. CHRISTIAN SCIENCE MONITOR 1:3, October 21, 1972, (Eastern, Midwestern, London and Overseas Editions); 1:3, October 24, 1972, (Western Edition).

UNTIED STATES v. JACKSON
  see: Cases Involving Capital Punishment
  The Law and Capital Punishment

WAR CRIMES
  Punishment of war crimes and crimes against humanity; Assembly adopts convention on non-applicability of statutory limitations; with text of resolutions. UNITED NATION'S MONTHLY CHRONICLE 5:85-90, December, 1968.

  Seven Nazis were hanged; the diary of a witness, by A. Settel. COMMENTARY 29:369-379, May, 1960; Discussion, 29:(a),459-460, May 30, 1960.

  —. COMMENTARY 30:66-68, July, 1960.

WEAVER, JAMES
  see: Cases Involving Capital Punishment

WEBER
  Weber's thesis as an historical explanation, by E. Sprinzak. HISTORY AND THEORY 11(3):294-320, 1972.

WILSON, J.
  see: Cases Involving Capital Punishment

WOMEN AND CAPITAL PUNISHMENT
  Capital punishment in the case of women and adolescents. JUSTICE OF THE PEACE 117:669, October 17, 1953.

NEWSPAPER ARTICLES

Former NYC HRA speech writer Nettie Leef comments on her reasons for changing stand against capital punishment; illus. of Carl Chessman. NEW YORK TIMES 33:2, July 30, 1975.

Michael Scott, Patricia J. MacDonald and D. Buonocore comment on Nettie Leef's July 30 article athat explained reasons why she has become a proponent of capital punishment (M). NEW YORK TIMES 28:3, August 12, 1975.

New Jersey League of Women voters, attending covention in Morris-town, reject resolution opposing reinstitution of death penalty. NEW YORK TIMES 67:7, April 14, 1975.

UN Assembly Committee completes draft of covenant reconciling statutes on imposing death sentence on pregnant women and those under legal age. NEW YORK TIMES 4:7, November 26, 1957.

Victoria state, Australia, abolishes death penalty for pregnant women convicted of murder. NEW YORK TIMES 141:1, December 10, 1967.

ZANZIBAR
NEWSPAPER ARTICLES

Zanzibar, Tanzania, introduces death penalty for persons convicted of stealing cloves, island's main income source. NEW YORK TIMES 73:3, April 20, 1969.

AUTHOR INDEX

277